EASY STYLE

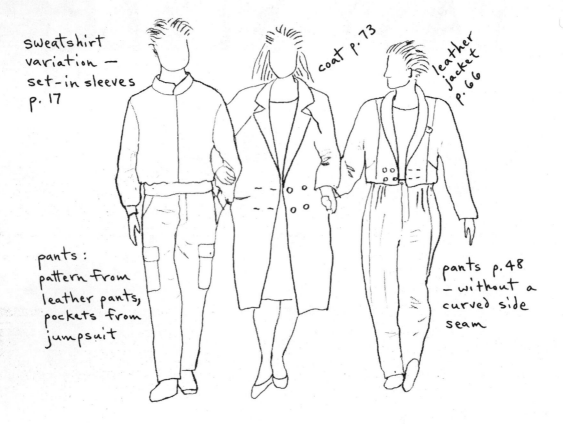

sweatshirt
variation —
set-in sleeves
p. 17

coat p. 73

leather
jacket
p. 66

pants:
pattern from
leather pants,
pockets from
jumpsuit

pants p. 48
— without a
curved side
seam

EASY STYLE

SEWING THE NEW CLASSICS

Elsebeth Gynther

Lark Books

Published in 1993 by Lark Books

Altamont Press
50 College Street
Asheville, North Carolina, U.S.A., 28801

First published in Denmark under the title of *Nyt Tøj*

Published in 1987 by Sterling Publishing Co., Inc., New York, NY

Translated from the Danish by Robin Hansen

Library of Congress Cataloging-in-Publication Data Available

ISBN 0-937274-68-2

Printed in Hong Kong by Oceanic Graphic Printing

Contents

Foreword 7

Introduction 8

EASY STYLE

Blouse with shawl collar 12

Shirt with facings 14

Sweatshirt 17

Jogging suit 19

Summer shirt 22

Tunic 24

Dress 27

Pullover or cardigan with dolman sleeves 29

Dressy slip-on coat 32

Straight skirt 34

Full skirt 35

Stretch pants 37

Culottes 38

Shorts/short pants with self-belt 40

Leather pants 43

Pleated pants with belt carriers 45

Buckled-up panel pants 48

Nylon jacket with elastic waist 50

Raincoat/spring coat 53

Lined leather-trimmed jacket 56

Coat lined to the edges 60

Kimono coat 63

Leather jacket 66

Raglan coat with shawl collar 69

Raglan coat or jacket with lapels 73

All-in-one jumpsuit 78

Jumpsuit with waistband 81

Robe 84

Pajamas 86

Leather belt 89

Beret 90

Cap with visor 91

Helmet 92

USING THE PATTERNS

    Patterns   94

    Measurement tables   96

    Basic patterns

        Tops   100

        Collars   104

        Pants   106

        Jumpsuits   110

        Skirts   111

        Pockets   112

        Headgear   112

    Drafting patterns   113

SEWING TECHNIQUES

    Sewing tools   118

    Fabrics   121

    Working with knits   125

    Working with leather   128

    Patterns and fabrics   131

    Pinning, basting, pressing, and fitting   133

    Stitches   136

    Pleats and tucks   138

    Gussets   141

    Pockets   142

    Finishing edges   149

    Waistbands   154

    Slits and cuffs   155

    Shoulder pads   158

    Linings   159

    Closures   164

    Straps and tabs   168

    Zippers and plackets   169

    Neck openings   173

    Collars   175

THE PATTERNS   178

    Index   191

Foreword

The clothes in this book were designed out of a desire to create classic clothing, or at least clothing that would be wearable for more than one or two seasons. Clothes that are ageless, and clothes that are so simple that they let the personality speak for itself.

This book is written for all who want to sew their own clothes.

It is quite possible to make all of one's clothing by beginning with the various basic patterns for tops, pants, and skirts and then combining them, varying them, for an infinite array of possibilities. At the same time, these patterns form a solid foundation for freely developing one's own ideas.

For most of the examples in this book, the patterns must be adapted to some extent before they can be used. Examples marked with * are fairly simple to make and demand very little experience, while examples marked with ** are for the more practiced hand. For both groups there are thorough directions for drawing the patterns and using them.

Some suggestions for variations are marked ***, indicating that you yourself must make the additional pieces and adjustments to the patterns and decide how to proceed.

This is a book to be used. There are no riddles, but, like all tools, one must know how to use it to get the best results. You must, therefore, read the section USING THE PATTERNS first of all, and then the more specific sections on materials and various sewing techniques as you need them.

It is important to keep in mind the material and the cut as a whole and let these two elements work together to support and accentuate each other. To these are added the body itself and its coloring. These elements taken together, along with the personality, create a complete picture. There is more on this on the following pages.

Elsebeth Gynther

The author designed the patterns in this book and wrote the sewing instructions using metric measurements. Although the metric system allows more precise measurement, and although sewing room tools now are marked with centimeters as well as inches, we realize there are many sewers who simply are not comfortable with the metric system. For their convenience we have given all measurements in inches as well. Exact conversion from one system to the other often produces fractions that are impossible to measure; therefore, adjustments have been made in some cases in order to present the measurements in a workable form. For this reason, IT IS VERY IMPORTANT TO CHOOSE ONE SYSTEM OF MEASURE-MENT OR THE OTHER, then to stay with it throughout a project. —Ed.

Introduction

Before we can begin to think about clothes as anything more than purely functional, we must accept the innate craving and love we have of ornamenting ourselves and surrounding ourselves with things we find beautiful—and accept that our clothing is part of the way we express ourselves as individuals.

Taste and style are very personal, whether or not the world in general values them as "personal." In fact, we express a great deal about ourselves in our outward appearance, through our clothes, our hair, our make-up, our body language, and our use of spoken language.

Clothes create the person, but first people create clothes, and we ourselves choose how we will express our personality—at least in our clothes and style.

But many people have trouble finding what one might call their "personal style," and their wardrobe consists of a lot of uncoordinated pieces of clothing in more or less random colors.

The body is the starting point upon which we base our choices of clothes. To this, add skin and hair tones and eye color. We can, to a certain extent, work with the body's form and carriage, which are essential for the overall impression as they are greatly influenced by health, personality, and radiance. But we can't change the body's basic form. And instead of being constantly unhappy with nature's gifts, we should work toward accepting ourselves as we are and using the existing material in the best possible way.

The body's proportions control which cut will complement each person. An outfit that is striking on a small, round person may be all wrong for a tall, thin person. This means that one must be cautious about using the ideas of people who have another starting point—different body proportions—from oneself, because it is always the overall picture that makes the impression.

Not only are height and weight important. The width of the shoulders, the waist, the width and shape of the hips, the comparative length of arms and legs and the shape and length of the neck—these are all details that influence the whole. And then, one can, according to one's taste and temperament, choose to emphasize, camouflage, or show the body as it is.

Two colors, each lovely in itself, can entirely ruin each other when put together. In the same way, a person's own coloring can be "ruined" by clothing of an uncomplimentary color. We have the colors which nature has given us: we get more out of building on them than from fighting them. The wrong color clothing can drain one's own coloring or give the face an unattractive cast. And then it's the color of the clothes others will notice instead of you. And there's not much point in that.

Color choice is also important if you use make-up. Colors that don't complement one's own can make one look almost sick. Try, therefore, to find tones you like and which best accent your own coloring, the way you want it to look.

It isn't my intention to set up rules for what is right or wrong, beautiful or ugly, as I have none and don't believe in rules anyway when it comes to personality. It must be your own individual taste, imagination and physical type that make your style. To use one's time and energy to find a personal style takes training, of course, and patience, and a genuine interest. In doing this, it is helpful to notice the small characteristics that create the whole, to be in a position to direct rather than to be directed in one's choices. Fashion can be hard to escape, and many people let themselves be led by it. But if we can regard fashion as a slate of choices, an inspiration at the points where we find it most attractive, then it will be fashion that is used, and not the person.

EASY STYLE

"It's said that women adorn themselves for men or for one another, but I don't believe this is correct. A woman's clothing only expresses the flowering of her personality."

— *Karen Blixen (Isak Dinesen)*

Blouse with Shawl Collar★

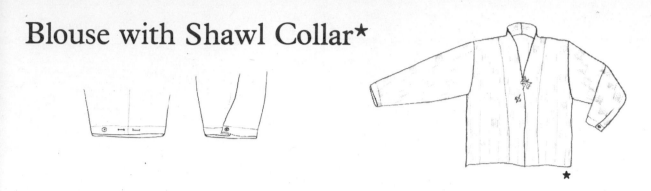

A blouse with a shawl collar made with Basic Pattern B with set-in sleeves. The front is closed with a big, handsome stickpin, and the sleeves are fastened at the wrists with two buttonholes and a button. The collar, which is part of the front pieces, can be varied widely. (See collars on pp. 29, 63, 66, and 69.)

The little shirt buttons in front and has a piped collar. It can also be made with a round neck and a sewn-on collar like the shirt on p. 22, which has a shirt collar and yoke.

• The fabric, viscose rayon, looks nice for festive occasions, but any light fabric will work well.

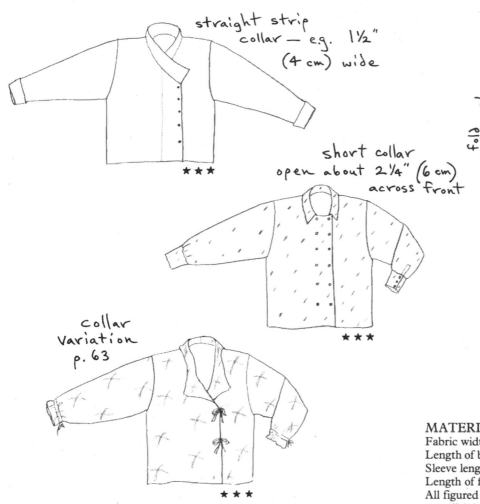

straight strip collar — e.g. 1½" (4 cm) wide

★ ★ ★

short collar open about 2¼" (6 cm) across front

★ ★ ★

collar variation p. 63

★ ★ ★

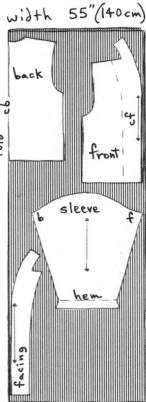

width 55" (140cm)

back
cb
fold
cf
front
sleeve
b
f
hem
facing

MATERIALS

Fabric width 55" (140 cm)
Length of blouse + 4" (10 cm) for collar x 1
Sleeve length (+ hem) x 1
Length of facing
All figured by size and exact fabric width,
   + 4" (10 cm) for seam allowances
2 buttons

CONSTRUCTION

1. Cut out all pieces, adding a ⅜" (1 cm) seam allowance and a 1¼" (3 cm) hem allowance at the bottom edge. Mark centerline of the sleeve and the center back.

2. Zigzag raw edges at the shoulders, armholes, sleeve caps, and the sleeve and side seams. If the fabric frays easily, zigzag all edges.

3. Stitch front/collar sections together at center back. Stitch center back seam in facing. Press seams open. Turn under the seam allowance on neckline edge of the collar facing; press. With right sides together, pin and sew facings to fronts at the collar, front edge, and bottom. Press seams open. Trim corners and notch all curves. Turn right side out. Pin and topstitch.

4. Sew shoulder seams and the neck/collar, right sides together (see p. 176).

5. Sew side and sleeve seams, right sides together, and press.

6. Pin sleeves into armholes, right sides together, matching underarm seam to side seam, and midpoint of sleeve cap to shoulder seam; stitch in place. Press seams open.

7. Turn the hem up double, press, and pin in place. Pin inner edge of facing to the blouse front. At neck back, fold raw edges under, out of sight. Stitch the facings down, and hem the bottom.

8. Turn up lower edges of sleeves ¼" (½ cm) then 1¼" (3½ cm), and hem. Make a buttonhole ⅝" (1½ cm) from each side of sleeve seam, in the middle of the hem. Sew a button to the middle of the hem in the center of sleeve back.

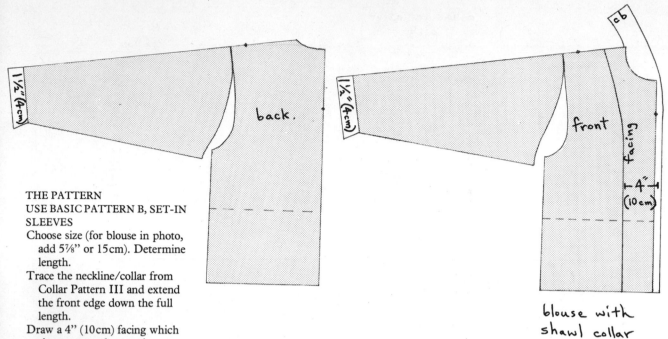

back.

front

facing

1½" (4cm)

1½" (4cm)

cb

4" (10cm)

blouse with shawl collar

THE PATTERN
USE BASIC PATTERN B, SET-IN
SLEEVES

Choose size (for blouse in photo, add 5⅞" or 15cm). Determine length.

Trace the neckline/collar from Collar Pattern III and extend the front edge down the full length.

Draw a 4" (10cm) facing which slants outward up to the shoulder line.

Allow a 1½" (4cm) hem at the wrist.

Pin front and back sleeve pieces together to make a one-piece sleeve.

Shirt with Facings★★

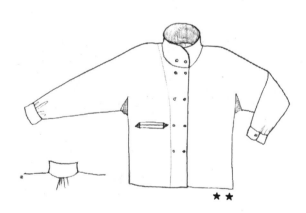

★★

A double-breasted shirt with a generous collar. Closes with snap fasteners, but can just as well be made with buttons if you prefer. Kimono-cut with sleeve gussets for easy movement (Basic Pattern C), it has extra fullness in back, and is gathered at the neckline. The facings, the inside of the collar, the insides of the cuffs and the gussets are in a darker tone, but the effect can be emphasized by using a contrasting color. The bound pocket is bracketed with two small triangles of the second color. Be careful not to put the pocket too low if the shirt is to be worn with a belt or tucked in at the waist.

• Here the design is made of cotton flannel, both warm and soft to wear. Cotton chamois or ordinary soft muslin would also work well, or it could be made up in raw silk, or in sweatshirt fabric, possibly with woven fabric for trim. There are many interesting possibilities in patterned fabrics as well—flowers and stripes might be an exciting combination.

• The design would work well lengthened into a smock (stopping at mid-thigh) or a dress, possibly with large inset pockets. And finally, it could be made in a heavier fabric and worn as a light jacket.

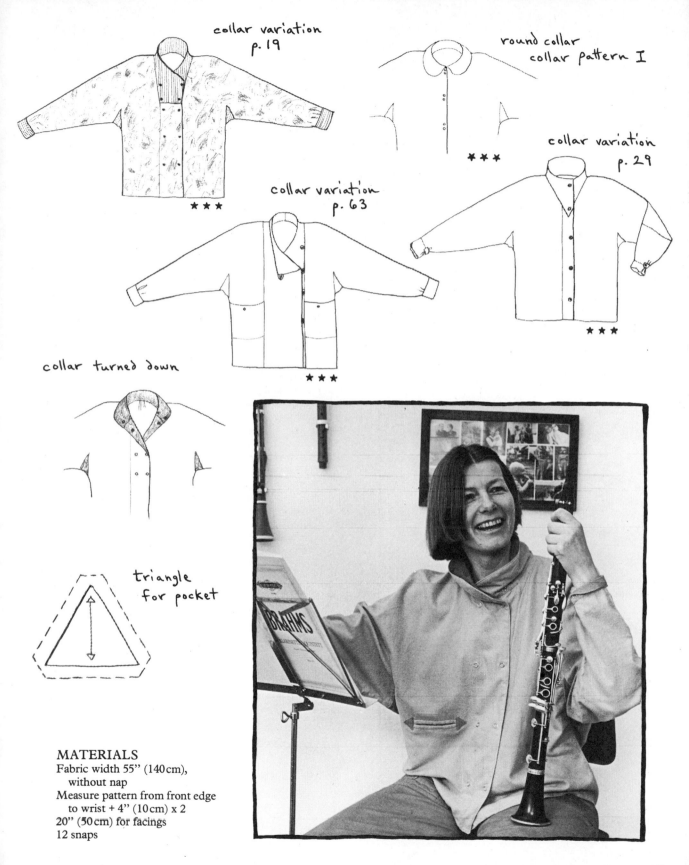

collar variation
p. 19

★ ★ ★

round collar
collar pattern I

★ ★ ★

collar variation
p. 63

★ ★ ★

collar variation
p. 29

★ ★ ★

collar turned down

triangle
for pocket

MATERIALS
Fabric width 55" (140 cm),
   without nap
Measure pattern from front edge
   to wrist + 4" (10 cm) x 2
20" (50 cm) for facings
12 snaps

CONSTRUCTION

1. Cut out all pieces, adding ⅜" (1 cm) seam allowance and ¾" (2 cm) for a hem at the bottom. Cut out under-arm gussets, cuffs (patterns for these are on pages 141 and 156), facings, and facings for cuffs and collar in a different color or shade. Mark center back, center front, pockets, and slits for underarm gussets.

2. Cut out and make the bound pocket, cutting the pocket bag and bindings in one piece (see p. 144). Sew a little triangle of the contrasting fabric at each end of the pocket.

3. Sew fronts to back at shoulder/sleeve seams. Zigzag, then stitch the seam allowance down.

4. Zigzag the edges of the sleeve/side seams and sew them. Zigzag edges of gussets and sew them in. Stitch the seams down.

5. Gather 2½" (6 cm) of the back at the neck, then sew the outer collar to the neckline, right sides together.

6. Sew facings and inner collar together from shoulder to front edge. Turn under and press a ⅜" (1 cm) seam allowance on the inner edge of the facing. Pin the shirt and the facing together at the collar, front edge, and lower edge, right sides together, and stitch. Turn right side out, tack inner edge of facing in place, and top-stitch. Slipstitch inner collar to neckline.

7. Sew triangular gussets in underarm seams (p. 156), and make the cuffs (p. 157).

8. Hem the bottom.

9. Measure in from the edge and mark for snaps or buttons in two rows 2" (5 cm) apart: place first pair on the collar ¾" (2 cm) above the collar seam, the next pair ¾" (2 cm) below it, then add three more pairs, about 5" (12-14 cm) apart. Set a snap in each cuff as well.

THE PATTERN
USE BASIC PATTERN C, KIMONO

Choose size (for shirt in photo, add 12" or 30 cm). Determine length.

Trace the pattern, marking the slit for the gusset.

Trace neckline and collar from Collar Pattern I and extend the front edge 1¾" (4½ cm) the full length.

Draw in a 3½" (9 cm) facing that slants toward the shoulder line.

On right side, mark placement lines for a pocket: 4" (10 cm) wide, 14-15" (35-38 cm) from shoulder, and 3¼" (8 cm) from center front.

Taper the sleeves to 4½" (11-12 cm) at the wrist (optional).

Add 1¼" (3 cm) to center back for pleat.

Mark slit for the gusset and draw cuffs following the drawing below.

Make gusset and triangle from patterns on p. 141 and p. 156.

Draw the pocket bindings and the pocket bag (see step 1 on this page.

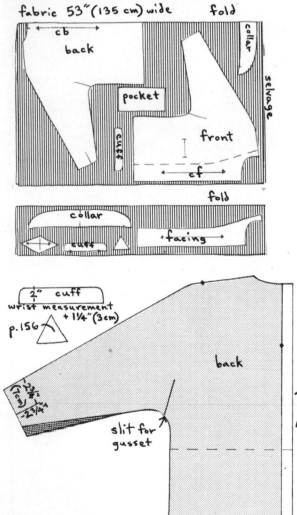

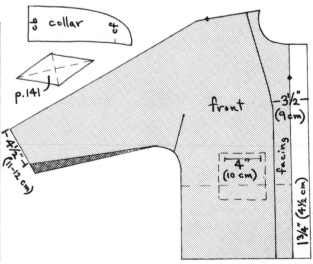

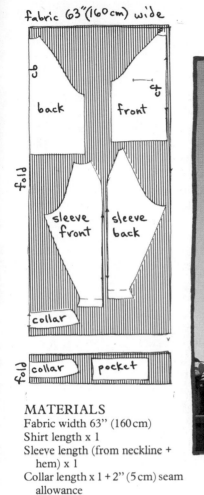

fabric 63" (160 cm) wide

back

front

fold

sleeve front

sleeve back

collar

fold collar   pocket

Sweatshirt★

MATERIALS
Fabric width 63" (160 cm)
Shirt length x 1
Sleeve length (from neckline + hem) x 1
Collar length x 1 + 2" (5 cm) seam allowance
Contrast fabric: appr. 6" (15 cm) for collar and pocket
3 snaps • 6" (15 cm) ribbing

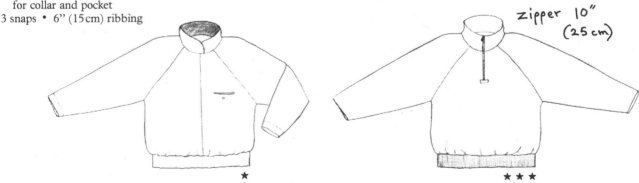

★

zipper 10" (25 cm)

★ ★ ★

A raglan pullover (Basic Pattern D) with an overlapping collar and a bound breast pocket in a contrasting color. The sleeves fasten with snaps at the wrists, but instead could have ribbing like that used for the bottom edge.

• The design here is made of sweatshirt material, the best possible fabric for this kind of shirt. It comes in heavy and light weights and with a waffled or rough inner surface. See the section on Working with Knit Fabrics, p. 125.

• There are many possible variations. Look over the suggestions here.

button or snap closure

★ ★ ★

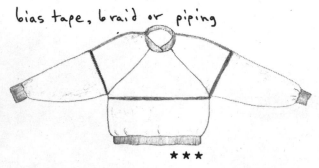

bias tape, braid or piping

★ ★ ★

CONSTRUCTION

1. Cut the raglan seams, upper sleeve seams, center front, collar and neckline, adding ⅜" (1 cm) seam allowance. The undersleeve/side seams are cut with ⅛-⅜" (½-1 cm) seam allowance, depending on the kind of seam to be used. The finished width of the ribbing is 2¾" (7 cm); see p. 127 for the length. In a contrasting color, cut out an inner collar and a pocket bag 4¾ x 9½" (12 x 24 cm) for a pocket 4" wide (10 cm). Mark center back on collar and on back.

2. Mark pocket placement (see p. 144) 8½-9½" (22-24 cm) from the neckline, and 2¼-3¼" (6-8 cm) from center front and at a right angle to it. Make the pocket.

3. Sew center front seam, zigzag the seam allowances and stitch them down. Sew front and back sleeve pieces together, and sew sleeves to front and back pieces the same way.

4. Sew underarm/side seams.

5. Sew inner collar to outer collar, right sides together. Turn, and topstitch. Pin collar to neck, right sides together, matching midpoints of backs. Front edges of collar will overlap about ¾" at center front. Sew with the most flexible seam possible, as the neck opening must slip over the head. Zigzag and stitch down seam allowances with zigzag or a stretch stitch.

6. Sew ribbed edging as described on p. 127. Turn up sleeve hems and snaps set near the lower edge, with the upper part ⅜" (1 cm) and the lower part 2" (5 cm) from the underarm seam.

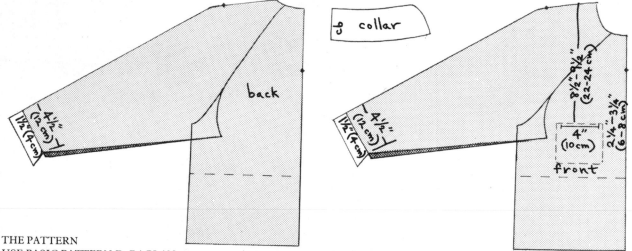

THE PATTERN
USE BASIC PATTERN D, RAGLAN
Choose size (for shirt in photo, add 6" or 15 cm). Determine length.
Taper sleeve to about 4¾" (12 cm) at the wrist and add 1½" (4 cm) for hem.
Mark breast pocket placement, 4" (10 cm) wide, 8½-9½" (22-24 cm) under the neckline and 2¼-3¼" (6-8 cm) from center front.
Trace neckline and collar from Collar Pattern I. It must be at least the head measurement minus 2" (5 cm).
For ribbing and pocket bag, see step 1 on this page.

18

A jogging suit of sweatshirt fabric, very simple, with dropped shoulders (Basic Pattern A)—the cut offering greatest freedom of movement. It features a sporty collar, trim on the sleeves, and ribbing at the wrists and waist. It can have, or do without, pockets at the side seams. See the section on Working with Knits, p. 125.

Jogging Suit*

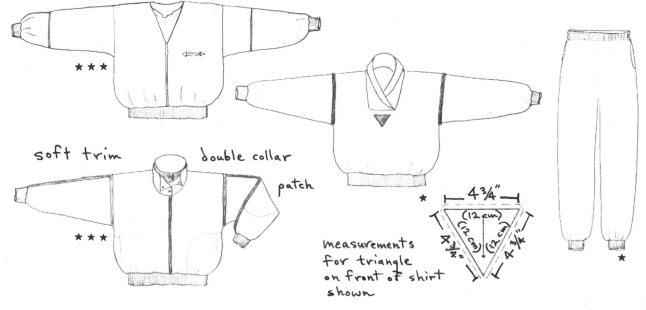

large inset triangle

★ ★ ★

soft trim

double collar

patch

★ ★ ★

measurements for triangle on front of shirt shown

* ┣━ 4¾" ━┫
(12 cm)
(12 cm)
4¾"
4¾"

*

CONSTRUCTION

Top:

1. Allow ⅜" (1 cm) seam allowance on all edges. Cut collar on double thickness of fabric. Mark the center on front, back, and collar pieces. Mark center line of sleeves. Ribbing at the waist and wrists is adjusted to fit the body measurements (see page 127). Cut two strips of ribbing for the trim, 1½" (4cm) wide and the length of the sleeve cap.

2. Sew shoulder seams with seam tape to lessen the stretch, and sew seam allowances down (optional).

3. Sew outer edges of collar together, with right sides together. Turn right side out and topstitch. Pin both layers of collar to center back and front corners of the neckline. Clip corners to seamline (see drawing, right). Sew the collar from one of these corners around the back of the neck to the other corner, but don't sew the horizontal seam in front yet. Overlap collar pieces in front, and pin them to the front. Be sure the corners lie flat. Stitch together and sew the seam down, stitching from the right side of the fabric all the way around.

4. Fold to ¾" (2cm) the ribbing to be used for trim. Lay the folded strip on the right side of the front/back armhole with the fold facing away from the edge. Pin, then sew, the sleeve on top of this, matching the center point to the shoulder seam.

5. Sew the sleeve/side seams.

6. Sew the ribbing to the sleeves and at the waist as described on p. 127.

7. Sew the triangle—or a decoration of your choice—to the front.

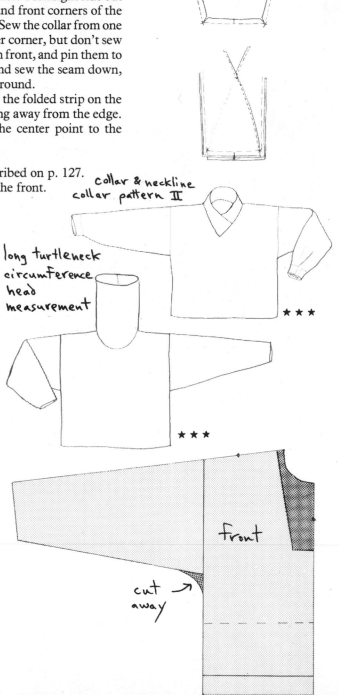

collar & neckline
collar pattern II

long turtleneck
circumference
head
measurement

* * *

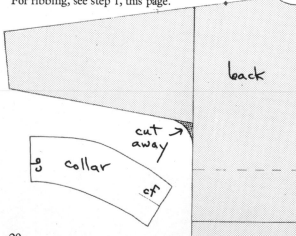

patches cut
with seam
allowance

* * *

PATTERN FOR TOP
USE BASIC PATTERN A, DROPPED SHOULDERS
Choose size (for version in the photo, add 9¾" or 25cm).
    Determine length.
Draw the sleeve seam by continuing the side seamline straight
    up to the shoulder. Add ease at the point where the sleeve
    joins the bodice at the underarm.
Use Collar Pattern II for the neckline and collar.
For ribbing, see step 1, this page.

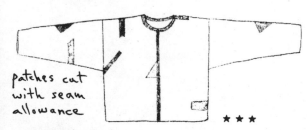

back

front

cut away

cut away

collar

cf

CONSTRUCTION: *Pants:*

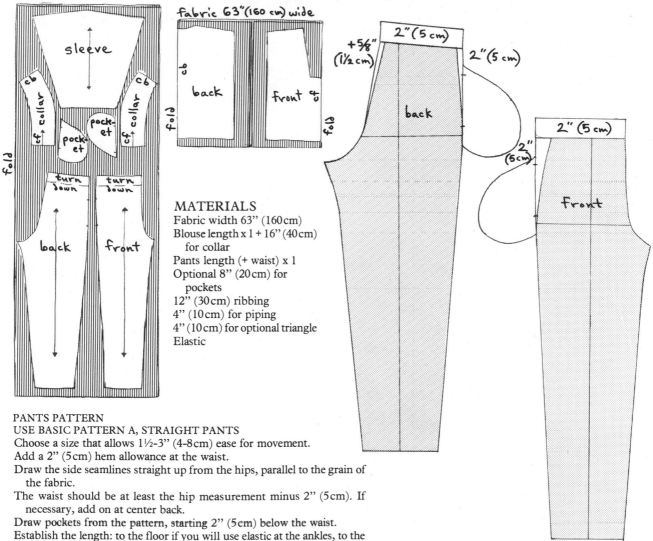

1. Cut out all pieces, adding ¼ to ⅜" (½-1 cm) seam allowance, depending on the kind of seam to be used. Cut length to the ankle if ribbing will be added, or to the floor if you plan a casing and elastic. Cut the ribbing (see p. 127). Pockets can be cut out as a part of the front and back pieces, or they can be cut separately and sewn in. Mark the waist and the placement of the pocket openings.
2. Sew the center back seam from the waist down. Sew the center front seam.
3. Sew pocket pieces on. Sew the side seams and the pockets together as shown in the drawing at left.
4. Sew the inseams.
5. Sew the upper edge: fold down, following your waist markings, and sew the casing for a single wide piece of elastic, or three rows of stitching for three narrow pieces. If using wide elastic, pull it through, then butt the ends and zigzag them together. Pull the elastic out, and distribute the fabric evenly along it, so that the waist lies smoothly. Pin, crosswise to the seam line, at the sides and centers. Sew three rows of stitching through the elastic, while stretching it out. If using three narrow pieces of pants elastic, pull each through its casing.
6. Sew ribbing, or elastic casing, at the ankles.

MATERIALS
Fabric width 63" (160cm)
Blouse length x 1 + 16" (40cm)
   for collar
Pants length (+ waist) x 1
Optional 8" (20cm) for
   pockets
12" (30cm) ribbing
4" (10cm) for piping
4" (10cm) for optional triangle
Elastic

PANTS PATTERN
USE BASIC PATTERN A, STRAIGHT PANTS
Choose a size that allows 1½-3" (4-8cm) ease for movement.
Add a 2" (5cm) hem allowance at the waist.
Draw the side seamlines straight up from the hips, parallel to the grain of the fabric.
The waist should be at least the hip measurement minus 2" (5cm). If necessary, add on at center back.
Draw pockets from the pattern, starting 2" (5cm) below the waist.
Establish the length: to the floor if you will use elastic at the ankles, to the ankle if you will add ribbing.
Taper the leg width at the bottom (p. 108) if desired.

Summer Shirt*

A shirt with set-in sleeves (Basic Pattern B), a little shirt collar, a buttoned front, a pleat in back, and short, cuffed sleeves. Here it's made of very summery fabric, but with long sleeves and another fabric it could as easily be a year-round shirt.

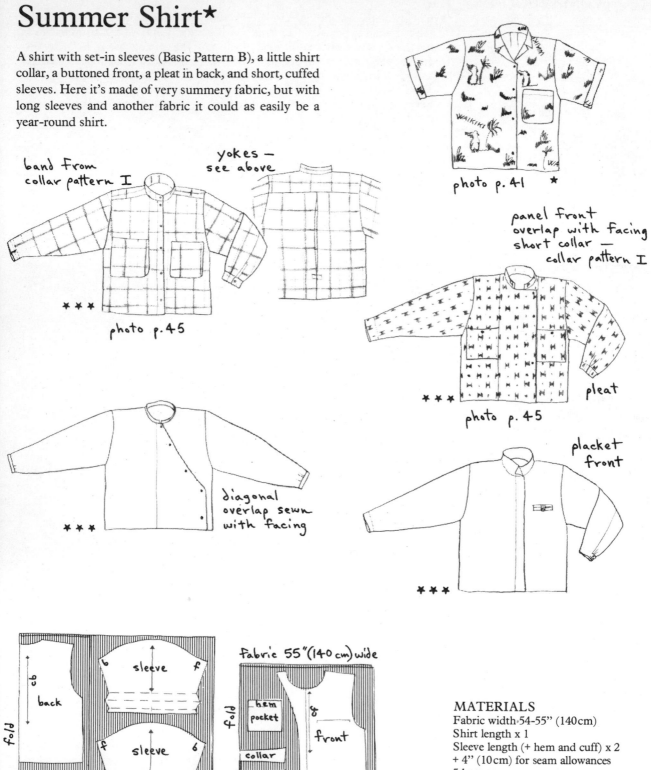

band from collar pattern I

yokes — see above

*** photo p. 45

photo p. 41 *

panel front overlap with facing short collar — collar pattern I

*** pleat

photo p. 45

diagonal overlap sewn with facing

***

placket front

***

Fabric 55" (140 cm) wide

fold

cb back

sleeve

sleeve

hem pocket

collar

collar

fold

fg

front

fabric doubled

single layer

MATERIALS
Fabric width 54-55" (140cm)
Shirt length x 1
Sleeve length (+ hem and cuff) x 2
+ 4" (10cm) for seam allowances
5 buttons

CONSTRUCTION:

1. Cut all pieces, adding ⅜" (1 cm) seam allowance and 1¼" (3 cm) hem at the bottom. Mark center front, the overlap of the fronts at top and bottom, the pleat in back, foldline for pocket hem, and foldlines for sleeve hems.
2. Fold and press the front edges (the raw edge of the facing, and the foldline), the pocket seam allowances and hem, the back pleat, the sleeve hems and cuff foldlines, and the neckline seam allowance on the inner collar.
3. Fold in the front facings with right sides together. If desired, pin a button loop, 1¼" (3 cm) long, into the seam (see drawing, upper right). Sew ⅝" (1½ cm) from the foldline to the center front line. Turn right side out, pin and stitch the lower front edges.
4. Pin the back pleat and stitch down about 4" (10 cm) from the top. Make stitching lines equal on both sides of pleat, as shown in the drawing below.
5. Sew shoulder seams, zigzag the seam allowance and stitch down toward the back.

6. Sew on the collar as a turned collar (p. 175).
7. Sew in the sleeves, right sides together, matching midpoint of sleeve to shoulder seam. Zigzag and stitch down the seam allowance.
8. Stitch pocket hem. Pin pocket to left front and sew it on.
9. Zigzag and sew sleeve/side seams. Press the seams.
10. Pin sleeve hems, folding up ⅜" (1 cm) then 2¼" (6 cm). Stitch. Fold a 1½" (4 cm) cuff, and tack in place at the underarm seam.
11. Turn up a double hem at the bottom edge; stitch.
12. Sew five or six buttonholes down the front (p. 164), the top one ¾" (2 cm) below the neckline, the others 4" (10 cm) apart. Sew buttons on the opposite front.

making a yoke

1   2

THE PATTERN
USE BASIC PATTERN B, SET-IN SLEEVES

Choose size (for version in photo, add 8" or 20 cm). Decide length and sleeve length.

Front edge: add ⅝" (1½ cm) at center front, fold the pattern on that line and draw the inner facing and the neckline, 1¼" (3 cm) wide at the lower edge slanting up to 2½" (6 cm) at the shoulder.

Add 1½" (4 cm) for a pleat at center back.

Shorten the sleeves to the desired length and add 1½" + 1½" + ¾" (4 + 4 + 2 cm) to that for a cuff and hem (p. 115).

Draw the pocket, about 6¼" (16 cm) wide and 6¾" (17 cm) high, + 1¼" (3 cm) for a hem.

Draw the collar pattern in the desired neck size from Collar Pattern I.

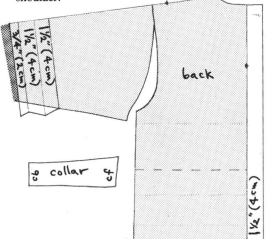

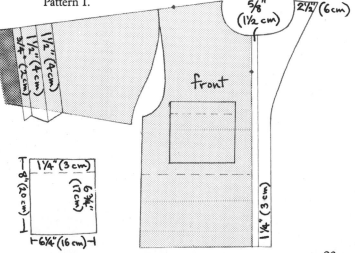

Tunic*

Made using Basic Pattern A with dropped shoulders, the tunic here has three-quarter length sleeves and is cut under the bust for the deep soft pleat that creates the drape in front. The slits in the side are 12" (30 cm) long. If the tunic is lengthened, the slits too should be lengthened, to 16" (40 cm). Although the design shown here is made of sweatshirt fabric, it could also be made of wool, mohair, knits, leather, heavy raw silk, or winter cottons. The stretch pants are described on p. 37.

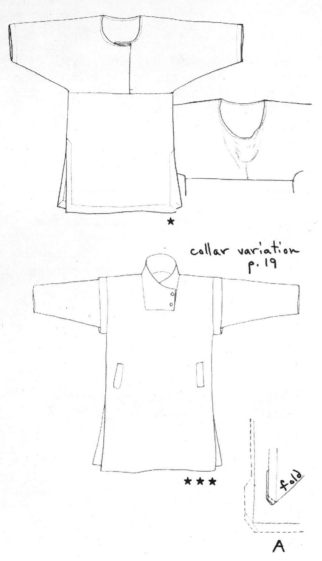

collar variation p. 19

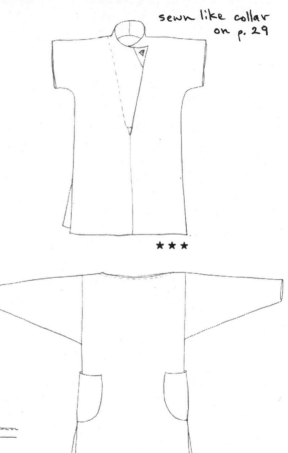

sewn like collar on p. 29

CONSTRUCTION

1. Cut pieces with ⅜" (1 cm) seam allowance at the shoulders/sleeves, sleeves/sides, slits/lower edge and the front horizontal cut. The neckline is cut with no seam allowance. Mark the top of the slit and the center front of the upper front piece for the pleat. Cut a strip 1½" (4 cm) wide and long enough to edge the neckline.
2. Zigzag all edges.
3. Fold the pleat at center front and, with right sides together, sew upper front to lower front. Stitch down the seam allowances, or press seam open.
4. Sew shoulder/sleeve seams and press seams open.
5. Zigzag one long edge of the neckline trim. Sew the other edge to neckline, right sides together. Turn, pin, and stitch on the right side in the seam furrow (see Trimming, p. 152).
6. Sew sleeve/side seams to the slit marking. Press.
7. Fold corners of slit hem together, mark the seam and sew (see diagram A). Press, turn and stitch down inner edge of slit (diagram B). For woven fabric, turn up the edge ¼" then 1¼" (1 + 3 cm). For knit fabric or leather, turn up a single hem.
8. Hem the sleeves.

THE PATTERN
USE BASIC PATTERN A, DROPPED SHOULDERS

Choose a size that allows 6-8" (15-20cm) ease at the hips.
   Determine length.

Draw in the crosswise cut 14-16" (35-40cm) below shoulder
   and at a right angle to center front line. Add 4" (10cm) to
   center front of the top part for a pleat.

Lower the front neckline by ¾" (2cm).

Draw in the sleeve length 25½-27½" (65-70cm) from the
   center front/center back lines, at a right angle to the sleeve/
   shoulder line and slanting toward the horizontal cut under
   the sleeves.

Trace the sleeve back from the sleeve front.

Add ¾" (2cm) width at the lower edge and slant the side line
   from that point up to the base of the sleeve line.

Draw the slit up to 10-12" (25-30cm) from bottom edge and
   add 1½" (4cm) hem allowance to slit, to bottom edge and at
   wrists.

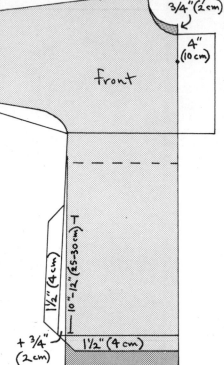

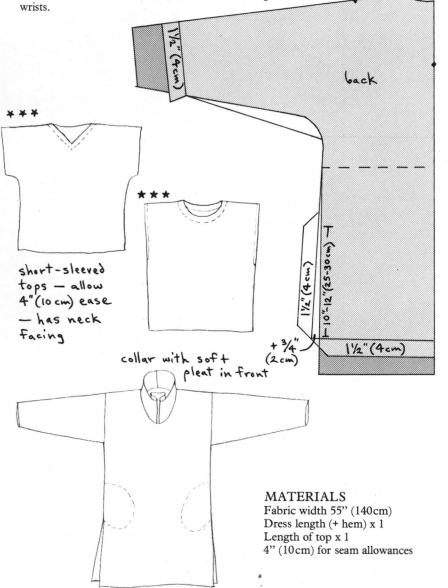

★ ★ ★

★ ★ ★

short-sleeved
tops — allow
4"(10cm) ease
— has neck
facing

collar with soft
pleat in front

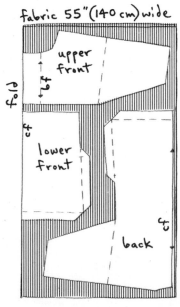

MATERIALS
Fabric width 55" (140cm)
Dress length (+ hem) x 1
Length of top x 1
4" (10cm) for seam allowances

★ ★ ★

26

Drcss*

As simple as can be, this dress is made with the kimono-cut Basic Pattern C. It has a round neckline with buttons on the shoulders and long sleeves that taper a little at the wrists so they can be pushed up. It is mid-calf length, and there are side slits with buttons. The dress can also be made with other basic patterns and with almost any of the collars, and could have pockets in the side seams like those in the jogging suit on p. 21.

• Sweatshirt fabric was used for this design, but the dress could also be made of woven fabric, possibly with a seam and a kick pleat in the back.

• The dress is slightly narrower toward the bottom. If you don't care for this look, you could make it straight up and down, or have it flare slightly at the hem.

photo p. 25

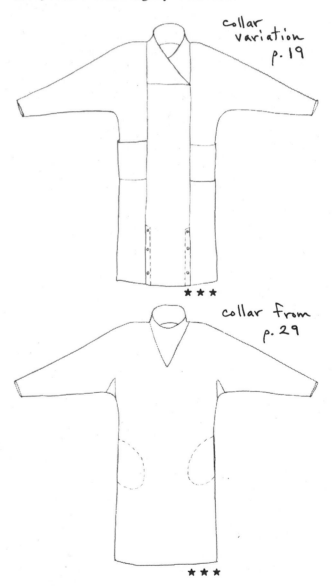

★

collar variation p. 19

★ ★ ★

collar from p. 29

★ ★ ★

CONSTRUCTION

1. Cut the sleeve/side and shoulder/sleeve seams, adding ⅛-⅜" (½-1 cm) seam allowance, depending on the kind of fabric and seam to be used (see Working with Knits, p. 125). Add ⅜" (1 cm) hem to the neckline, sleeves, and bottom edge. The button strips for the shoulders and sides are cut with no seam allowance.

2. If seams are to be pressed open, all edges should be zigzagged. If they are to be sewn with an overlock, zigzag only those edges that will not be sewn together.

3. Sew sleeve/shoulder seams up to the slits, using seam tape from the neck to the rounding of the shoulder. The slit at the neck is sewn like the slit in the two-part sleeve on p. 156, and with the overlap to the back. If desired, press fusible interfacing onto the overlap to support the buttonhole. Fold the overlap on the foldline, right sides together, and stitch along the neck seamline. Turn right side out and sew as instructed. For sweatshirt fabric, just turn the edge up once, as a double hem would make the edge too bulky.

4. Turn in ⅜" (1 cm) at the neckline, or sew seam tape or a narrow piece of bias tape to the neck edge to prevent stretching. Stitch the edge down and press.

5. Sew sleeve/side seams and make the slits according to directions given for shoulder slits.

6. Hem the bottom and sleeves.

7. Make a buttonhole on each shoulder, parallel with the shoulder seam. Make three buttonholes in each side slit, also parallel with the seam. Press all seams. Sew on buttons.

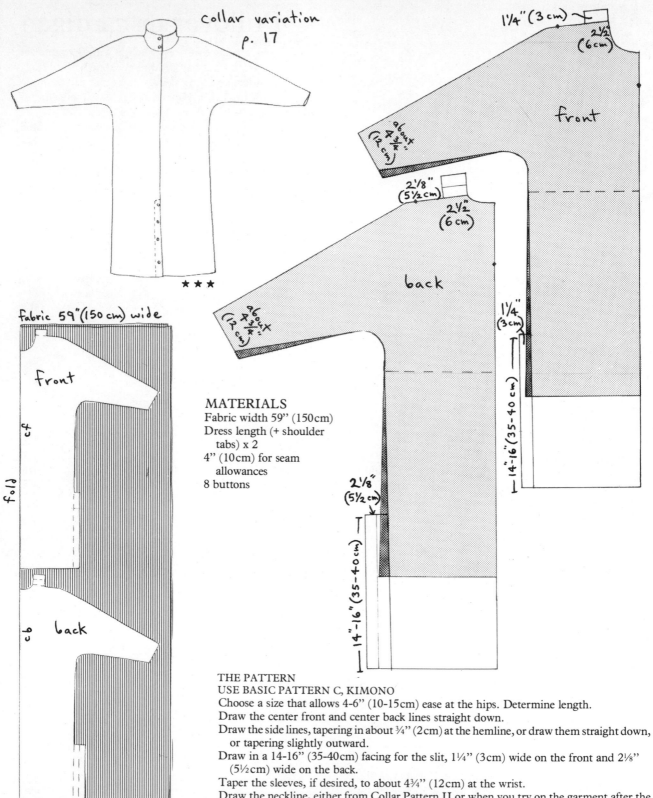

collar variation
p. 17

1¼" (3 cm)

2½" (6 cm)

front

about 4¾" (12 cm)

2⅛" (5½ cm)

2½" (6 cm)

back

1¼" (3 cm)

14"-16" (35-40 cm)

about 4¾" (12 cm)

2⅛" (5½ cm)

14"-16" (35-40 cm)

★ ★ ★

fabric 59" (150 cm) wide

fold

front

cf

back

cb

MATERIALS
Fabric width 59" (150cm)
Dress length (+ shoulder
 tabs) x 2
4" (10cm) for seam
 allowances
8 buttons

THE PATTERN
USE BASIC PATTERN C, KIMONO
Choose a size that allows 4-6" (10-15cm) ease at the hips. Determine length.
Draw the center front and center back lines straight down.
Draw the side lines, tapering in about ¾" (2cm) at the hemline, or draw them straight down,
 or tapering slightly outward.
Draw in a 14-16" (35-40cm) facing for the slit, 1¼" (3cm) wide on the front and 2⅛"
 (5½cm) wide on the back.
Taper the sleeves, if desired, to about 4¾" (12cm) at the wrist.
Draw the neckline, either from Collar Pattern II or when you try on the garment after the
 shoulder seams are sewn.
Draw in the shoulder openings, 2½" (6cm) along the shoulder line, 1¼" (3cm) wide on the
 front and 2⅛" (5½cm) wide on the back.

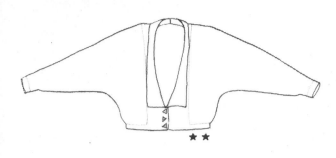

Pullover or cardigan with dolman sleeves ★★

★ ★

★ ★

The cardigan has a shawl collar, the pullover has a soft cowl, cut as a shawl collar. Both reach to the waist and fit quite snugly there, just as the sleeves fit snugly at the wrists. Both are made of a wool and mohair knit, which is available in many weights and with different percentages of wool, mohair, and sometimes polyester. It's wise to find a blend that doesn't itch, especially if you're sensitive to wool. The designs here are just as well suited to sweatshirt knits, but wool knit seems to hang more gracefully. See the section on Working with Knit Fabrics, p. 125. "Round" shoulder pads are sewn into both the pullover and the cardigan, but both also look nice without them (see Shoulder Pads, p. 158).

CONSTRUCTION

1. Cut out pattern pieces, adding ⅜" (1 cm) seam allowance all around, and 1½" (4 cm) hem allowance at wrists and bottom edges. Facing for the pullover is cut out along a fold in the fabric, and a 2½ x ¾" (6 x 2 cm) strip is cut for a button loop.

2. *Pullover:* Make and turn the button loop and pin it in place on the front seam, 3" (8 cm) from the upper edge. Sew the fronts together, zigzag seam allowances and stitch down.

   Both sweaters: Stitch back seams on collar and facing; zigzag inner edge of facing.

3. Pin back and front together at shoulder/neck seam, right sides together. If the fabric frays or ravels easily, sew a length of seam tape into the neck seam. Stitch, then zigzag the seam allowances and stitch down toward the back.

4. Zigzag the lower edges. Zigzag the sleeve/side seams unless they are sewn with an overlock stitch.

5. *Pullover:* Pin facing and sweater together along the upper edge, right sides together. Sew, turn facing to the inside and topstitch ¼" (¾ cm) from the edge with a narrow zigzag stitch. Pin and sew down the inner edge of the facing with a narrow zigzag.

   Cardigan: Pin the collar/front edge to facing with right sides together. The fabric should not be stretched during sewing: if it has a tendency to do so, stay stitch just inside the seamline with a soft thread, such as embroidery cotton. Seam tape would be a little heavy in these very light fabrics. On the other hand, be careful that the stitching doesn't pucker; it must lie completely flat. If there are to be buttonholes in the front, baste a piece of grosgrain ribbon (preshrunk so that it doesn't shrink later in the laundry), or other firm but soft ribbon, into the facing, right up to the seamline, and topstitch in place. Sew in the facing as described on p. 150.

6. Pin and sew the sleeve/side seams, right sides together.

7. Pin up the hems at the lower edge and the wrists and sew with a narrow zigzag stitch.

8. *Pullover:* Sew a button 1¼-1½" (3-4 cm) from the center front.

   Cardigan: Sew buttonholes and buttons down the front, or use decorative snaps.

9. If desired, make shoulder pads and sew them in place (p. 158).

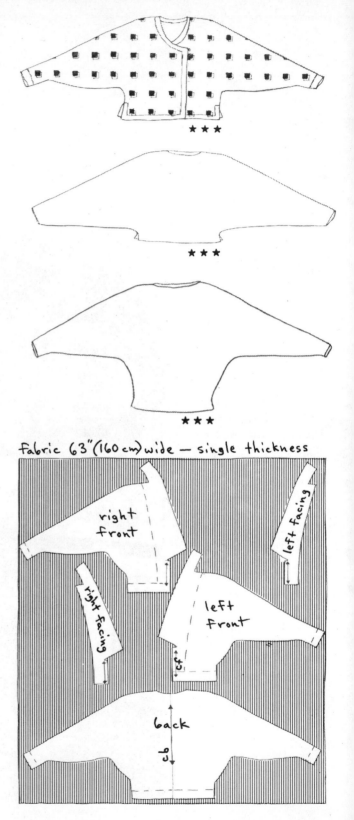

Fabric 63" (160 cm) wide — single thickness

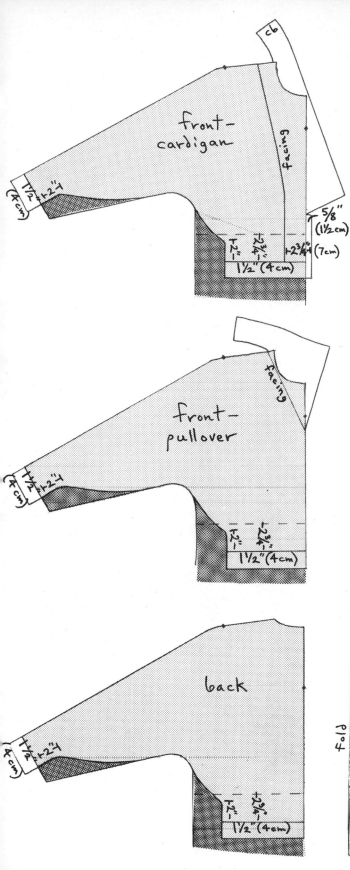

CARDIGAN PATTERN
USE BASIC PATTERN C, KIMONO

Choose size (for sweaters in photo, add 4¾" or 12cm).

Mark the length at about 2¾" (7cm) below the waistline.
  Measure the hips, divide by 4, and draw a line this length
  on the length line.

Draw straight up from this line for 2" (5cm), then draw a
  curved diagonal to the base of the sleeve.

Measure around the hand, divide by 2 and draw in this
  measurement at the wrist edge. Draw straight up for 2"
  (5cm), then curve gently to the lower edge of the sleeve.

Extend the sleeve/side seamline over onto the back, so that
  the front and back are the same.

Trace collar from Collar Pattern III.

Widen front by ⅝" (1½cm) from below collar to hem.

Draw a facing 2¾" (7cm) wide at the lower part and slanting up
  to the shoulder line.

Add a 1½" (4cm) hem at the wrists and bottom.

PULLOVER PATTERN

Draw the pattern just like the cardigan, except for the neckline,
  collar, and facings, which are found with Collar Pattern III.

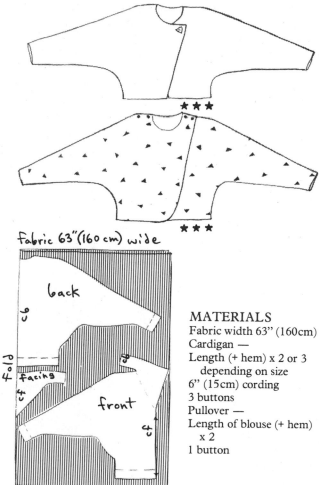

★ ★ ★

★ ★ ★

Fabric 63" (160 cm) wide

MATERIALS
Fabric width 63" (160cm)
Cardigan —
Length (+ hem) x 2 or 3
  depending on size
6" (15cm) cording
3 buttons
Pullover —
Length of blouse (+ hem)
  x 2
1 button

31

Dressy Slip-on Coat**

This open coat has broad tucks in the shoulders, waist-high slits in the sides and a wide, pointed collar. It comes to just above the knees, has generously wide sleeves, and has shoulder pads. It's made with Basic Pattern B with set-in sleeves, but could also be made with Basic Pattern A.

• The coat shown here is made of silk with a light, soft drape, but it could be made up in any fabric that drapes softly. In firmer fabrics, the tucks could be narrowed, or eliminated altogether.

★★

fabric 35"(90 cm)wide—double thickness

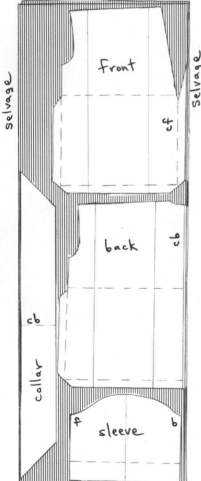

MATERIALS
Fabric width 35" (90 cm)
Length of coat (+ hem) x 4
Sleeve length (+ hem) x 2

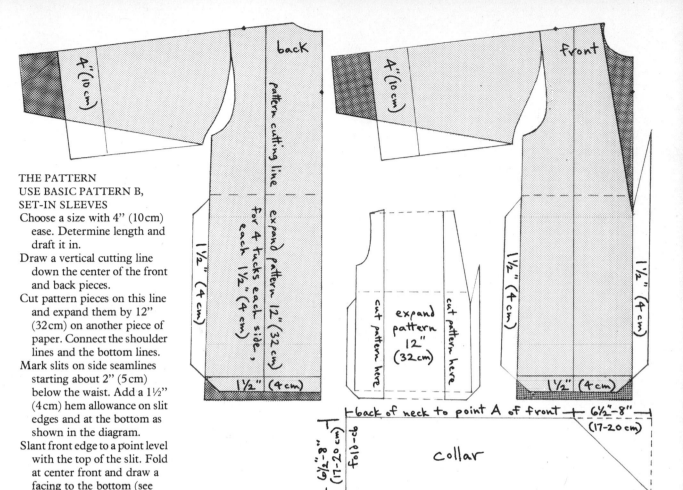

THE PATTERN
USE BASIC PATTERN B,
SET-IN SLEEVES

Choose a size with 4" (10cm) ease. Determine length and draft it in.

Draw a vertical cutting line down the center of the front and back pieces.

Cut pattern pieces on this line and expand them by 12" (32cm) on another piece of paper. Connect the shoulder lines and the bottom lines.

Mark slits on side seamlines starting about 2" (5cm) below the waist. Add a 1½" (4cm) hem allowance on slit edges and at the bottom as shown in the diagram.

Slant front edge to a point level with the top of the slit. Fold at center front and draw a facing to the bottom (see diagram).

Shorten sleeves to the midpoint of the underarm seam and add a 4" (10cm) hem allowance. Measure the width at the armhole and carry it straight down to the bottom edge.

Draw the collar according to the diagram at right.

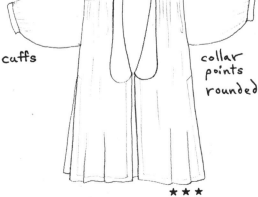

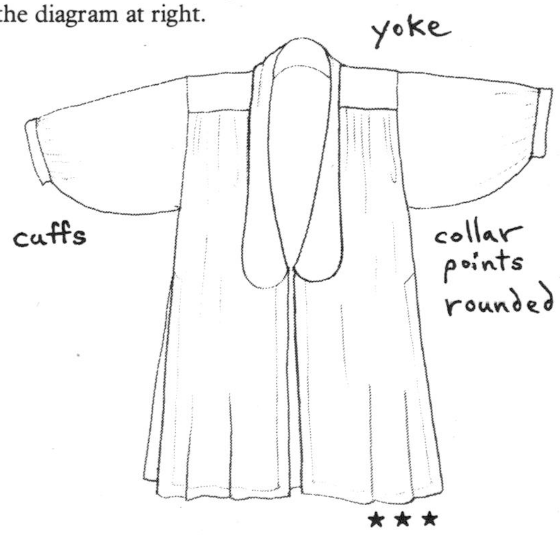

yoke

cuffs

collar points rounded

CONSTRUCTION

1. Cut all pieces, adding ⅜" (1cm) seam allowance to all edges except where hem allowances were added for slit, lower edge, front edge and sleeves, as shown in the pattern diagram. Mark center back.

2. Zigzag all raw seam allowances.

3. Sew center back and shoulder seams, and press. Mark tucks. This design has 4 tucks, each 1½" (4cm) deep, placed 1¼" (3cm) apart and so that the fold of the outermost tuck just reaches the shoulder seam. On front and back, pin and sew tucks to a point 6¼" (16cm) below shoulder seam.

4. Sew on the sleeves and sew sleeve/side seams down to the slit.

5. Press edges under, first ¼" (½cm), then 1¼" (3½cm). The front corners are sewn as on the dress on p. 24. Hem all the way around. Press sleeve hems up, first ¼" (½cm) then 3¾" (9½cm), and stitch.

6. Stitch the collar together and sew it on (p. 175).

7. If desired, make shoulder pads and sew them in place (p. 158).

Straight skirt*

A skirt made from Basic Pattern C, except for the pleats. It hangs to mid-calf, with a box pleat in front and back, a hidden zipper and a waistband. It can be varied in many ways: one way would be to expand the pattern to allow for pleats—about 4" (10 cm), as in the pants on p. 107. Another would be to make a fly front and inset pockets, or to make side slits as in the dress on p. 27. The design shown here was made of heavy raw silk and could be made of any fairly heavy fabric, as well as soft, light leathers, which work very well.

• See also the section on Lining Skirts, (p. 159).

photo p. 29*

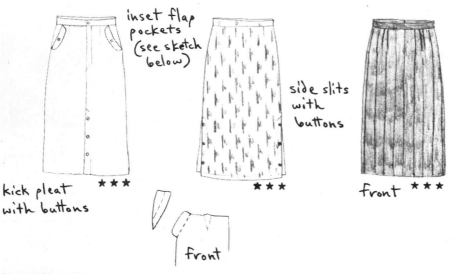

inset flap pockets (see sketch below)

side slits with buttons

kick pleat with buttons ★★★

★★★

front ★★★

back ★★★

front

fabric 35"(90 cm) wide

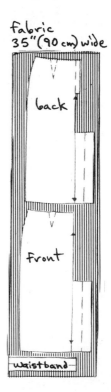

CONSTRUCTION

1. Cut out pieces, adding ⅜" (1 cm) seam allowance at the waist, sides, and center front and back. Cut the zipper placket with ¾" (2 cm) seam allowance, and the bottom edge with 1¼" (3 cm). Mark the foldlines of the pleats, and of any darts, with two notches at the waistline and a chalk mark at the bottom. Cut the waistband the length of the waist measurement + ¾" (2 cm) for overlap, and with a finished width of 1¼-1½" (3-4 cm) x 2. Add ⅜" (1 cm) seam allowance all the way around.
2. Zigzag all edges.
3. Pin and sew the darts and press them. Sew back sections together from the bottom of the zipper placket to the pleat. Sew in a hidden zipper (see p. 169).
4. Sew front sections together from waist to pleat. Make the pleats in front and back, folding fabric with right sides together. Press seams open. Fold and press on foldlines to form a box pleat (p. 139).
5. Sew side seams.
6. Sew on waistband (p. 154). Make the buttonholes and sew on buttons.
7. Hem the bottom. Topstitch folded edges of the pleats and stitch diagonally across the tops of the pleats on the outside with 2 lines of stitching as shown in the drawing above.

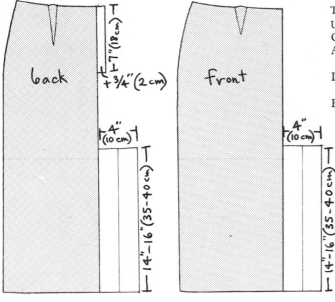

THE PATTERN
USE BASIC PATTERN C, STRAIGHT SKIRT
Choose size and determine length.
Add 4" (10 cm) for pleats at center front and center back, 14-16"
    (35-40cm) long.
Draw in a zipper placket, 7" (18cm) long, ¾" (2cm) wide, at the
    top center back.
For waistband, see step 1.

MATERIALS
Fabric width 35" (90cm)
Skirt length x 2
+ 4" (10cm) for waistband
+ 4" (10cm) for seam allowances
+ interfacing
7" (18cm) zipper • 1 button

Full Skirt★

A skirt made from Basic Pattern D—a full skirt, with narrow, soft pleats at the waist, bound pockets with loose flaps and a waistband that fastens in back. This design is pleated tightly all the way around, which means that the waist measurement must be multipled by 3 to get adequate fabric. If you have fairly ample hips, it would probably be more flattering to place the pleats a little further apart, in which case multiply the waist measurement by only 2 or 2½ and reduce the pattern accordingly (p. 97).
• The example shown is made of a medium weight nubby wool tweed. The thinner the fabric, the more width the skirt can bear. With very thin fabric the pleats can even be laid in so that they overlap.
• This skirt can also be combined with the top part of the straight skirt pattern for a yoke effect around the hips. Look over the suggestions.

buttoned inset pockets ★★

piped pockets with flaps ★★★

pockets as on culottes ★★★

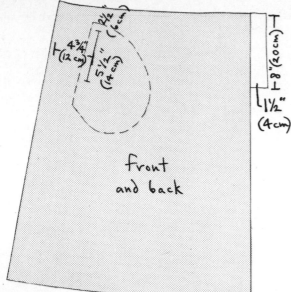

front
and back

4¾" (12 cm)

5½" (14 cm)

2½" (6 cm)

8" (20 cm)

1½" (4 cm)

THE PATTERN

USE BASIC PATTERN D, FULL SKIRT

Choose a size and determine the length.

The bottom edge should be at right angles to the side seams and
center lines.

Draw in a 1¼" (4 cm) wide, 6¼" (20 cm) long placket at top
center back.

Mark the pocket: 5½" (14 cm) wide, 2½" (6 cm) below the waist,
and 4½" (12 cm) from the side seam.

Make the pocket bag according to the pattern piece. For
waistband and pocket bindings, see step. 1

buttoned
side
opening

yoke
at hips
p. 112

★ ★ ★   ★ ★ ★

MATERIALS

Fabric width 59" (150 cm)
Skirt length x 2
+ 4" (10 cm) for waistband
+ 4" (10 cm) for seam allowances
10" (25 cm) fabric for pocket bag
Interfacing • 3 snaps • 1 button

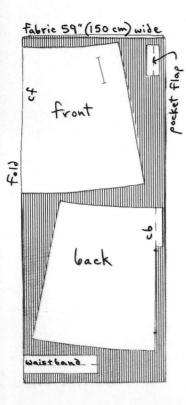

fabric 59" (150 cm) wide

fold

front

back

pocket flap

waistband

CONSTRUCTION

1. Cut out skirt, adding ⅜-⅝" (1-1½ cm) seam allowance at sides and at center back.
   Allow ⅜" (1 cm) at the waistline and 1¼" (3 cm) hem allowance. Cut waistband
   3½" (9 cm) wide for a finished width of 1¾" (4½ cm). Length = waist measure +
   1½" (4 cm) for overlap. Add ⅜" (1 cm) seam allowance all the way around. Cut
   the pocket bindings 3 x 7" (8 x 18 cm) for a pocket opening approximately 5½"
   (14 cm). Cut the pocket flaps 6 x 4" (15 x 10 cm) plus seam allowances. From
   thinner fabric, cut pocket bags and one facing for placket extension, 1½ x 8" (4 x
   20 cm) plus seam allowance.
   Mark center front, center back, and pocket openings.

2. Zigzag all edges.

3. Sew the pockets following the procedure for Pockets with Free-standing,
   Upturned Flaps (p. 147).

4. Sew the center back seam from ⅜" (1 cm) above the slit to the bottom edge. Turn
   placket extension to one side of center back line and stitch it down. Sew facing to
   placket extension, right sides together; turn, and topstitch. Sew the inner edge to
   the center back line.

5. Sew side seams.

6. Make 5-7 pleats, 1¼" (3 cm) deep. Pleat from the centerlines out toward the
   sides, so that the pleats "meet" at the sides. Try to make the pleats fall naturally
   around the pocket and the center back.

7. Sew on the waistband (p. 154). Make skirt hangers: sew a folded piece of twill
   tape about 8" (20 cm) long into the waistband seam at each side seam.

8. Hang skirt and hem the bottom.

9. Sew snaps on placket. Make buttonhole in waistband; sew on button.

Stretch Pants*

Stretch pants, or long underwear if you wish, are nice and warm to wear, whether under skirts, dresses, and pants, or as warm-up clothes for yoga, dancing, aerobics, etc. They can be made of any lighter weight knit fabric, like jersey, interlock, or a wool-mohair blend. As the fabric is most elastic in the crosswise direction, the pattern must be made somewhat tighter than the actual body measurements or the pants will be baggy after being worn a few hours. On the other hand, the length should not be changed unless you want the pants legs to lie in folds around the ankle, in which case add 4" (10cm) to the length.

CONSTRUCTION

1. Cut the fabric with ¼-⅜" (½-1 cm) seam allowance at center front, center back, side, and inseams, depending which kind of seam you're using (see Working with Knit Fabrics, p. 125). At the waistline, allow an extra 1¼" (3cm) to fold into a channel for the elastic. At the lower edge, allow ¾" (2cm) hem allowance, unless you are adding ribbed cuffs. The optional ribbing can be cut to the ankle measurement minus 1½" (4cm) and twice as long as the finished length. (Check to be sure it will slide over the heel.)
2. Sew center front and center back seams.
3. Sew side seams.
4. Sew inseams of the legs.
5. Sew the channel for the waist with a double needle seam, and pull elastic through. Sew the ends of the elastic together, then finish by closing the channel.
6. Hem the bottom with a row of double needle stitching, or sew on ribbed cuffs (see ribbed edging, p. 127). Try on the pants before putting on the ribbing, to be sure of length.

MATERIALS
Fabric width 50" (130cm)
Pants length (+ hem) x 1
Elastic

photo p. 25   ★

fabric 50"(130cm) wide

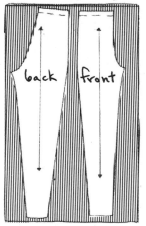

back   front

THE PATTERN
USE BASIC PATTERN A, STRAIGHT PANTS
Choose a size that fits your hip measurement.
Determine length.
Reduce the pattern by making a pleat ¾" (2cm) deep in front and back pattern pieces (overall reduction = 6" or 16cm).
Deduct 1⅛" (3cm) at back crotch point and ¾" (2cm) at front crotch point.
Narrow the ankle width on the back by 1⅛" (3cm) at side seam and inseam, and on the front by ¾" (2cm) on both sides.
Add ¾" (2cm) to waist at side seamline and draw a line to that point from the hip.
Connect the lines as shown at right.
The pattern should measure 2¼" (6cm) less at the calf than the actual calf measurement. If you have heavy calves, reduce the pattern by less below the calf and use ribbing at the ankles. For ribbing, draw a pattern 8" (20cm) long (finished length 3¾" or 9½cm) and as wide as the ankle measurement minus 1½" (4cm).
Add 1¼" (3cm) height at the waist for the elastic channel.

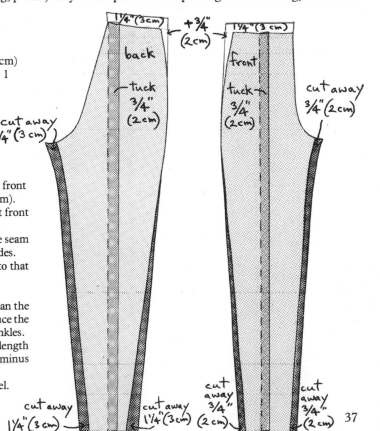

1¼"(3cm)   +¾" (2cm)   1¼" (3cm)

back   front

tuck 3¾" (2cm)   tuck 3¾" (2cm)

cut away 1¼" (3cm)   cut away ¾" (2cm)

cut away 1¼" (3cm)   cut away 1¼"(3cm)   cut away ¾" (2cm)   cut away ¾" (2cm)

37

Culottes★★

Culottes are a combination of Basic Pattern B—Full Pants—and Basic Pattern C—Straight Skirt. They have enough fullness to function as an ordinary skirt. This design has inset pockets, and opens on the side fronts. The fullness is drawn up into 5 pleats in front, and 2 narrow pleats and a deep one in back. They can be made fuller or slimmer, depending how far you place the skirt pattern from the center line. Any softly draping fabric will work well. This design was made in a fairly heavy, ikat-woven cotton.

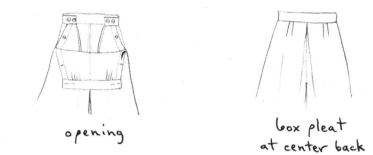

photo p. 67★★

opening

box pleat
at center back

THE PATTERN: USE BASIC PATTERN B, FULL PANTS, and BASIC PATTERN C, STRAIGHT SKIRT

Choose a size and enlarge and trace Basic Pattern B, full pants (remember markings for hipline and grain of fabric line), and enlarge and trace Basic Pattern C, skirt, in the desired length.

Place center front of skirt onto pants front, 2" (5cm) from grain of fabric line, top (waist) edges even.

Measure distance from waist to hipline, and transfer this measurement to skirt back. Place skirt center back on pants back, 2" (5cm) from grain of fabric line, and aligned vertically so transferred hipline matches hipline of pants back.

Correct waistline of pants back by trimming ⅝-¾" (1½-2cm). Draw inseam of pants front straight down from crotch point.

Add 1¼" (3cm) fullness at point of the back crotch, and draw inseam straight down from it.

Correct length of pants to match skirt.

Add about 1½" (3cm) fullness at waistline at each side edge so curve of the hip is straightened.

Add 2" (5cm) fullness at bottom of side seams, and slant side seams to meet that point (see p. 111, fig. A).

Draw pockets from the pattern, and draw in pocket openings and hem on front. For waistband, see step. 1.

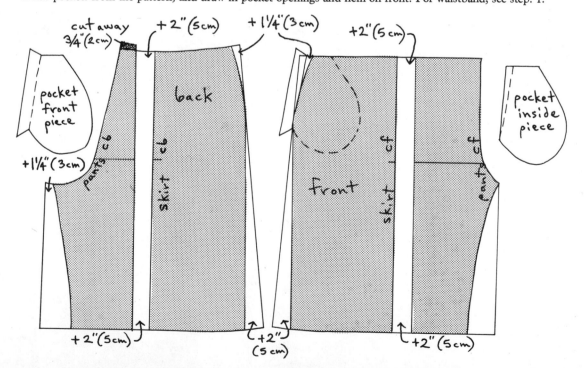

CONSTRUCTION

1. Cut out all pieces, adding ⅝" (1½cm) seam allowance and 1½" (4cm) hem at the bottom. Cut pocket bags. Cut the back waistband 4" (10cm) wide (the finished width is 2½" or 5cm) x ½ the waist measurement + 6¼" (16cm), and front waistband the same width and ½ the waist measurement minus 1½" (4cm). Mark center front, the pleat at center back, and pockets.
2. Zigzag all edges.
3. On wrong side of front and pocket, if desired, press a strip of fusible interfacing into the foldline. Turn under the raw edges, first ⅜" (1cm) then on the foldline. Stitch down and topstitch. Cut a small notch in the seam allowance of the hem to release it. Sew pocket sections together, with the finished edges outward. Edge the finished pocket bags with bias tape. Pin pockets to fronts and topstitch a short anchor seam at the bottom of the opening, and at a right angle to it.
4. Sew side seams and inseams and press the seams open. Hem the legs.
5. Pin and sew the center front and center back seams, right sides together, first turning one leg right side out and putting it down into the other leg. Turn everything right side out.
6. Make 5 pleats in each side of the front, 1-1⅛" (2½-3cm) deep and ⅜" (1cm) apart, starting 2¾" (7cm) from center front, to make each front section equal to ¼ the waist measurement. If desired, stitch the pleats down 1½-2" (4-5cm) from the top (p. 138).
7. Fold a pleat 1" (2½cm) deep on each side of the center back seam, so they meet at the seam. Sew, from wrong side, about 2" (5cm) down from the top so a box pleat is formed (p. 139). Fold 2 more pleats, about 1" (2-3cm) deep and 3½-4" (9-10cm) from center back, to make each back section equal to ¼ of the waist measurement. If desired, stitch these pleats down, depending on how "flat" you are in back.
8. Sew the longer waistband section to the back/pockets as described on p. 154, and sew the shorter section to the front.
9. Make buttonholes in the front waistband, ⅜" (1cm) from the edge, in the vertical center of the waistband, and in the center of the hem of the pocket opening. Sew on buttons.

MATERIALS

Fabric width 45" (120cm)
Skirt length x 2
+ 8" (20cm) for waistband
+ 4" (10cm) for seam allowances
Interfacing • 6 buttons

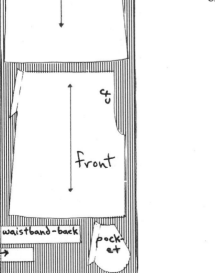

fabric 45" (120 cm) wide

buckles & belt tabs

pocket in side seam

★ ★ ★

belt tabs on side

★ ★ ★

Shorts/Short Pants with self-belt★★

Pants sewn using Basic Pattern A for straight pants, with the front expanded 4¾" (12cm) for pleats. The waistband has a two-part self-belt long enough to wind all the way around the waist and buckle in front. The pants button in front and have a little tab in back to hold the belt. This design is made without pockets, but it could be made with inseam pockets in the side seams, with bound pockets, or with inset pockets. Here the design is made in a heavy jacquard-woven cotton-linen blend, but any kind of fabric suitable for pants would work.

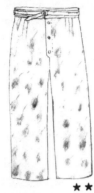

★★

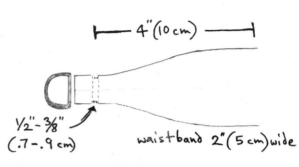

button & tab

4" (10 cm)

½"-⅜" (.7-.9 cm)

waistband 2" (5 cm) wide

CONSTRUCTION

1. Cut fronts and backs, adding ⅜" (1cm) seam allowance and 1½" (4cm) hem at the bottom. Mark center front and foldlines. Cut the waistband 4¾" (12cm) wide x the waist measurement + 1¼" (3cm) for overlap and with ⅜" (1cm) seam allowance. From a double thickness of fabric, cut 4 belt sections, two 30-35" (80-90cm) and two 35-40" (90-100cm) long, as wide as the waistband, and tapering inward so the ends will fit D-rings (see drawing above). Also cut a tab for the back, 3¼ x 1" (3 x 2½cm).
2. Zigzag all edges, except at the waist.
3. Sew center fronts together up to the button placket. On the side that is to overlap, fold under 1⅛" (3cm), with right sides together, ⅝" (1½cm) from center front. Sew diagonally from fold to center front. Turn right side out and press the fold. Fold and press the underlap, also ⅝" (1½cm) from center front. Stitch down the inside edges. Lay the overlap on top, matching center fronts. Pin, and cut a small notch in the seam allowance where the seam pulls. Stitch down the base of the overlap side in a V.
4. Pin and sew center back and center front seams.
5. Sew side seams and inseams and press seams open.
6. Make 2-3 pleats in each front section, about 2½" (6-7cm) from center front, taking up the fullness allowed for pleats. If desired, stitch the pleats down 1-2" (2-5cm) from the top.
7. Sew the belt pieces together, with right sides together, press the seams, turn right side out, and topstitch. Sew belt ends into the seams at the ends of the waistband, with the shorter belt on the overlap side. If making a bound buttonhole in the side seam of the waistband (the overlap side for the belt), make it before sewing down the inside of the waistband (see Waistbands, p. 154 and Buttonholes, p. 164).
8. If desired, make a machine buttonhole instead of a bound one. Make buttonholes and sew buttons on the front, and sew a D-ring onto the overlapping belt end.
9. Sew the wide belt loop for the back as a turned strap (p. 168) and make a buttonhole in it. Sew the belt loop to the top of the waistband at center back. Sew a button at the bottom edge of the waistband, center back (see drawing, above).
10. Hem the legs.

high-waisted
+ 1½" (3 cm)
elastic

★ ★ ★

narrow
pants
legs

★ ★ ★

drawstring

★ ★ ★

★ ★

cut shorts in
a light knit using
a pair of briefs
as a pattern

SHIRT p. 22, SHORTS VARIATION p. 47, JACKET VARIATION OF JUMPSUIT p. 79

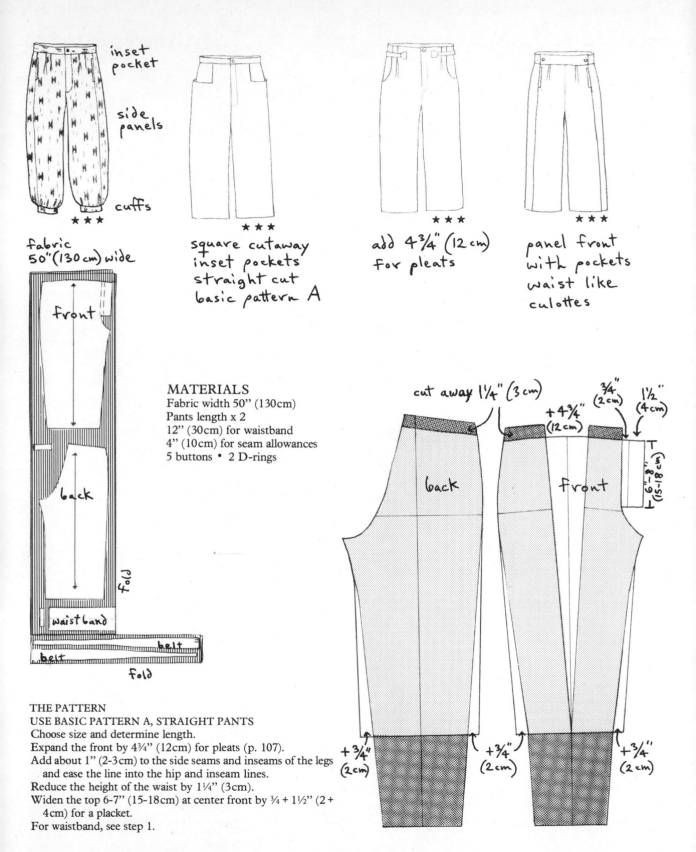

inset pocket

side panels

cuffs

★ ★ ★

fabric 50"(130cm) wide

★ ★ ★

square cutaway inset pockets straight cut basic pattern A

★ ★ ★

add 4¾" (12cm) for pleats

★ ★ ★

panel front with pockets waist like culottes

front

back

waistband

belt

belt

Fold

Fold

MATERIALS
Fabric width 50" (130cm)
Pants length x 2
12" (30cm) for waistband
4" (10cm) for seam allowances
5 buttons • 2 D-rings

cut away 1¼" (3cm)

+4¾" (12cm)

¾" (2cm)

1½" (4cm)

6-8" (15-18cm)

back

front

+¾" (2cm)

+¾" (2cm)

+¾" (2cm)

THE PATTERN
USE BASIC PATTERN A, STRAIGHT PANTS
Choose size and determine length.
Expand the front by 4¾" (12cm) for pleats (p. 107).
Add about 1" (2-3cm) to the side seams and inseams of the legs
    and ease the line into the hip and inseam lines.
Reduce the height of the waist by 1¼" (3cm).
Widen the top 6-7" (15-18cm) at center front by ¾ + 1½" (2 +
    4cm) for a placket.
For waistband, see step 1.

Pants with a simple line, made using Basic Pattern A for straight pants, expanded 2¼" (6cm) at the waist for 2 pleats on each side of the front. They have bound hip and front pockets, a fly opening, and a waistband. Whether or not the pants legs should be pieced depends on the size of the skins. Piecing should be either above or below the knee, and can be either straight or diagonal. The pants could also be made without pleats and with inset pockets at the sides.
• This design is in rather heavy calfskin, lined with lining satin.
• Read the section on Working with Leather, p. 128, and follow the pattern and cutting suggestions.

Leather Pants★★

pocket bag

cut away 1¼" (3cm)

+ 2¼" (6cm)

1½" (4cm)

2½" (6cm)

1¼"

1¼"
5½-6½"
(14-17cm)

7-8"
(18-20cm)

back

front

★★

straight pants piped pockets

fly with snaps as in pants on p. 40

★★★

piped pockets with snap — add 4" (10cm) for pleats

diagonal closure with facing

★★★

THE PATTERN
USE BASIC PATTERN A, STRAIGHT PANTS
Choose a size and determine length.
Lower the waist by 1¼" (3cm).
Expand the front 2¼" (6cm) for pleats (p. 107).
Draw in the fly, 1½" (4cm) wide and 7-8" (18-20cm) long.
Mark the front pockets, 1¼" (3cm) below the waist and 1¼" (3cm) from the side seamline. The pocket opening is 5½-6½" (14-17cm).
Mark the hip pocket at the center of the back piece, 2½" (6cm) from the top edge and square with the grain of the fabric.
Make the pocket bags from the pattern. For waistband and pocket bindings, see step. 1

CONSTRUCTION

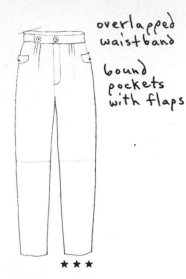

overlapped waistband

bound pockets with flaps

★ ★ ★

add 2¼" (6 cm) for pleats

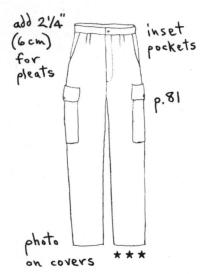

inset pockets

p. 81

photo on covers

★ ★ ★

1. Cut all pieces, adding ⅜" (1 cm) seam allowance and a ¾" (2cm) hem at the bottom. Cut bindings for 2 side pockets and 1 hip pocket (p. 145). Cut the waistband 3" (8cm) wide for a finished width 1½" (4cm), and as long as the waist measurement + 1" (2½cm) for the overlap and ⅜" (1 cm) seam allowance. The lining is cut without any lengthwise piecing, and 2-4" (5-10cm) shorter than the pants (see Linings in Pants, p. 160). Also cut a strip 1½" (4cm) wide and as long as the waistband. The pocket bags are cut of lining fabric, or of sturdier fabric if the lining seems too thin.
Mark center front and pocket opening.

2. Make bound pockets in the sides and a welt pocket on the right side of the back (p. 145). The pocket bags for the front pockets, which are marked before the pattern is expanded for pleats, are sewn along with the pleats so that the smaller pocket bag lies closest to the body and the larger, which is later sewn into the fly, lies away from the body (see Inset Pockets in Pants, p. 147).

3. If necessary, piece the legs together. Stitch or glue down the seam allowances.

4. Stretch the center back seam and the front inseams by dragging the leather down across the edge of a table. Press a strip of fusible interfacing along the seamline at center back, or sew a strip of narrow twill tape into the seam. Glue or stitch the seam allowances down.

5. If the leather seems very soft, press narrow strips of lightweight interfacing onto the seamlines.

6. Sew the center front seam to the fly. Press interfacing into the center front line. Sew a zipper into the fly (p. 170). Remember to sew the pocket bags into this seam. The topstitching line around the fly can be marked, if desired, by scoring the line with a canvas needle or other semi-sharp object so the stitching line will be very neat and will end in a curve under the zipper.

7. Clip and sew the side seams and stitch or glue the seam allowances down. Clip and sew the inseams and glue the seam allowances down.

8. Clip 2 pleats, each roughly centered on the 2 front sections, to make the waist edge correspond to the waist measurement.

9. Press interfacing onto the waistband back. Sew the waistband sections together at the ends (p. 154). Don't turn up the seam allowance as described, as it will be cut off afterward. Clip and sew the waistband to the waist edge. If the lining is to be removable, sew a waist strip into the waistband seam as described under Linings in Pants (p. 160).

10. Make the lining (p. 160), and sew it to the waist strip by hand.

11. Place a snap at center front, and hem the legs.

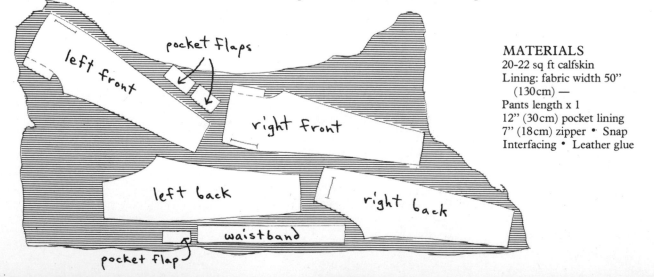

left front

pocket flaps

right front

left back

right back

waistband

pocket flap

MATERIALS
20-22 sq ft calfskin
Lining: fabric width 50" (130cm) —
Pants length x 1
12" (30cm) pocket lining
7" (18cm) zipper • Snap
Interfacing • Leather glue

LEATHER PANTS p. 43, SHIRT VARIATIONS p. 22

Pants with inset pockets on the sides, a bound hip pocket, closed with a fly and a snap fastener. There is no waistband, but there are belt carriers for a narrow belt. This means that the waistline of the pants can be ¾-1½" (2-4cm) wider than the actual waist measurement, to create a little fullness to gather up. If you prefer pants with a waistband, shorten the height of the waist by 2" (5cm) and sew on a separate waistband as described on p. 154. If you do this, remember to fold the pleats to get the correct waist meaurement.

• Pants with a lot of fullness for pleats work best in fabric that drapes softly. Soft cottons, blends of cotton/linen/rayon, and heavy raw silk are all good, and a light calfskin would also work well with this design.

CONSTRUCTION

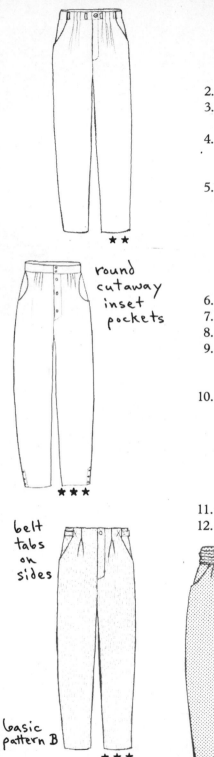

round
cutaway
inset
pockets

belt
tabs
on
sides

basic
pattern B

cut away 3"(8 cm) leg width

1. Cut out the pants, adding ⅜" (1 cm) seam allowance and a 1½" (4 cm) hem allowance at the lower edges. Mark center front and matching points for front and back pocket locations. Cut a facing 2" (5 cm) wide and as long as the waist measurement (+ the extra fullness to gather up) + 1¼" (3 cm) for overlap. Cut a separate fly extension as long as the fly and 3¼" (8 cm) wide. Cut a strip for belt loops, 14" (35 cm) long and 1½" (4 cm) wide. Cut the pocket bags out of a lighter weight fabric.
2. Zigzag all edges.
3. Sew in the inset pockets (p. 148) and the bound hip pocket, adding a buttonhole tab and button, if desired (p. 145).
4. Stitch the center front up to the fly, and sew in the zipper with a separate extension, as described on p. 170. The zipper extends to 2" (5 cm) below the finished upper edge.
5. Make three pleats in each front section. The first is made ⅝" (1½ cm) from the pocket, the last 3⅛" (8 cm) from the center front line. Subtract ¼ of the waist measurement plus ¼ of the extra fullness from the extra fullness of the front piece, measured from the center front to the side seam. The remainder is fullness for pleats, which should be divided by 3, so the pleats will be equal in depth. Pin and, on the wrong side, sew them down about 2" (5 cm) from the top. (See p. 138). Press the folds toward the sides.
6. Sew the center back seam and, if desired, stitch down the seam allowances.
7. Sew the side seams and stitch the seam allowances toward the back.
8. Sew the inseams and press the seams open.
9. Sew the strip for the belt carriers (p. 168) and cut 7 pieces, each 2" (5 cm) long. They can be sewn on with the waist facing or can be sewn on later so they lie a little below the top edge.
10. Turn under the seam allowances on the lower edge of the waist facing and on the ends; press. If desired, pin the belt carriers into the waist seam, 1½" (4 cm) from the center front, just where the pocket ends, about 1" (2-3 cm) behind the side seams and at the center back. Pin the waist facing to the upper edge, right sides together, and sew. Press the seams open and turn right side out. Pin and stitch down the lower edge. Sew or slipstitch the ends. Turn under the ends of the belt carriers ¼" (½ cm) and stitch them down.
11. Set a snap at center front, or make a buttonhole and sew on a button.
12. Hem the legs.

wide
waistband
with
narrow
belt tabs
and D-rings

waistband
& wide
belt loops

welt
"back"
pockets
on sides

wide
legs
with cuffs
p. 78

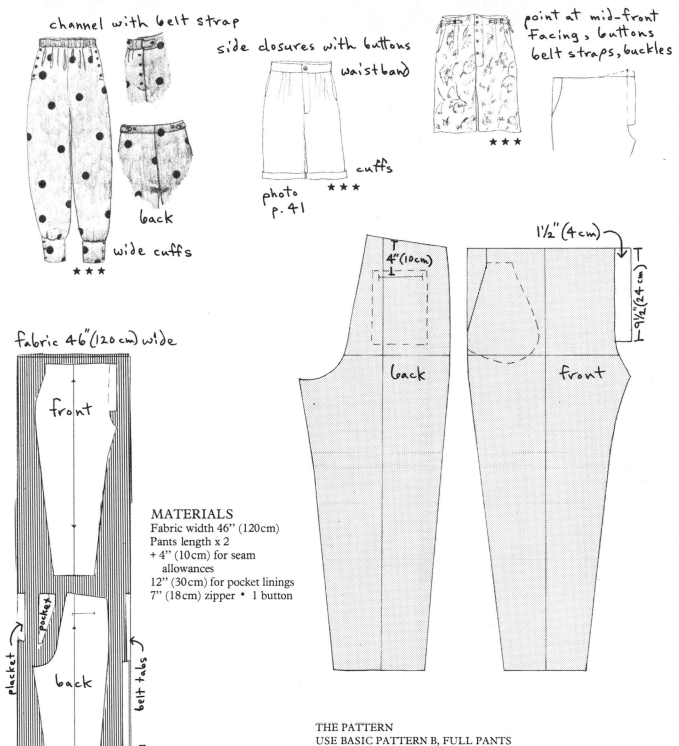

channel with belt strap

side closures with buttons

waistband

photo p. 41

cuffs
★ ★ ★

point at mid-front
Facing, buttons
belt straps, buckles
★ ★ ★

back

wide cuffs
★ ★ ★

fabric 46" (120 cm) wide

front

back

placket

Pocket

belt tabs

facing

MATERIALS
Fabric width 46" (120cm)
Pants length x 2
+ 4" (10cm) for seam
  allowances
12" (30cm) for pocket linings
7" (18cm) zipper • 1 button

4" (10cm)

1½" (4cm)

9½" (24cm)

back

front

THE PATTERN
USE BASIC PATTERN B, FULL PANTS
Choose a size and determine length.
Make the pockets from the pattern.
The hip pocket is placed in the center of the back piece, about 4"
   (10cm) down from the waist and square with the grain of the fabric.
Draw in the fly at center front, 1½" (4cm) wide and 9½" (24cm) long.
For facings, hip pocket, fly extension, and belt tabs, see step. 1.

Buckled-Up Panel Pants★★

CONSTRUCTION

1. Cut out all pieces, adding ⅜" (1 cm) seam allowance and 1¼" (3 cm) hem allowance on the legs. If desired, cut the pockets out of a lighter weight fabric. Cut a double button strip as wide as the fly and to 1½" (4 cm) below the waist edge. Cut a waist facing 2" (5 cm) wide and as long as the waist measure + ¾-1½" (2-4 cm) (to gather) + overlap. Cut belt tabs: 4 for the ankles and center front for a finished size of 1 x 1⅜" (2½ x 3½ cm); for the sides, 4" (10 cm) long with a finished width of ¾-1" (2-2½ cm), to fit your buckles, and one the length of ½ the waist measurement plus 4¾" (12 cm). Cut a 4 x 1¼" (10 x 3 cm) double belt channel for the back (see straps, p. 168). Mark center front, a 5½" (14 cm) pocket opening starting 2¾" (7 cm) below the waist, and points to match the front and side panels.
2. If all seam allowances are to be sewn down, they can be zigzagged as they are sewn. Otherwise, zigzag all edges now.
3. Make the two 4" (10 cm) tabs. Set buckles into each, folding the tab double.
   Sew the 4 small tabs for the center front and the ankles, and make buttonholes in them.
   Make the half-belt for the back and set 3 grommets in each end, ⅜" (1 cm) apart.
   Sew the back belt channel sections together and topstitch the ends.
4. Sew each pocket bag piece to a pocket facing (edge), and sew the pockets as a pocket in a panel cut (p. 148), sewing the side panel and the front together in the same seam. Pin the 2 belt tabs into the seam ⅝" (1½ cm) from the top edge and the 2 ankle straps 1¼" (3 cm) from the bottom (in both cases, measurement does not include the seam allowance). If desired, stitch down the seam allowances either separately or together and toward the front.
5. Sew the center back seam.
6. Sew the center front seam up to the fly, and sew in a fly with a button strip (p. 171).
7. Sew the side and inseams.
8. Fold and pin 3 pleats on each front section, 2¼" (6 cm) from center front, so that each front from side seam to center front equals ¼ of the intended waist measurement. Stitch down the pleats 2" (5 cm) from the top (p. 138).
9. Sew on the waist facing. Follow the instructions in step 10, p. 46, but leave off the belt tabs. Stitch buttonhole tabs between the facing and the pants on both sides of center front overlap. Machine stitch the ends.
10. Pin and sew the belt channel at center back ⅜" (1 cm) below upper edge, and slide the half-belt through it.
11. Sew buttons on fly and waistband, and at the ankles. Hem legs.

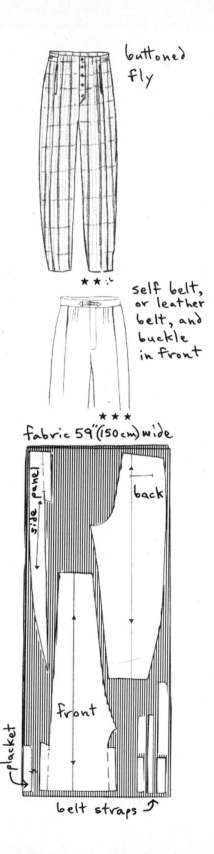

buttoned fly

★★ ∴ self belt, or leather belt, and buckle in front

★ ★ ★
fabric 59" (150 cm) wide

side panel

back

front

placket

belt straps ↗

Pants adapted from Basic Pattern B—full pants, with a panel cut and pockets on the front. The panel cut line is shown on the printed pattern. Side seams are slightly bowed, for a baggy look, but this can be eliminated if you find it hard to draw, or if you don't feel this look works with your fabric. The design has waist facing, belt tabs and buckles at the waist, and 3 pleats on each side of the front. The fly here is buttoned, but it could just as well have a zipper. The ankles are much narrower than the rest of the pants legs: the length is 2" (5 cm) longer than usual and the ankle fullness is gathered in with buckled straps. The fabric should drape softly, or the pants could be made of, for example, a light calfskin. A striped, lightweight wool/rayon blend was used for this design.

MATERIALS

Fabric width 59" (150 cm)
Pants length x 1½
+ 2" (5 cm) for seam allowances
10" (25 cm) for pocket lining
6 buttons • 2 buckles

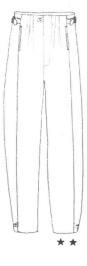

back

FROM LEATHER JACKET PATTERN p. 66—MADE HERE OF LINEN AND COTTON

★ ★

49

THE PATTERN
USE BASIC PATTERN B, FULL PANTS

Choose a size and determine the length. If desired, add 2" (5cm) to normal length.

Trace the pattern with the panel cut line (the same for all sizes).

Draw in the same grain of fabric line on the side panel as for the front, and draw matching points on the line.

Widen both pieces by 1½" (4cm) at the top 10" (25cm) of the panel cut line for pocket facings (see the cutting layout).

Mark the pocket opening 2¾" and 8¼" (7 and 21 cm) down from the top.

Draw the fly at center front, 1½" (4cm) wide and 9½" (24cm) long for a 7" (18cm) zipper.

If desired, add ⅝-¾" (1½-2cm) to the side seamlines at knee height, and bow the line as shown in the diagram, perhaps tapering the ankle by ¾" (2cm) at the side seamline.

Draw the hip pocket placement, about 4" (10cm) below the waistline in the center of the back, square with the grain of fabric.

Make pockets from the patterns.

For facings, tabs, etc., see step 1.

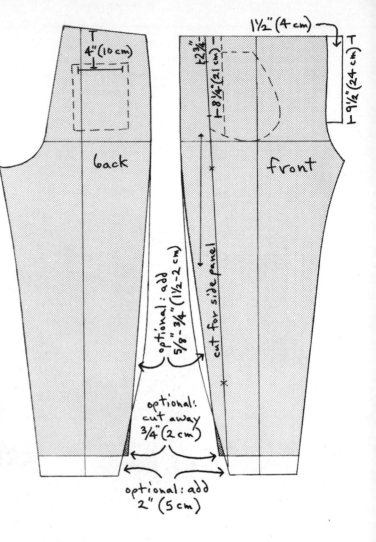

Nylon Jacket with Elastic Waist★★

Made of crinkle nylon, a jacket with a slightly irregular surface, lined with a brushed cotton, very light and soft. It's made from Basic Pattern A, with dropped shoulders. The larger pockets are sewn-on bags, two pockets in one, one accessible from the side, the other from above, and the smaller one is a bound pocket with a flap. All 3 pockets have Velcro fasteners. The collar band has a flap closing and the front edge, a sewn-on extension with snaps.

• It could also be made of downproof ticking, poplin, or chintz, and the lining of terry or sweatshirt fabric.

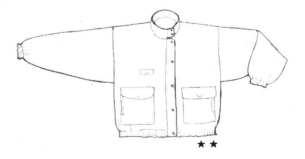

★ ★

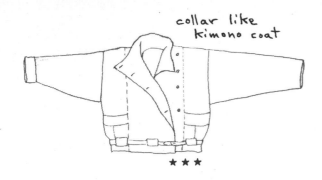

collar like
kimono coat

★ ★ ★

loose yoke
front & back
sewn into sleeve
& neckline seams

flap pockets
with piping

★ ★ ★

MATERIALS
Fabric width 55" (140cm)
Outer fabric —
Jacket length (+ hem) x 1
Sleeve length (+ hem) x 1
20" (50cm) for pockets
4" (10cm) for seam allowances
For sizes larger than 48"
   (120cm) —
Jacket length (+ hem) x 2
4" (10cm) for seam allowances
Zipper, the length of front edge
7 snaps • 4" (10cm) Velcro
1-2/3 yds (1½m) wide elastic
Lining fabric 55" (140cm)
   wide —
Jacket length x 1
Sleeve length x 1

outer fabric
55" (140 cm) wide

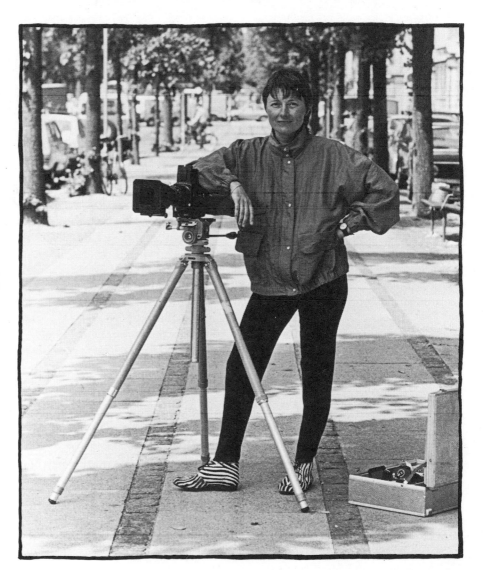

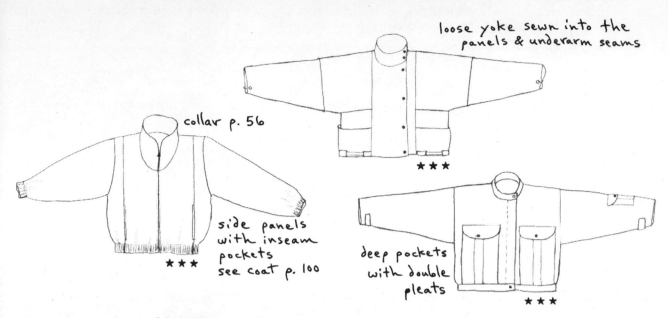

loose yoke sewn into the panels & underarm seams

★ ★ ★

collar p. 56

side panels with inseam pockets see coat p. 100

★ ★ ★

deep pockets with double pleats

★ ★ ★

CONSTRUCTION

A

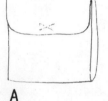

B

C

1. Cut all pieces, adding ⅜" (1cm) seam allowance. Sleeves are sewn in two pieces, with an extended shoulder, but could as well be cut as one piece. The front edge extension, collar band, and pockets are cut from doubled outer fabric. If desired, a layer of lining can be added as an interlining. Mark pocket locations. Lining pieces can also be cut with ⅜" (1cm) seam allowance, but 3" (8cm) shorter than outer fabric at wrists and lower edge. Cut pocket bag pieces for the small bound pocket (p. 144).

2. Pin and sew small pocket flap sections together, turn, topstitch, and sew on a 1" (3cm) strip of Velcro tape. Make bound pocket, sewing Velcro to the front before assembling it.

3. Sew optional upper sleeve to the lower sleeve, right sides together, and double welt the seam. Sew shoulder seams in the same way. Sew on sleeves, matching fronts and backs, shoulder seam to centerline, and welt seam toward the sleeve.

4. Make the lining just like the jacket. If desired, stitch the seam allowances open.

5. Sew on the front extension, right sides together (use lining fabric if desired), turn, and sew a double line of topstitching on the outside edges.

6. Pin extension to jacket on the desired side, ⅜" (1cm) from the top edge, with raw edges flush.

7. Make buttonhole tab like the front extension. Sew collar band sections together, but don't fold in the seam allowance on neckline edge (see Collars, p. 175). Turn and sew a double line of topstitching on outside edges. Pin to neck edge of jacket, so flap lies on the overlapping side.

8. Pin the lining to the jacket, right sides together, at neck and front edges, so collar and buttonhole tab are between the 2 layers. Stitch, trim corners and notch neckline curve. Turn right side out and topstitch front edges and neckline.

9. Turn lining to the outside and make a double hem at the bottom and on the sleeves, turning under ½" then 1½" (1 then 4cm). Pin and sew. Leave front edges open to receive elastic.

10. Sew pocket pieces together, right sides together. Leave 4" (10cm) open on each pocket, turn right side out, and sew a double line of topstitching. Fold the pocket as shown in A, and pin a 1" (3cm) strip of Velcro on the front as a fastener. Sew on the Velcro with a cross. Sew the pocket together at side/opening as shown in B. Pin and sew pockets in place on the front as in C, so the pocket is open between the 2 layers from the top, and open on the side between pocket and jacket.

11. Pull a wide elastic through the channel at the bottom of the jacket and sew it in place.

12. Place snaps in the overlap and collar tab (see p. 167).

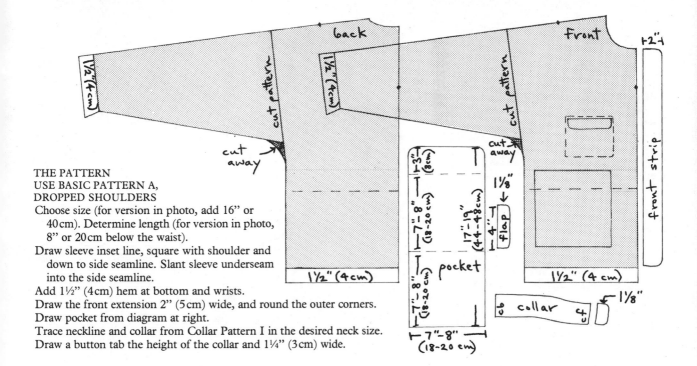

THE PATTERN
USE BASIC PATTERN A,
DROPPED SHOULDERS

Choose size (for version in photo, add 16" or
  40cm). Determine length (for version in photo,
  8" or 20cm below the waist).
Draw sleeve inset line, square with shoulder and
  down to side seamline. Slant sleeve underseam
  into the side seamline.
Add 1½" (4cm) hem at bottom and wrists.
Draw the front extension 2" (5cm) wide, and round the outer corners.
Draw pocket from diagram at right.
Trace neckline and collar from Collar Pattern I in the desired neck size.
Draw a button tab the height of the collar and 1¼" (3cm) wide.

Raincoat/Spring Coat★

An unlined coat, made of water-repellent nylon. It was
adapted from Basic Pattern A with dropped shoulders,
and has a sharply angled, diagonal front closure, a big
lapel collar, cut pockets with flaps and a long kick pleat
in the back. It's fastened with shiny snaps in front. It
could also be made of heavy duck, poplin, a light
plastic cloth, heavy chintz or wool, of which, however,
only the plastic would be waterproof. If you prefer to
line the coat, see p. 163.

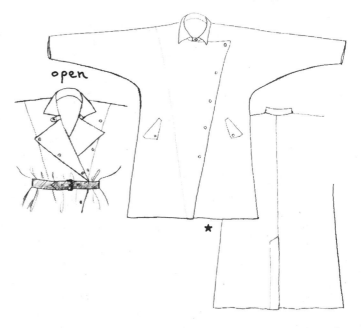

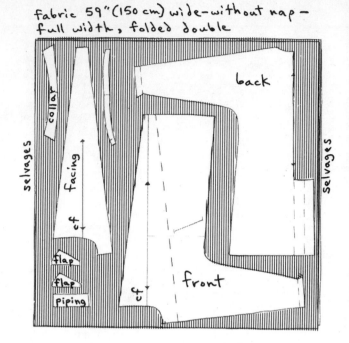

fabric 59" (150 cm) wide—without nap—
full width, folded double

THE PATTERN
USE BASIC PATTERN A, DROPPED SHOULDERS

Choose size (for version in photo, add 16" or 40 cm). Determine
  length.

Extend the center front/center back. Add 1½" (4 cm) width at
  the bottom of each side seamline, and draw the bottom edge at
  a right angle to both side and center lines.

Trace neckline and collar from Collar Pattern I in the desired
  neck size.

Draw the front edge: add 6" (15 cm) at the throat and 1¼" (3 cm)
  at the bottom edge. Connect these points.

Draw the facing, following the same lines, and slant the inner
  side up to the shoulder.

Add a 1¼" (3 cm) hem at the wrists.

Add 4 x 16" (10 x 40 cm) for a kick pleat at center back.

Mark pocket placement: 6" (15 cm) wide, 2" (5 cm) from side
  seamline, with the highest point about 2½" (6 cm) below the
  waist. Draw the flap according to the diagram below, and the
  pocket bag from the pocket pattern.

MATERIALS
Fabric width 59" (150 cm),
  without nap
Coat length x 2
+ length from underarm to
  shoulder x 2
8 snaps

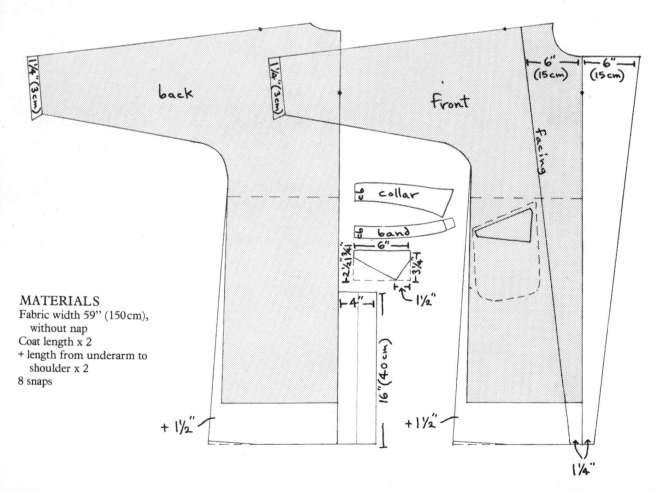

54

collar p.29

extra width for gathers

optional fold

★ ★ ★

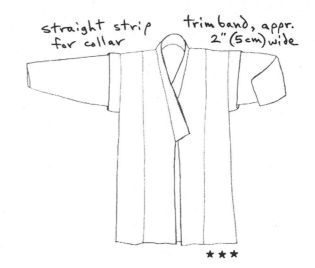

straight strip for collar

trimband, appr. 2" (5cm) wide

★ ★ ★

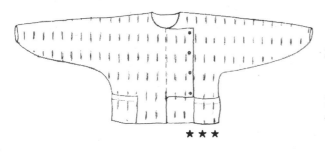

rounded at wrists

★ ★ ★

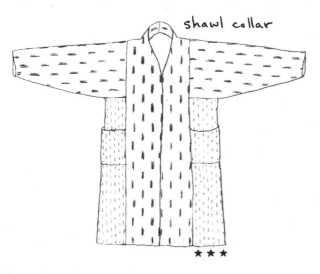

shawl collar

★ ★ ★

CONSTRUCTION

1. Cut out all pieces, adding ⅜-¾" (1-2cm) seam allowance at shoulders and sides, and 1½" (4cm) hem at the bottom and wrists. For the front edges, neckline, buttonhole tab, and pocket flaps, allow ⅜" (1cm). Cut the buttonhole tab from doubled fabric, 1½" (4cm) long and 1" (2½cm) wide. Cut pocket bags from thinner fabric. Mark center front, pocket placement, and the kick pleat.

2. Sew center back seam down to ¾" (2cm) below the base of the slit, and make pleat according to directions on p. 138.

3. Make bound pockets with downturned flap (p. 146).

4. Sew sleeve/shoulder seams, with epaulets, if desired (p. 168). Zigzag the seam allowances, and stitch them to the back.

5. Sew sleeve/side seams. Zigzag the seam allowances together, and sew 2 rows of topstitching from the right side. Starting at the underarm, sew down the side seam. Starting at the underarm again, sew the sleeve seam.

6. Pin and sew on the facing, with right sides together. As the front edge is on the diagonal, it's a good idea to sew a piece of seam tape into that seam (see Facings, p. 150).

7. Hem the bottom and sleeves.

8. Stitch the tab and collar, and sew on as a collar with stand (p. 176). The tab is sewn onto the collar stand on the overlap side.

9. Mark and set snaps in the points of the pocket flaps, in the sleeve tabs, if desired, and on the front edge, starting with one at the upper corner and placing 4 down the front, 6-6½" (15-17cm) apart.

Lined Leather-Trimmed Jacket★★

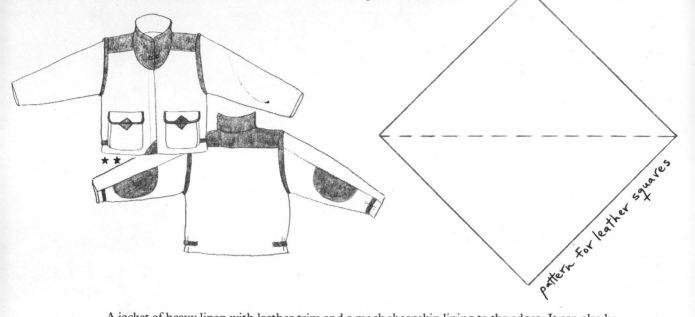

pattern for leather squares

A jacket of heavy linen with leather trim and a mock sheepskin lining to the edges. It can also be made entirely of leather or entirely of fabric with trim in a contrasting color. Mock sheepskin is wonderfully warm for winter, but quilted fabric, or even a wool lining, will give the same results. For a lighter version, a soft cotton would be good, perhaps with the inner collar sewn of the same cloth as the outer, as it's quite visible. The jacket has set-in sleeves (Basic Pattern B) and visible edging. There are big patches on the elbows; the pockets have accordian sides. The jacket front fastens with a zipper, and the pockets and tabs have snaps. See the section of Working with Leather (p. 128).

pleated pockets

elastic at waist ★ ★ ★

collar variation p. 63

waistband ★ ★ ★

pockets in panel seam ★ ★ ★

***

collar
variation p.56

box pleat
in back

waistband

***

COAT p. 53

optional
leather trim
★ ★ ★

decorated
with leather
★ ★ ★ patches

CONSTRUCTION

1. Cut out the pieces for the outer jacket with ⅜" (1 cm) seam allowance at all edges, and 1¼" (3 cm) hem allowance at the tops of the pockets and their side strips. The leather trim is cut out with a seam allowance at the shoulder seam, sleeve edge, the straight edge of the elbow patches, and the collar. Cut out tabs for the sleeves and sides, 2 each in the following sizes: sleeves 1½ x 3½" and 1½ x 3¼" (4 x 9 and 4 x 8 cm); sides 1½ x 3¼" and 1½ x 4" (4 x 8 and 4 x 10 cm); one piece for center front 1½ x 2" (4 x 5 cm). Squares for the pocket trim measure 2¼ x 2¼" (5½ x 5½ cm). Cut four, and cut 2 of these in half diagonally. Leather strips for the armhole trim and pocket flap are cut 1½" (4 cm) wide and are measured against the pattern for length. Cut interfacings (for leather) for the tabs and collar.

2. The lining is cut like the outer jacket, with ⅜" (1 cm) seam allowances. The sleeve lining could be cut as one piece, without a back seam.

3. Zigzag lining and jacket pieces, if the fabric frays.

4. Sew the leather yoke trim together at the shoulder seams; sew or glue down the seam allowances. Sew collar sections at center back, stitch or glue down the seam allowances. Press fusible interfacing onto the collar and all tabs.

5. Fold each tab to ¾" (2 cm) wide and stitch around the edge to make a diagonal tip (p. 168). Trim the seam allowances.

6. Pin or glue the leather patches to the small sleeve pieces, about 4¾" (12 cm) from the wrist. Stitch around the edges. Pin sleeve sections, with right sides together, and stitch the longer tab section into the seam, 1½" (4 cm) from the wrist edge and with the folded edge up. Sew together, and stitch seam allowances to the larger sleeve piece. Pin the underarm seam and the other tab section at the same height as the first, stitch, and press seam open.

7. Sew shoulder seams. Clip/glue the leather yoke and stitch it on. Pin and sew on the collar, matching center backs, and front edges.

8. Sew the pocket front and sides as described on p. 143. Glue and sew on the decorative squares 1¼" (3 cm) below the top edge, in the center. Pin the longer side tab at the bottom of the pocket side edge. Pin and sew on the pocket 1½" (4 cm) from jacket bottom edge and 1½" (4 cm) from the side seam. Sew one of the half-square pieces (a triangle) onto the center of each double pocket flap, and edge the flaps (p. 152). Pin and stitch.
The pocket and flap can instead be sewn on when the jacket and lining are sewn together and turned, to keep the layers from slipping.

9. Sew half-squares onto the lower corners at center front. Sew side seams, with right sides together, and press seams open.

10. Pin and sew on sleeves, with wrong sides together. Finish seam allowance with leather strips, sewn on from bodice side (p. 152).

11. Make the lining, sewing with right sides together.

12. Pin lining to jacket, right sides together, at collar, front edge, and bottom edge, and sew all the way around, leaving an opening of 10" (25 cm) in back, along the bottom edge. Trim corners and turn. Fold and pin the opening closed and topstitch all the way around. Use bobbin thread the color of the lining, and top thread the color of the jacket, changing color of the top thread, if you wish, when you sew into the leather. Fold up lining and jacket ⅜" (1 cm) at wrists, baste and topstitch together.

13. Pin, baste and stitch the zipper in place (p. 171). It should be long enough to end just under the collar.

14. Try on jacket and pin the back side tabs to the bottom edge.

15. Pin on collar tab and sew on all 3 tabs with crosses. Set snaps on pockets and at center front. Sew 2 snaps on each side tab to regulate fullness.

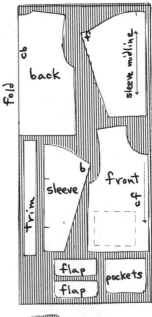

outer fabric 55" (140 cm) wide

THE PATTERN
USE BASIC PATTERN B, SET-IN SLEEVES

Choose a size (for jacket in photo, add 12" or 30 cm). Determine length.

Draw a panel cut the length of the sleeve, about 2" (5 cm) down from the top of the sleeve back. (Pin this strip to the sleeve front.)

Draw a yoke (trim), 3–4" (8–10 cm) down the front and parallel with the shoulder line, and the same distance down the back but at a right angle to the center back line.

Draw the patch on the sleeve back following the pattern diagram.

Use the neckline and collar from Collar Pattern II.

Add ¾" (2 cm) along the front edge.

Draw the pocket and pocket flap from the diagram below. For tabs, see step 1.

MATERIALS
Fabric width 55" (140 cm)
Outer layer —
Jacket length x 2
Pocket length x 1
+ 4" (10 cm) for seam allowances
Lining —
Jacket length x 2
Collar length x 1
2" (5 cm) for seam allowances
Leather —
Appr. 5 sq ft
Zipper the length of front edge to collar
12 buttons

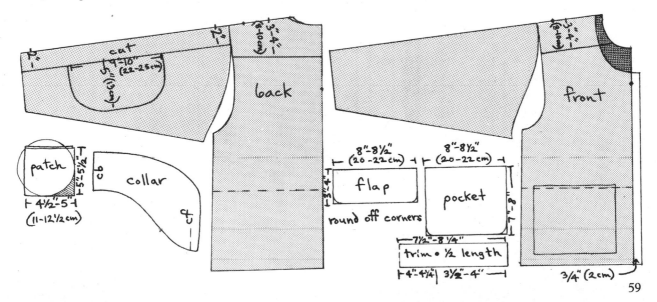

59

★ ★

Coat Lined to the Edges★★

A coat made of a soft, blanket-weight wool, with heavy chintz serving as both facings and lining, hence "lined to the edges." It has vertical panel cuts in front and back, a large, high collar, a deep overlap in front and roomy patch pockets.
• The buttonholes are hand worked, and there are large "straight" shoulder pads—both these features are optional.
• Most heavier fabrics will work, and if you don't like the idea of the lining extending to the edges, the coat can certainly be made with traditional facings (see the section on Linings, p. 163).

CONSTRUCTION

1. Cut the coat pieces, adding ⅝" (1½cm) seam allowance (⅜" or 1cm if using duck or other canvas) on all edges. Add 1½" (4cm) hem allowance at top edge of pocket and at bottom edge of coat. Mark matching points on vertical seams, center front, center back, midpoint of sleeve, and pockets. The lining is cut without the vertical panel cuts in front and back: lay the coat pattern pieces close together for this. Allow ⅜-⅝" (1-1½cm) seam allowance all the way around. For pocket lining, cut fabric without seam allowance.
2. Zigzag all edges, if the fabric frays.
3. With right sides together, pin and sew coat front and back panel cuts, then side seams. The seam allowances are sewn open as you go along, from the right side, a presser foot's width from the seamline and with a long stitch. Press the seams. Sew the shoulder seams in the same way.
4. Sew sleeve seams, with right sides together. It's easiest to sew seam allowances down from inside sleeves and to turn right side out afterward. Pin and sew sleeves into armholes, stitch seam allowances down, and press.
5. Press and pin the pocket hems. Press in seam allowances at sides and bottom. If making a lining, lay it in place under seam allowances. Pin pockets onto front sections, so back edges extend 1-2" (2-5cm) over side seams. Sew on with a single line of stitching, a presser foot's width from the edge.
6. Sew the lining as you did the coat, and sew it in as described under Lining to the Edges, p. 162.
7. Mark 5 buttonholes: 1 at the vertical center of the collar, one 1¼-1½" (3-4cm) below the seam, and 3 down the front, 6-7" (15-18cm) apart. The buttons on this design are 1½" (4cm) wide. Work buttonholes by hand (p. 164). Pin the coat together in front, mark and sew on buttons.

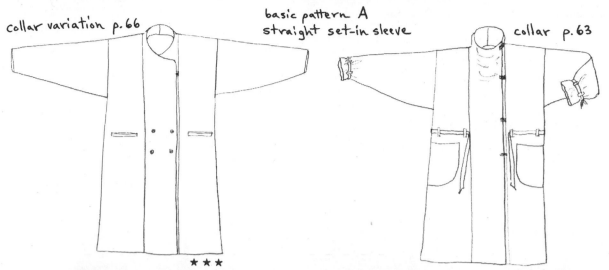

collar variation p.66

basic pattern A
straight set-in sleeve

collar p.63

★ ★ ★

★ ★ ★

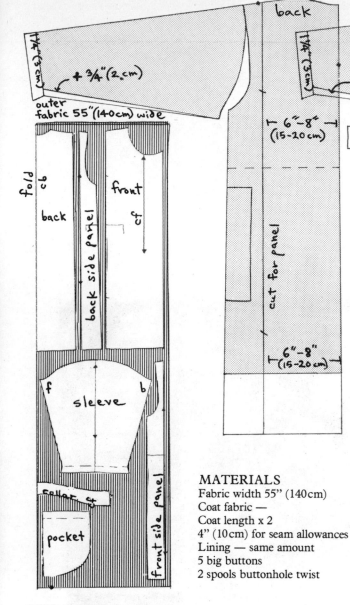

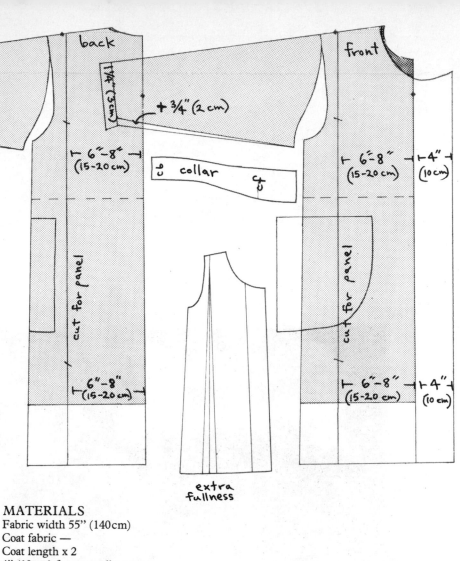

back

+ ¾" (2 cm)

1¼" (3 cm)

front

+ ¾" (2 cm)

1¼" (3 cm)

outer fabric 55" (140 cm) wide

6"–8" (15–20 cm)

6"–8" (15–20 cm)

4" (10 cm)

collar

cut for panel

cut for panel

6"–8" (15–20 cm)

6"–8" (15–20 cm)

4" (10 cm)

extra fullness

fold

cb

back

back side panel

front

cf

f   sleeve   b

collar   cf

pocket

front side panel

MATERIALS
Fabric width 55" (140 cm)
Coat fabric —
Coat length x 2
4" (10 cm) for seam allowances
Lining — same amount
5 big buttons
2 spools buttonhole twist

THE PATTERN
USE BASIC PATTERN B, SET-IN SLEEVES
Choose size (for version in photo, add 16" or 40 cm).
   Determine length.
Extend the center front/center back line and draw the
   bottom edge.
(If fullness of hips is markedly greater than bust measurement,
   extra fullness can be added at the panel cut as shown in the
   drawing above.)
Add 4" (10 cm) along front edge.
Use neckline and collar from Collar Pattern II.
Draw the vertical panel cuts 6-8" (15-20 cm) from center front/
   center back lines.
Mark matching points. Make pockets from pattern and mark as
   shown in the drawing.
If desired, add ¾" (2 cm) to sleeve width at wrist. Add
   1¼" (3 cm) hem allowance to sleeve.

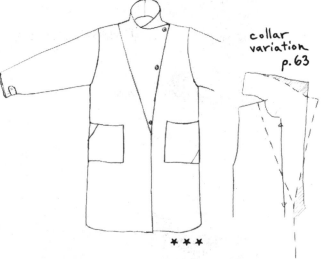

collar variation p. 63

collar variation p. 63

✶ ✶ ✶

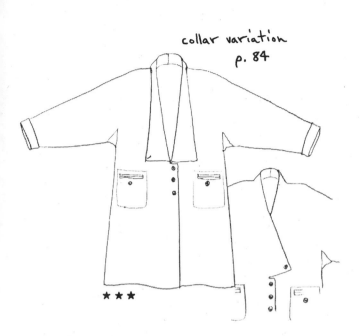

collar variation
p. 84

★ ★ ★

Kimono Coat★

★

CONSTRUCTION

1. Cut out all pieces, adding ⅝" (1½cm) seam allowance at sleeve/shoulder and sleeve/side edges and no seam allowance at the front edges and wrists. Allow 1½" (4cm) hem at the bottom. Cut pockets with seam allowances except on the flap. Cut two gussets from the pattern on p. 141. Cut leather strips for trim, 5-5½ yds (4½-5m), depending on coat length, x 1½" (4cm) wide, plus about 1 yd (1m) for the front edge (see step 9). Mark center front and gusset slit.

2. Zigzag all edges if the fabric frays, otherwise only the "inside" edges.

3. Sew the sleeve/side seams and sew in the gussets according to the instructions on p. 141. Pin and sew center back seam, and stitch down seam allowances.

4. Sew center back seam of collar with wrong sides together, and sew a leather strip over seam allowance. Pin and sew front and back together at sleeve/shoulder/neck seams (p. 176). Stitch seam allowances down to the back.

5. Hem the bottom edge.

6. Sew lining the same as the coat, and make a ¾" (2cm) hem at the bottom. (The lining is cut without hem allowance). Stitch lining to coat, wrong sides together, at collar and front edges.

7. Position the leather strips with spring clips (right sides together) at front edges, collar, and wrists. Be careful when clipping that the edges neither strain nor bunch up. Sew as described on p. 152.

8. Trim the pocket flap. Fold in seam allowance of pocket. Position, pin, and sew it onto the coat (p. 143).

9. If using very thin leather, cut button loops 1¼" (3cm) wide. Finished width will be about ¼" (¾cm). In heavier leather, cut them ⅝" (1½cm) wide. They should be long enough for the button to pass through the loop. On the design, the toggles are 1½" (4cm) long, the button loops 3" (8cm) long and sewn into the seam of the trim. If the holes on the buttons are large enough, the buttons can be sewn on with leather strips. Place the top button about 1" (2-3cm) from the top edge and the remainder 6" (15cm) apart.

63

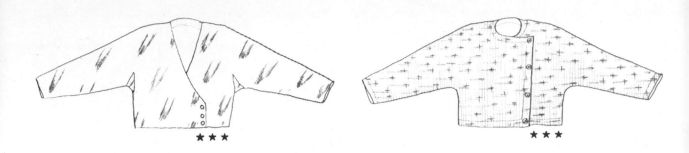

★ ★ ★   ★ ★ ★

A kimono-style coat (Basic Pattern C) with a wide overlap and a big, high collar. Gussets are added under the arms to give freedom of movement. It's made of heavy, soft cotton upholstery fabric, but could just as well be made of wool—blanketing, for example—or leather (see suggestions for panel cuts). It's trimmed with leather and buttoned with leather loops and toggles. D-rings or ties are other possible fasteners. This design is sewn with no lining; if you want the coat lined, see the section on p. 161.

★ ★ ★

* * *

MATERIALS
Fabric width 50" (130cm), without
  nap
Coat length (+ collar) x 2
+ 4" (10cm) for seam allowances
Leather for strips, 6½ yds (6m),
  1½" (4cm) wide
5 buttons

fabric 50"(130 cm) wide —
without nap, 2 layers, full width

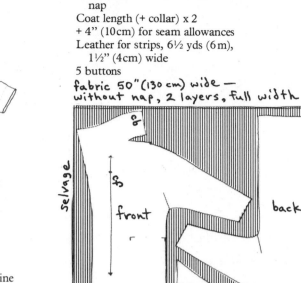

THE PATTERN
USE BASIC PATTERN C, KIMONO CUT
Choose size (for version in photo, add 12" or 30cm). Determine
  length.
Draw in the length and draw the sidelines straight down to it or
  slanted slightly outward.
Draw the gusset slit and draw the gusset pattern from p. 141.
Draw the collar from Collar Pattern III and extend the front
  edge.
Draw the pocket pattern from the illustration below.

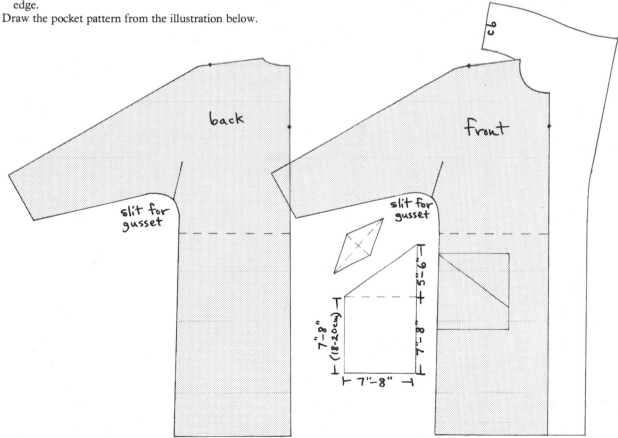

65

Leather Jacket★★

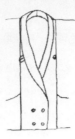

★ ★

★ ★ ★

collar variation
p. 69

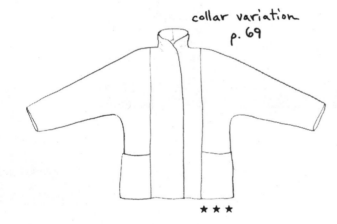

★ ★ ★

A kimono-style jacket, from Basic Pattern C, in thin, soft calfskin. It's double-breasted and has a shawl collar that can be turned down or buttoned up. There are panel cuts both front and back, and pockets in front. It can be fastened with buttons and bound buttonholes as shown here, or with snaps. Lined with thin cotton broadcloth, it can be worn in spring and summer as an outergarment, and as an indoor jacket in winter, so is truly an all-season coat.

• Made of fabric, the jacket can be completely reversible, perhaps with a light interlining. In this case the facings are not attached at the bottom edge, and the sleeves could be cut long enough to allow a little turn-up. The pockets can be made with bound openings on one side, so they are accessible from both sides.

• See the section on Working with Leather, p. 128, and follow the pattern and cutting directions.

MATERIALS
About 25 sq ft calfskin
Lining, fabric width 50"
  (130 cm) —
Jacket length x 3
Interfacing • 5 buttons
Leather glue

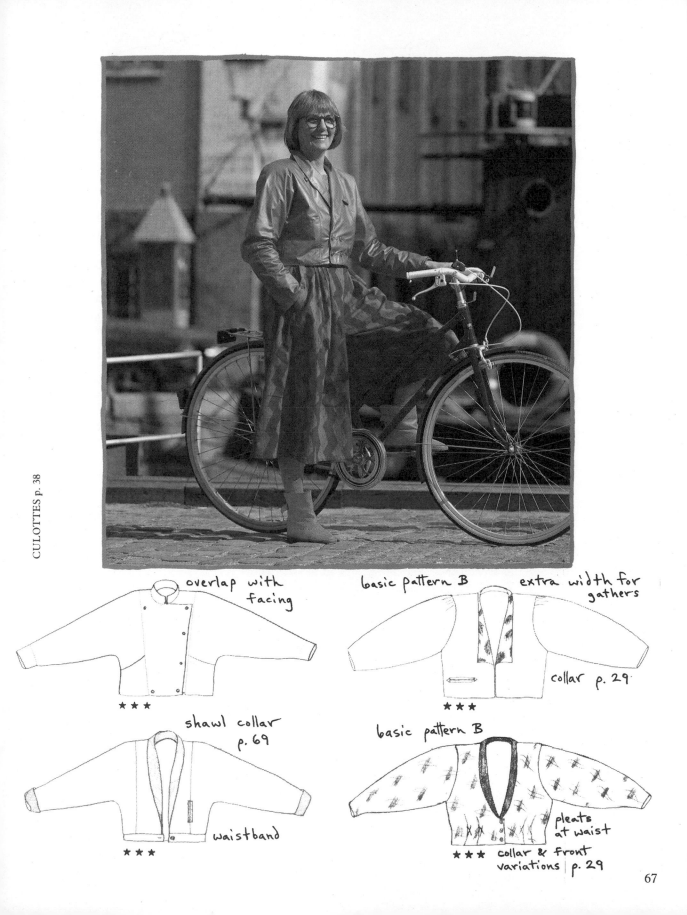

CULOTTES p. 38

overlap with facing

basic pattern B

extra width for gathers

collar p. 29

★ ★ ★

★ ★ ★

shawl collar p. 69

waistband

basic pattern B

pleats at waist

★ ★ ★

★ ★ ★ collar & front variations | p. 29

CONSTRUCTION

back   front

3/4" 3/4" 1⅛"
(2cm) (2cm) (3cm)

1. From *leather*, cut out 2 right and 2 left center front/collar pieces (jacket and facing), 1 whole back, and a total of 4 sleeve/side pieces for right and left, front and back. Cut 2 pockets. Cut facings 1¼" (3cm) wide for top edges of pockets, for sleeves (cut in one piece with seam at the underarm seam) and for bottom edges of side pieces and center back, as well as a tab 1½" (4cm) square. Cut all pieces with ⅜" (1cm) seam allowances and ⅜" (1cm) hems. Also cut strips for binding 5 buttonholes (p. 165).

2. On *lining* fabric, lay the center back of pattern ⅝" (1½cm) from the fold to widen for a pleat. Cut side/sleeve pieces ⅜" (1cm) shorter at the wrists and about 1" (2-3cm) shorter at the bottom edges than the jacket (see drawing), so the bottom edges of the front slant about 1" (2-3cm) for comfort. Cut pocket linings, cutting off 1¼" (3cm) at the top edge.

3. Mark center back on both leather and lining, mark pleat, and mark buttonhole tab placement on front edge.

4. Mark 4 buttonholes on outside front on the overlap side, 1¼-1½" (3½-4cm) from the bottom edge then 2" (5cm) apart lengthwise, ⅜" and 2⅜" (1 and 6cm) from the front edge seamline, and centered under buttonhole tab. Make the buttonholes. Make and turn buttonhole tab and pin it to front edge where marked.

5. Sew pocket lining and facing together, right side to smooth side. Sew inner and outer pocket pieces together at top, turn and topstitch.

6. Clip pockets to sleeve/front pieces. Clip and sew these to the center fronts. Stitch seam allowances open. Sew center back seams of collar and glue the seam allowances down.

7. Clip and sew center back and sleeve/back seams and stitch seam allowances down.

8. Clip and sew fronts and back together at sleeve/shoulder/neckline (see Collars, p. 176). Thread tension should not be too tight, as there will be some strain on these seams. Stitch seam allowances down.

9. Sew sleeve/side seams to include sides of pockets. Notch seam allowances at underarm and glue seam allowances down. Sew in shoulder pads.

10. Press the pleat in lining center back; stitch it 2" (5cm) from both top and bottom. Sew center back panel to sleeve/back, leaving an opening of about 8" (20cm) for turning. Sew front and back together at sleeve/side seams. Sew facing at bottom edge to lining. Sew center front panels to lining. Sew collar together at center back and glue seam allowances down.

11. Sew sleeve/shoulder/neck seam. It might best be sewn with a narrow zigzag because of the diagonal cut of the sleeve. Sew sleeve facing together and sew it to sleeve edge of the lining. If desired, press a strip of fusible interfacing into the front edge of the collar.

12. Clip jacket and lining together at all outside edges, matching seams. Be sure the tab and pockets lie flat. Stitch all the way around. Trim seam allowances and turn right side out through opening in lining back.

13. Work a little with the edges to make them lie flat, and topstitch all the way around on the right side. Finish the buttonholes.

14. Fold and glue the hems. With wrong sides together, clip edges of facings to hems so that the facings extend beyond the folded edges by ⅜" (1cm). Edgestitch on right side, and trim off facing seam allowance very close to the stitching.

15. Slipstitch opening in lining back, and stitch layers together at back of neck. Sew on buttons, preferably with a smaller flat button under each one on the inside of the jacket.

68

THE PATTERN: USE BASIC PATTERN C, KIMONO

Choose size (for version in photo, add 6" or 15cm). Determine length (in photo, 2" or 5cm below the waist) and
   draw it in.
Trace collar from Collar Pattern III and extend front edge to the jacket bottom. The facing is identical to the
   center front/collar panel.
Draw a vertical panel cut 4-4¾" (10-12cm) from center front/center back.
Cut a narrow wedge from both front and back, starting 10-11" (25-28cm) below the shoulder line, widening to
   ⅜" (1 cm) on each side of the panel cut.
Cut another wedge from center back, ⅜" (1 cm) wide at bottom, tapering to a point 2/3 of the way up.
Taper sleeve to 5-6" (13-15cm) at wrist.
Draw the pocket using the side front panel and the drawing at right.
Draw facings for sleeve and bottom hems, 1¼" (3cm) wide.

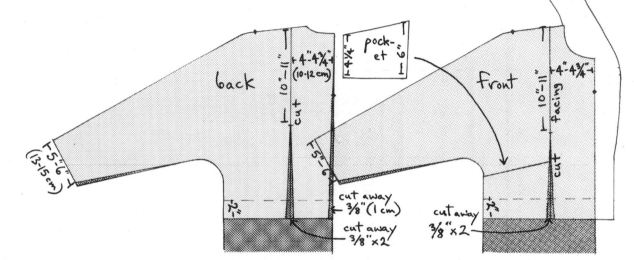

Raglan Coat with Shawl Collar★★

★★

A coat in a classic cut with raglan shoulders (Basic Pattern
D) and a shawl collar. It has bound pockets with flaps, and
a kick pleat in back. As there are no buttons or other
fasteners, the front edge falls cleanly, and the coat is held
closed with a belt.

• This design is made in a heavy, wool-embroidered canvas intended for upholstery, but because of its simple lines
it can be made of almost any kind of fabric, from heavy
cotton print for a summer coat to fake fur as a short coat
for winter. This one is lined with lining satin. For a winter
coat, underlining can be added.

★ ★ ★

pattern
alteration

zipper closure

collar
variation
p. 50

bound pocket
with upturned
flap

★ ★ ★

half belt
sewn into
side seams
& buttoned
in back

French tack

CONSTRUCTION

1. Cut all coat pieces, adding ⅝" (1½cm) seam allowance on the raglan, sides, sleeves, center back, front edge, and facings. For lighter fabrics ⅜" (1cm) would be enough. Add 1¼" (3cm) for hem at the bottom edge and ⅜" (1cm) on the pocket flaps.

2. Cut lining with ⅜" (1cm) seam allowance, and ¾" (2cm) at wrists and bottom edge. Cut lining fronts only to edge of facing and minus the 2¼" (6cm) hem in the straight front edge. Mark edge of facing. Remember to mark matching points for facings and lining. Cut pocket bags from lining fabric.

3. Cut interfacing for the front edges and collar, depending on the weight of the fabric.

4. Zigzag side seam allowances, bottom edges, and inner edge of facing on both coat and lining pieces. Zigzag all edges if the fabric frays easily.

5. Sew center back seam to ⅜" (1cm) into kick pleat. Zigzag and stitch down seam allowances toward overlap side of kick pleat.

6. Pin and sew front and back sleeve pieces together, with right sides together, and stitch seam allowances down to back.

7. Pin and sew sleeves to back. Zigzag and stitch seam allowances down to back.

8. Mark pocket placement, and make pockets following the procedure for bound pockets with standing flap (p. 146). If you are not sure of placement, make the pockets after you try on the coat.

9. Sew front collar pieces to facings at center backs, with right sides together. Press seams. Press fusible interfacing along front collar edge, inside seam allowance. On the straight edges, press interfacing up to the foldline. If you don't interface the coat, you may have to use seam tape or a strip of interfacing material along the seamline to prevent the edge from stretching out of shape.

10. Pin and stitch facings to fronts, turning up the hems of the facings before sewing. Press the seam and turn facings to the inside. Baste all the way down, close to the edge.

11. Pin and sew sleeve/back to front/collar, matching center backs. Be sure the rounding of the sleeve front and the curve of the collar lie smoothly (p. 103). Zigzag and stitch down the seam allowances.

12. Sew the sleeve/side seams and press the seam.

13. Hem the coat at bottom and wrists with a catch stitch or by machine.

14. Sew the lining together just like the coat. These instructions call for sewing in the lining by hand. If you prefer to sew it in by machine, follow the procedure on p. 163. Turn under the seam allowance around the neck; baste. Hem the bottom by machine: the lining should be ⅝" (1½cm) shorter than the coat.

15. Have someone else try on the coat, or hang it wrong side out on a hanger. Pin in the lining, right side out, matching seams and markings. Slipstitch it in place.

16. Sew the kick pleat as described on p. 162.

17. Topstitch the front edge/collar. Slipstitch lower edges of facings to the hem. Stitch layers together at the back of the neck.

18. Turn up lining ⅜" (1cm) at wrists. Pin folded edge of lining ⅜" (1cm) above edge of sleeve so that the lining will form a ¾" (2cm) pleat for ease.

19. Remove basting threads. Make French tacks at the bottom of each side seam to hold the lining to the coat (see drawing above).

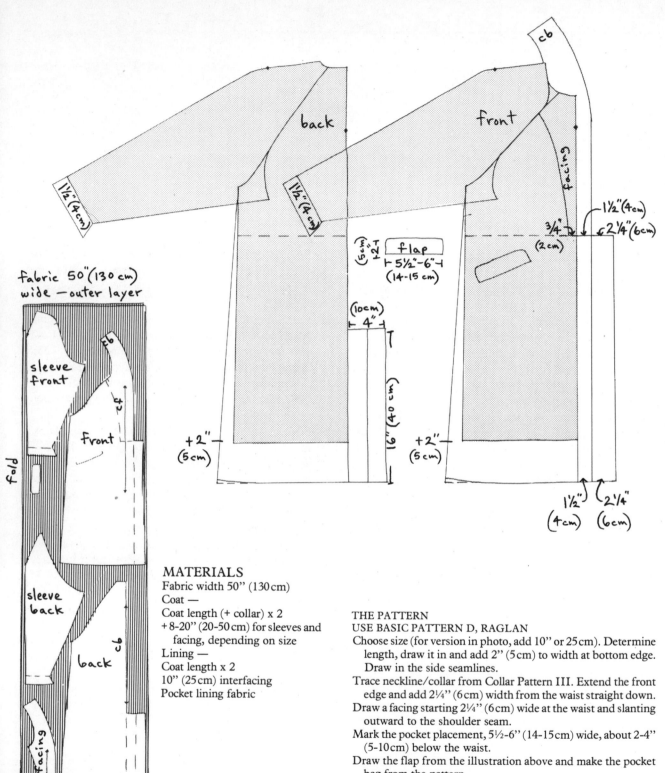

fabric 50" (130 cm)
wide — outer layer

fold

sleeve front

front

sleeve back

back

cb

facing

back

front

cb

facing

flap

5½"-6"
(14-15 cm)

2"
(5 cm)

4"
(10 cm)

16" (40 cm)

+ 2"
(5 cm)

+ 2"
(5 cm)

1½" (4 cm)

1½" (4 cm)

3/4"
(2 cm)

1½" (4 cm)

2¼" (6 cm)

1½"
(4 cm)

2¼"
(6 cm)

MATERIALS
Fabric width 50" (130 cm)
Coat —
Coat length (+ collar) x 2
+ 8-20" (20-50 cm) for sleeves and
   facing, depending on size
Lining —
Coat length x 2
10" (25 cm) interfacing
Pocket lining fabric

THE PATTERN
USE BASIC PATTERN D, RAGLAN
Choose size (for version in photo, add 10" or 25cm). Determine
   length, draw it in and add 2" (5cm) to width at bottom edge.
   Draw in the side seamlines.
Trace neckline/collar from Collar Pattern III. Extend the front
   edge and add 2¼" (6cm) width from the waist straight down.
Draw a facing starting 2¼" (6cm) wide at the waist and slanting
   outward to the shoulder seam.
Mark the pocket placement, 5½-6" (14-15cm) wide, about 2-4"
   (5-10cm) below the waist.
Draw the flap from the illustration above and make the pocket
   bag from the pattern.
Add 4" (10cm) for a kick pleat at center back, about 16" (40cm)
   long.
Add 1½" (4cm) hem allowance at the wrists.

Raglan Coat/Jacket with Lapels★★

Both jacket and coat have classic lines that have been popular, in different variations, for at least 50 years. The coat is made in a firm twill, and the jacket in heavy canvas. Chintz, tweed, polyester worsted and cambric would also work well.

• Leather would be a striking material—the design would require about 60 square feet of leather. The examples here are not lined, but could be made as fall coats with light quilted lining. See the section on Linings (p. 159). The coat is double-breasted with bound pockets; the jacket is single-breasted with patch pockets. Both designs feature a pleat in back, and the coat also has a half belt. It could, instead, be worn with a full belt. There are many ways to vary the details and still maintain the classic flavor. The lapels can be made wider/narrower/higher/lower. You could make a collar and a button placket front, and the pocket could be sewn with a down-turned or standing flap.

coat:

use 4 or 6 buttons

1) buttonholes in just the edge of the rt. front & decorative buttons for the 2nd row (photo p.73), or

2) buttonholes for both rt. front rows & two rows of buttons on the left front (photo on cover)

1⅛" (3cm) 4" (10cm)
4" (10cm)
2¼" (6cm)
cf

Fabric 59" (150cm) wide

half belt of doubled fabric — sew together, turn right side out & topstitch

1⅛" (3cm)
1⅛" (3cm)
2¼"–3¼" (6–8cm)
A 18"–22" (45–55cm)

B

epaulet turned & topstitched

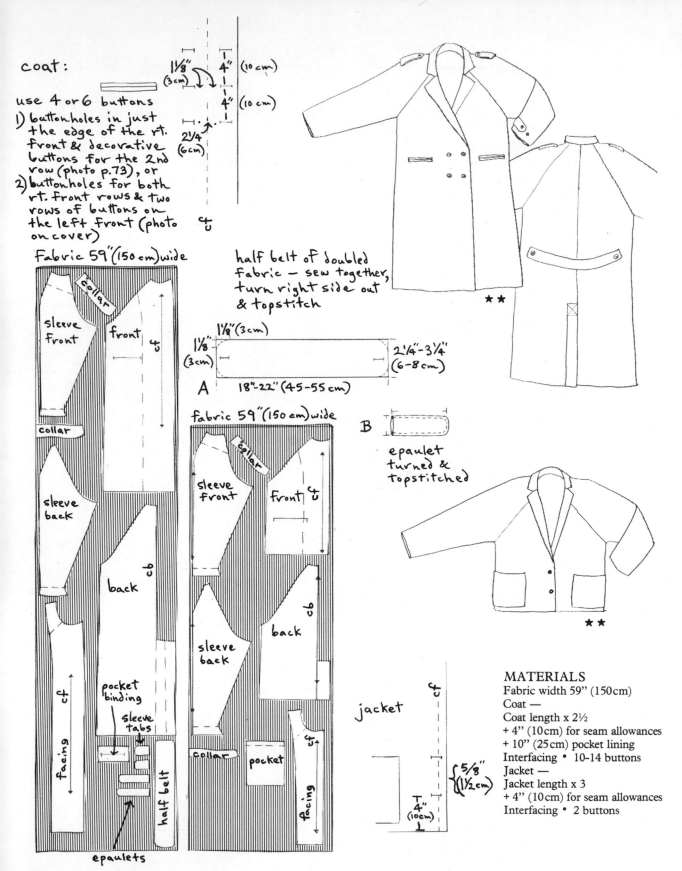

collar
sleeve front
front
cf
collar
sleeve back
back
cb
cf
facing
pocket binding
sleeve tabs
half belt
epaulets

fabric 59" (150cm) wide

collar
sleeve front
front
cf
sleeve back
back
cb
collar
pocket
facing
cf

jacket
cf
5/8" (1½cm)
4" (10cm)

MATERIALS
Fabric width 59" (150cm)
Coat —
Coat length x 2½
+ 4" (10cm) for seam allowances
+ 10" (25cm) pocket lining
Interfacing • 10-14 buttons
Jacket —
Jacket length x 3
+ 4" (10cm) for seam allowances
Interfacing • 2 buttons

★ ★

★ ★

CONSTRUCTION

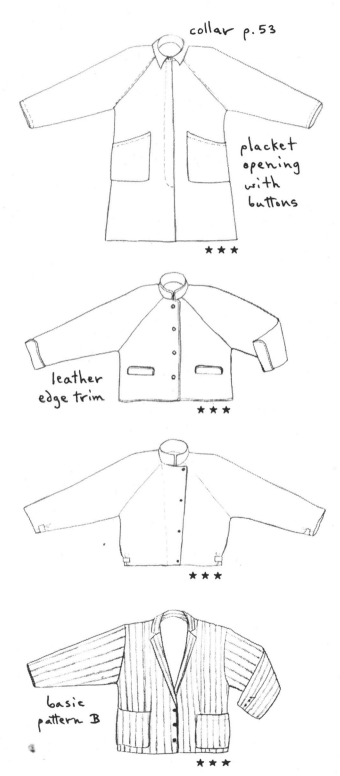

collar p.53

placket opening with buttons

★ ★ ★

leather edge trim

★ ★ ★

★ ★ ★

basic pattern B

★ ★ ★

1. Cut all pieces, adding ⅜" (1 cm) seam allowance and a 1½" (4 cm) hem at the lower edge. Cut the under collar on the bias, and the outer collar on a fold, a shade larger at the outer edges. If the kick pleat can't be cut as part of the back (due to the fabric width), cut it as a separate facing, 4" (10 cm) wide and as long as the pleat + 1¼" (3 cm). Cut pocket bags and bindings for, say, a pocket opening 6¼" (16 cm) wide and 8" (20 cm) deep (p. 145), or cut patch pockets (p. 142).

2. Cut sleeve tabs (and epaulets, if you wish) for a 2" (5 cm) finished width (p. 168). Cut them 2¾" (7 cm) long for sleeves and 6" (15 cm) long for the shoulders. Optional tabs on the pockets are also cut 2" (5 cm) long. Cut the half belt 18-20" (45-55 cm) long and 4-4¾" (10-12 cm) wide, double thickness.

3. Cut interfacing for collar and front edge. Mark center front, center back and pockets.

4. Sew and turn tabs, and make buttonholes in them. Sew front and back sleeve sections together, with right sides together, including tabs in the seams 1½-2" (4-5 cm) above the wrists. Zigzag and double-welt the seams toward the front.

5. Make bound pockets on the front (p. 145).

6. Sew the optional separate pleat facing to the center back (if the fabric stretches, press a narrow strip of fusible interfacing up to the seamline). Sew center back seam, zigzag and double-welt the seam toward the overlap side. Pin up the coat hem. Make the kick pleat as described on p. 140.

7. Sew in the sleeves. Zigzag and double-welt the seams.

8. Zigzag and sew the sleeve/side seams, or sew first, then zigzag and stitch down.

9. Sew lapels as described on p. 177.

10. Hem the bottom and sleeves.

11. Make optional epaulets and then make half belt. See drawings A and B, and Straps/Tabs (p. 168). Sew epaulets onto the shoulders and sew on buttons to fasten them down. Try on the coat and mark placement of the half belt. Sew the buttons onto it.

12. Sew on optional patch pockets.

13. Mark buttonholes on the coat front, following the drawings at left. Make these and sew on buttons.

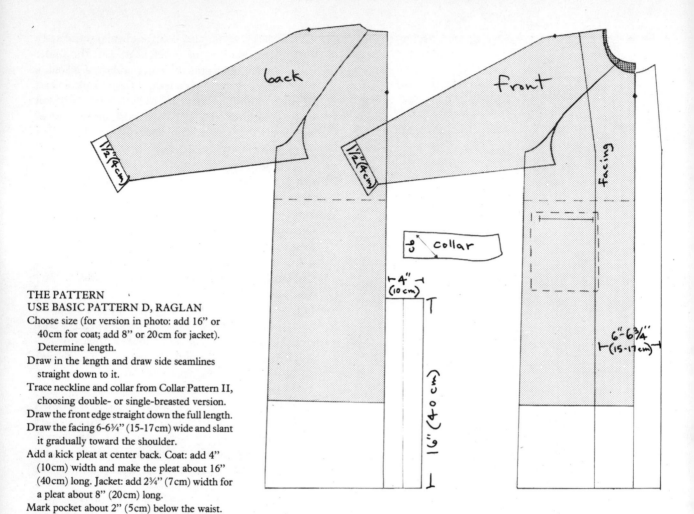

THE PATTERN
USE BASIC PATTERN D, RAGLAN

Choose size (for version in photo: add 16" or
    40 cm for coat; add 8" or 20 cm for jacket).
    Determine length.

Draw in the length and draw side seamlines
    straight down to it.

Trace neckline and collar from Collar Pattern II,
    choosing double- or single-breasted version.

Draw the front edge straight down the full length.

Draw the facing 6-6¾" (15-17 cm) wide and slant
    it gradually toward the shoulder.

Add a kick pleat at center back. Coat: add 4"
    (10 cm) width and make the pleat about 16"
    (40 cm) long. Jacket: add 2¾" (7 cm) width for
    a pleat about 8" (20 cm) long.

Mark pocket about 2" (5 cm) below the waist.
    Make pocket or pocket bag from the pattern.

For tabs, etc., see step 1.

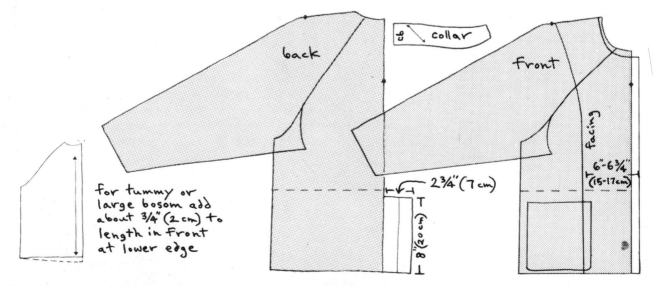

for tummy or
large bosom add
about ¾" (2 cm) to
length in front
at lower edge

JUMPSUIT WITH WAISTLINE SEAM, p. 81   ALL-IN-ONE JUMPSUIT, p. 78

All-in-One Jumpsuit*

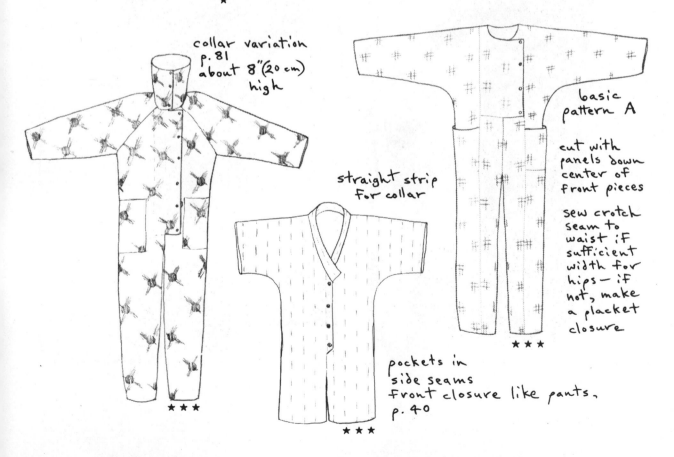

photo p. 77

A raglan-style jumpsuit with a collared Y-neck, buttoned down the front. It has patch pockets and wide, cuffed legs, and is otherwise as simple as can be. It can be varied with almost any collar, or made without one like the summer jacket on p. 41. The pockets can also be changed, and it can be made with set-in sleeves or dropped shoulders, and worn with or without a belt. It could be made as a summer playsuit with shortened sleeves and legs.

• This design is made in thin, satin-weave cotton, but shiny satin, crepe de Chine, sweatshirt fabrics, gingham, or a gorgeous big floral print would also work well.

★

collar variation
p. 81
about 8"(20 cm)
high

★ ★ ★

straight strip
for collar

pockets in
side seams
front closure like pants,
p. 40

★ ★ ★

basic
pattern A

cut with
panels down
center of
front pieces

sew crotch
seam to
waist if
sufficient
width for
hips — if
not, make
a placket
closure

★ ★ ★

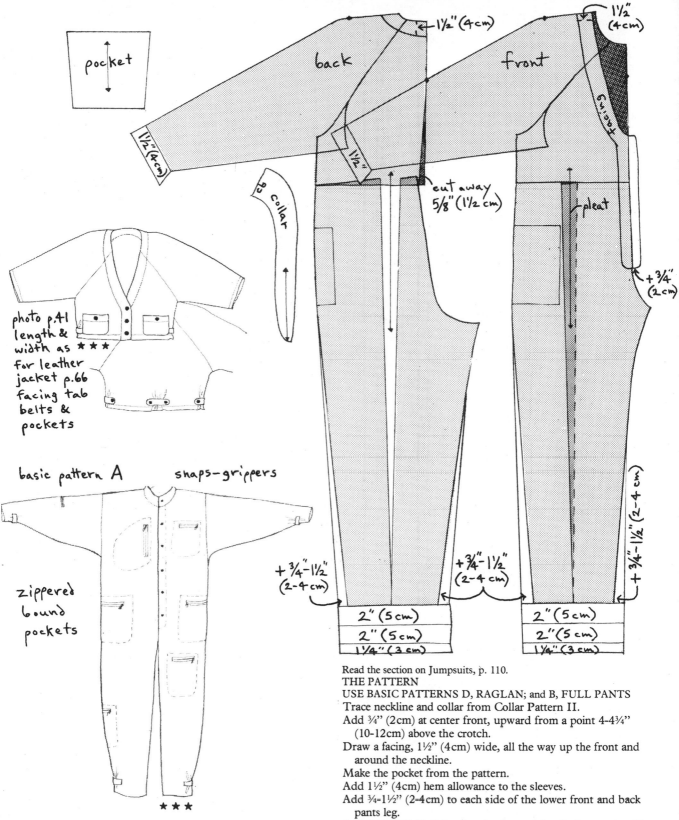

pocket

1½" (4cm)

back

front

1½" (4cm)

1½" (4cm)

facing

1½"

collar

cut away
5/8" (1½ cm)

pleat

+ ¾"
(2cm)

photo p.41
length &
width as ★★★
for leather
jacket p.66
facing tab
belts &
pockets

basic pattern A   snaps-grippers

zippered
bound
pockets

+ ¾"-1½"
(2-4 cm)

+ ¾"-1½"
(2-4 cm)

+ ¾"-1½" (2-4 cm)

2" (5cm)
2" (5cm)
1¼" (3cm)

2" (5cm)
2" (5cm)
1¼" (3cm)

★★★

Read the section on Jumpsuits, p. 110.
THE PATTERN
USE BASIC PATTERNS D, RAGLAN; and B, FULL PANTS
Trace neckline and collar from Collar Pattern II.
Add ¾" (2cm) at center front, upward from a point 4-4¾"
   (10-12cm) above the crotch.
Draw a facing, 1½" (4cm) wide, all the way up the front and
   around the neckline.
Make the pocket from the pattern.
Add 1½" (4cm) hem allowance to the sleeves.
Add ¾-1½" (2-4cm) to each side of the lower front and back
   pants leg.
Add 2, 2, 1¼" (5, 5, 3cm) at leg bottom for the hem and cuff.

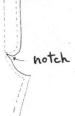

notch

CONSTRUCTION

1. Cut all pieces, adding ⅜" (1 cm) seam allowance at all edges. Cut facings for front edges and neckline, and for collar and pockets. Cut interfacing without seam allowance for the collar and facings. Cut pockets from single thickness fabric with 1½" (4 cm) hem allowance, or from double thickness fabric with no hem.

2. Zigzag inseams of the legs and the underarm seams. If the other seams are to be sewn down, zigzag them as they are sewn. Otherwise, zigzag all seam edges now.

3. Sew center back and side seams.

4. Sew sleeve sections together.

5. Pin and sew sleeves to fronts and back. Sew seam allowances toward the bottom.

6. Pin and sew center back seams in under and outer collars, press the seams, and sew the collar pieces together at the outer edges. Turn and topstitch. Pin collar to neckline, right sides together, matching center backs and front edges. Sew the facing together at center back and press in ⅜" (1 cm) seam allowance on collar's inner edge.

7. With right sides together, pin and sew facing to neckline/front edge, with collar between the 2 layers. Notch the seam at bottom of front opening (see drawing above), and sew as described on p. 150. Sew center front seam from the notch down. Lay overlapping side over underlying side. Pin and sew together in a curve.

8. Make the pockets (p. 142). Try on the suit, pin and sew on pockets.

9. Sew leg inseams and press seams.

10. Hem sleeves and legs, turning up a cuff, if desired.

11. Mark placement of buttons or snaps ¾" (2 cm) below the collar and ¾" (2 cm) from the bottom, and space 3-4 more buttons evenly between these.

MATERIALS
Fabric width 55" (140 cm)
Length of suit (+ hem and cuff) x 2
+ 4" (10 cm) for seam allowances
5-6 buttons

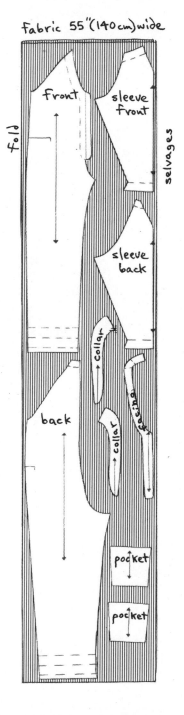

Fabric 55"(140cm)wide

Jumpsuit with Waistband**

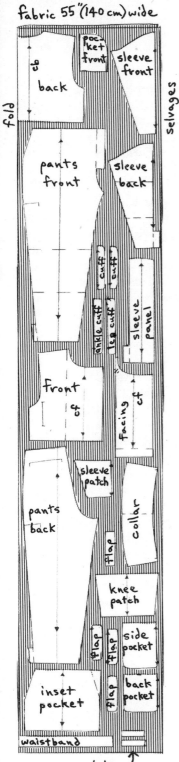

fabric 55"(140cm)wide

fold

selvages

back
pocket front
sleeve front
pants front
sleeve back
cuff
cuff
ankle cuff
leg cuff
sleeve panel
front cf
facing cf
sleeve patch
collar
pants back
flap
inset pocket
flap
flap
flap
flap
knee patch
side pocket
back pocket
waistband

tabs

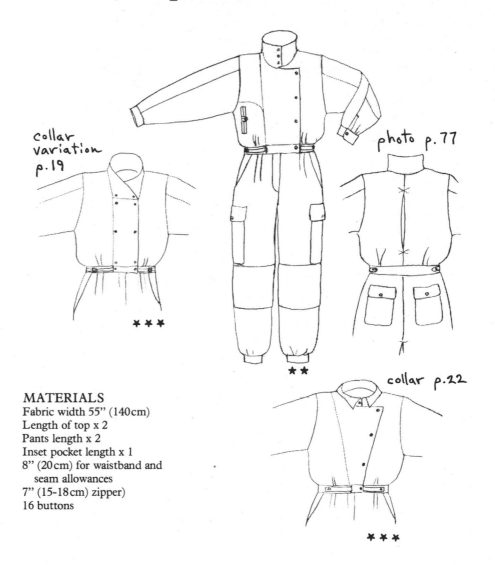

collar variation p.19

★ ★ ★

photo p.77

★ ★

collar p.22

★ ★ ★

MATERIALS
Fabric width 55" (140cm)
Length of top x 2
Pants length x 2
Inset pocket length x 1
8" (20cm) for waistband and
   seam allowances
7" (15-18cm) zipper)
16 buttons

A jumpsuit made as 2 pieces and joined with a waistband. The top has set-in sleeves (Basic Pattern B), a deep overlap and a high collar. It has bound pockets in front, a pleat in back, and 3-seam sleeves with cuffs and elbow patches.

• The pants have inset pockets, patch pockets with flaps on the thighs, patches on the knees, and cuffs at the ankles. The waistband has tabs and buttons on the sides.

• Because there are many details, this design takes a little time to make, but it can be made in a simpler version—for example, elasticized at the wrists and ankles, with one-piece sleeves and a simple front opening closed with a zipper or a button placket.

• This example is made in a firm, soft cotton. Crinkle nylon and flannel, pinwale corduroy, and cambric would also work well.

• The jumpsuit opens to the left in these instructions.

CONSTRUCTION

1. Cut out all pieces, adding ⅜" (1 cm) seam allowance. Add a hem at the lower pants leg for a slit ¾" (2 cm) wide and 3¼" (8 cm) long in the outer seam. Cut front facings 1½" (4 cm) longer than the fronts, because of the waistband. Cut the waistband from a single thickness of fabric, the waist measurement + 3-4" (8-10 cm) for ease and overlap, x 1½" (4 cm) wide. Cut cuffs for the legs the length of the ankle measurement + 1¼" (3 cm) x 1½" (4 cm) wide. Cut pocket bags and bindings for the upper front pockets (p. 144). Cut inset pockets, perhaps from thinner fabric (p. 148), and patch or bound pockets with flaps (p. 83 and p. 146) for back and sides. Also cut belt tabs for the waistline, 3-4¾" (8-12 cm) long and 1¼" (3 cm) wide (p. 168). Mark center front on all front sections, the pleat at center back, and pocket and patch placements.

2. If seam allowances are to be stitched down, zigzag only sleeve/side seams and inseams and outer seams of the legs, doing the others as you go along.

3. *Top:* Fold and sew the pleat at center back, stitching it down 4" (10 cm) from the neck and up 2¾" (7 cm) from the waist. Fold as a box pleat and press. Sew a cross at the top and bottom of the pleat opening.

4. Make a bound pocket on the right front, with button loop, flap, or zipper. Sew shoulder seams with right sides together. Zigzag and stitch down seam allowances.

5. Press under the seam allowances at the top and bottom of the sleeve patches. Pin and sew at the elbows.

6. Sew sleeve seams, except for underarm seams. Leave an opening at the bottom of the center back seam.

7. Sew sleeves to the top, with right sides together, matching center to shoulder seam. Zigzag and stitch down the seam allowances.

8. Sew the sleeve/side seams and hem the sleeves. Make 1-2 pleats in each front and back section, so each equals ¼ the waist measurement. On the fronts, take into account the inner edge of the facing.

9. *Pants:* Make inset pockets at the sides, and patch or bound hip pockets.

10. Sew the center front seam to the fly, but wait to sew in the zipper.

11. Sew center back seam, zigzag and stitch down.

12. Press under the seam allowance at top and bottom of knee patches, pin and sew them at the knees.

13. Sew the sides seams, leaving a slit at the bottoms (p. 155).

14. Sew the thigh pockets on at mid-thigh (p. 142). Sew the inseams.

15. Pleat the waist so that each front section equals ¼ of the waist measurement.

16. Pin top to pants at the waist, with wrong sides together. Try on and adjust length at the waist if necessary. Mark placement of waistband, either right on, just below, or just above the waist seam.

17. Sew zipper into the fly with overlap on right side. Sew together at the waist, still with wrong sides together. Trim the seam allowance if there's more than ⅜" (1 cm), and press seam open, or up, or down, depending where the waistband will be.

18. Cut a small notch at center front of the waistband bottom seam allowance. Turn under and press the top ⅜" (1 cm) seam allowance, and press under the bottom seam allowance out to the notch. Pin and baste the waistband on, making sure all layers lie smoothly and evenly. Stitch down both sides.

19. Turn under and press the inside seam allowance of the facing. Adjust length, and trim the seam allowance. Notch the seam allowance at bottom center front. Make belt tabs and pin them to the edges of the waistband. Pin and sew on the overlap, from facing center front to center front of the waist. Trim seam allowances, turn, and topstitch. Make a bound buttonhole, 1¼" (3 cm) long, in the right side of the waistband just before the end of the facing (p. 156). Pin and stitch down the inner edge of the facing and finish the buttonhole.

20. Sew the collar sections together from center front around ends and outside edges to center front, and sew it on as described on p. 175.

21. Mark buttonholes: 3 on the collar—top, center, and bottom—and 4 on the front edge—¾" (2 cm) from top and bottom, with 2 spaced evenly between them. Sew 1 or 2 on each belt tab at the waist. The buttons on the waistband are marked when the garment is fitted. Make buttonholes and sew buttons on the sleeve and leg cuffs.

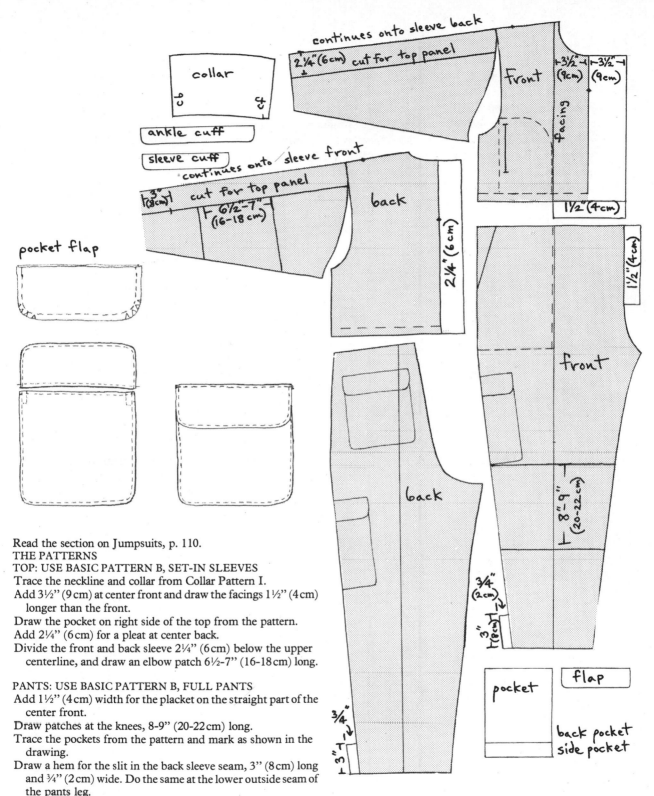

collar

ankle cuff

sleeve cuff

pocket flap

continues onto sleeve back

2¼" (6cm) cut for top panel

Front

facing

3½" (9cm) 3½" (9cm)

1½" (4cm)

continues onto sleeve front

cut for top panel

3" (8cm)

6½"-7" (16-18 cm)

back

2¼" (6cm)

1½" (4cm)

front

back

8"-9" (20-22cm)

¾" (2cm)

3" (8cm)

¾"

3"

pocket

flap

back pocket
side pocket

Read the section on Jumpsuits, p. 110.

THE PATTERNS

TOP: USE BASIC PATTERN B, SET-IN SLEEVES

Trace the neckline and collar from Collar Pattern I.

Add 3½" (9 cm) at center front and draw the facings 1½" (4 cm)
    longer than the front.

Draw the pocket on right side of the top from the pattern.

Add 2¼" (6 cm) for a pleat at center back.

Divide the front and back sleeve 2¼" (6 cm) below the upper
    centerline, and draw an elbow patch 6½-7" (16-18 cm) long.

PANTS: USE BASIC PATTERN B, FULL PANTS

Add 1½" (4 cm) width for the placket on the straight part of the
    center front.

Draw patches at the knees, 8-9" (20-22 cm) long.

Trace the pockets from the pattern and mark as shown in the
    drawing.

Draw a hem for the slit in the back sleeve seam, 3" (8 cm) long
    and ¾" (2 cm) wide. Do the same at the lower outside seam of
    the pants leg.

Draw cuffs for sleeves and legs following the diagram above.

For tabs, see step 1.

Robe*

A bathrobe in a raglan cut. This one is made with Basic Pattern D, but it could just as well be made using A with dropped shoulders. The bathrobe is made of terry cloth with a shiny satin brocade on the collar and sleeve cuffs.

• When putting together two fabrics as dissimilar as terry and satin, the fabrics must be washed separately before cutting to preshrink them and to prevent the colors from bleeding together. Later, when the bathrobe itself is laundered, it is washed according to the more delicate fabric, satin.

• There are many other fabric combinations that would work: smooth-finish cotton and flannel work well if the entire bathrobe is of both layers of fabric. A classic combination for bathrobes is light wool and lining satin. And sweatshirt fabric could be used alone, with a doubled collar and sleeve turn-up.

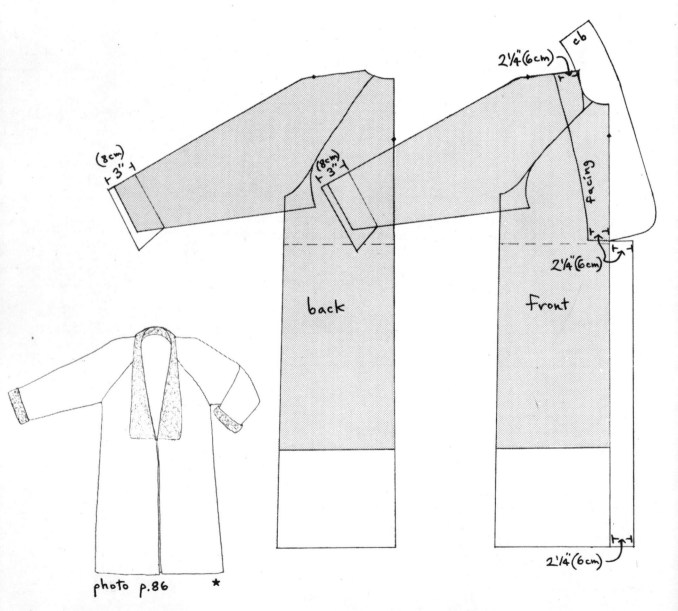

photo p.86   *

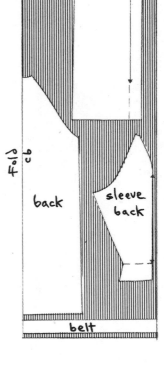

THE PATTERN
USE BASIC PATTERN D, RAGLAN
Follow the description for the raglan coat with shawl collar, p. 72.
The sleeve here is shortened, and 3" (8 cm) is added for a cuff.
Draw the facings for the sleeves and front edges.
If desired, add 1¼-2" (3-5 cm) to the width at the bottom.

CONSTRUCTION

1. The edges to be sewn together are cut with ⅝" (1½ cm) seam allowance added. Allow ⅜" (1 cm) at collar/front edge and sleeve seam, and a 1½" (4 cm) hem at the bottom and along the straight front edge. The sleeves can either be cut as 2 pieces or in one piece with a shoulder dart (p. 103). The facing and sleeve turn-up are cut with ⅝" (1½ cm) seam allowance, of which ¼" (½ cm) is "filling." Cut a sash 5 ft (150 cm) long and 4" (10 cm) wide + seam allowance, for a finished width of 2" (5 cm). Make the sash longer if you wish.

2. Zigzag the side seams, sleeve/seams, bottom edge, and straight front edge.

3. Sew the shoulder dart, or sew front and back sleeve pieces together. Zigzag seam allowances and stitch down to the back.

4. Press under ⅜" (1 cm) on the inside edge of the facing. Sew the center back collar seams on the front sections and the facings, and press the seams open. Pin and sew facing to robe with a ⅜" (1 cm) seam allowance, right sides together, from center front to center front. Be careful the fabric doesn't stretch, as it's cut on the bias. You may wish to use seam tape (p. 124). Turn facing to inside and topstitch. If the facing is quite thin compared to the robe, sew a second line of topstitching a presser foot's width in, while pulling the robe fabric out a little and letting the facing fabric lie loosely.

5. Pin and sew the back and sleeves at the raglan, zigzag and stitch down the seam allowances. Pin and sew the front/collar to the back/sleeves, matching center back seams (p. 177). Sew a hanger loop into the seam, if desired. Zigzag and stitch the seam allowances down.

6. Sew the sleeve/side seams.

7. Hang the robe on a hanger or try it on someone else. Turn the collar out so it lies smoothly, and pin down the inner edge of the facing so that none of the layers strain or bunch. Fold the straight front edge in and pin. Pin the facing down onto the hem edge where they meet, and sew by hand or machine. Pin, baste, and sew the facing to the robe. Depending on the fabric, you may have to sew another line of stitching ⅜-¾" (1-2 cm) from the foldline.

8. Sew the seams in the sleeve facings, with right sides together, and press the seams open. Sew facings to the lower edges of the sleeves, with right sides together. Turn and topstitch. Fold back the cuffs and pin the inside edges. Fold cuffs down again and sew according to the pinning. In lighter fabrics it's unnecessary to pin with the cuff folded back.

9. Make the sash as a strip 5 ft (150 cm) long (see p. 168), and make belt loops at the sides of the robe.

MATERIALS
Fabric width 55" (140cm)
Robe length (+ collar) x 1
+ length from armhole to lower
   edge, depending on size
+ 4" (10 cm) for seam allowances
+ 4" (10 cm) for belt
Length of facing in contrasting
   fabric

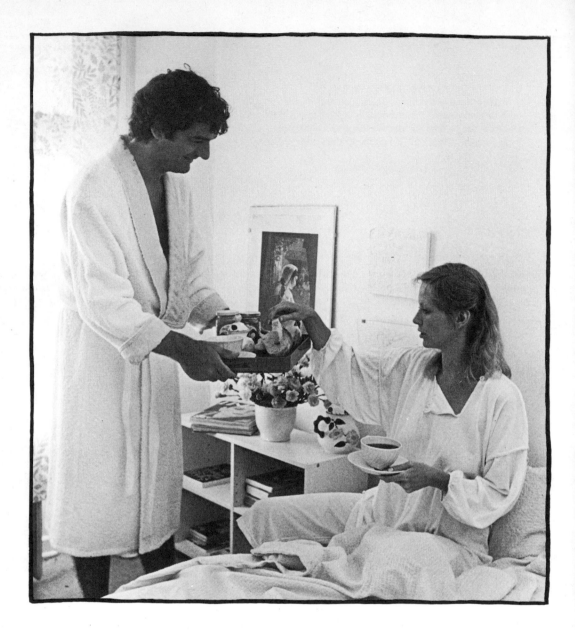

Pajamas*

Pajamas consisting of a full top falling to mid-thigh and a pair of three-quarter-length pants. Sewn in cotton-acetate jersey, they get their luster from the acetate. Thin cotton interlock or lightweight woven cottons will also work well.

• The top is trimmed with satin bias tape at the shoulder seam and the sleeve cap, but it can also be made without this feature, if you prefer.

• The pants are simplicity itself, without side seams and with elastic at the waist. Choose a size 1-2 sizes larger than your actual size, because night clothes are best if they're a little roomy. If the pants are made of woven fabric, be sure the waist equals the hip measurement + ¾" (2 cm), so you can get into them easily. If using knit fabric, read the section on p. 125.

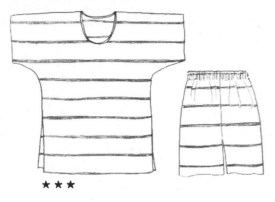

★ ★ ★

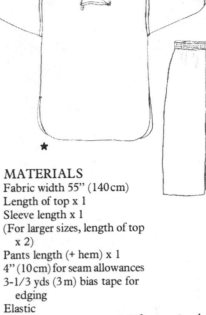

★

CONSTRUCTION

1. *Top:* Cut the pieces, adding ¼" (½ cm) seam allowance for knits or ⅜" (1 cm) for woven fabrics on all edges to be sewn together. Add ⅝" (1½ cm) at the bottom edge and the slit. Don't add a seam allowance at the neck.

   • *Pants:* Cut the pieces, adding ¼" (½ cm) seam allowance for knits or ⅜" (1 cm) for woven fabrics at center front, center back, and inseams. Add ¾" (2 cm) hem at the bottom. Allow ⅜" (1 cm) at the waist in addition to the 1¾" (4½ cm) hem for the channel. Mark the channel.

2. *Top:* Pin the shoulder seams with wrong sides together. Lay the fabric out smoothly, pin on bias tape, and sew it on the seamline. Fold the tape over the seam allowance and stitch the other side (p. 152).

   • Cut a slit 4" (10 cm) long down from the left side of the neckline and finish it with bias tape. Sew a button loop into the upper front corner of the slit (p. 156).

   • Pin and sew on the sleeves with wrong sides together, and finish with bias tape like the shoulder seams. For woven fabric, zigzag the edges. Pin and sew the sleeve/side seams down to the slit. Zigzag the slit and bottom edge. Pin and hem with a row of double-needle stitching or make a doubled hem.

   • Sew two gathering lines at each wrist. Gather to about 10" (25 cm) and edge with bias tape. Sew a button at the neck.

3. *Pants:* For woven fabric, zigzag all edges first. Sew center front and center back seams. Leave 1½" (4 cm) open at the top center back to insert elastic.

   • Pin and sew the inseams.

   • Zigzag the waist and the bottom edge.

   • Make a hem ¾" (2 cm) at the bottom with double needle stitching, or turn up and sew a doubled hem.

   • Turn down the waist edge and make 3 channels, each ⅝" (1½ cm) wide, and pull elastic through. Sew elastic together at the ends and slipstitch the opening.

MATERIALS

Fabric width 55" (140 cm)
Length of top x 1
Sleeve length x 1
(For larger sizes, length of top
   x 2)
Pants length (+ hem) x 1
4" (10 cm) for seam allowances
3-1/3 yds (3 m) bias tape for
   edging
Elastic

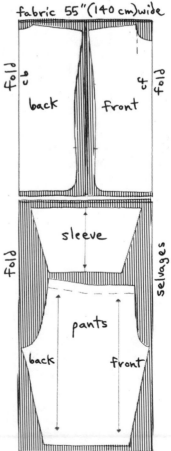

fabric 55" (140 cm) wide

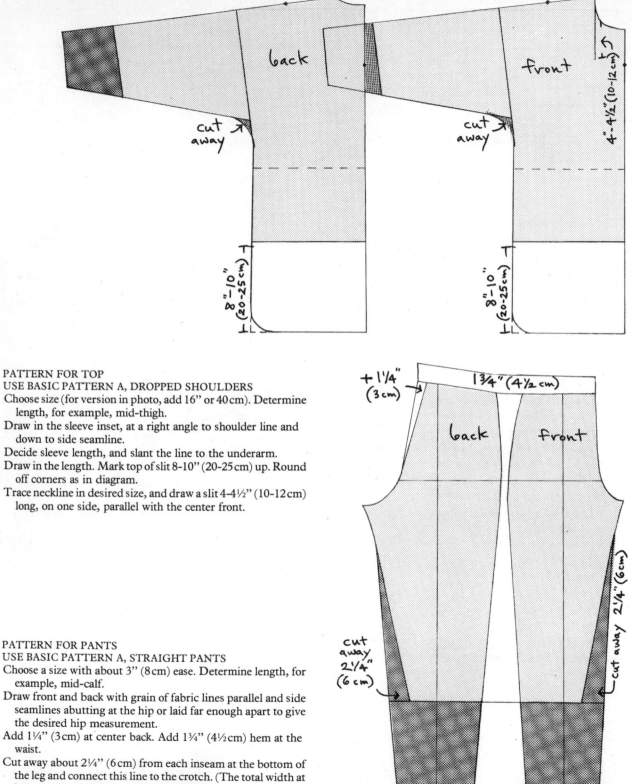

PATTERN FOR TOP
USE BASIC PATTERN A, DROPPED SHOULDERS

Choose size (for version in photo, add 16" or 40 cm). Determine length, for example, mid-thigh.

Draw in the sleeve inset, at a right angle to shoulder line and down to side seamline.

Decide sleeve length, and slant the line to the underarm.

Draw in the length. Mark top of slit 8-10" (20-25 cm) up. Round off corners as in diagram.

Trace neckline in desired size, and draw a slit 4-4½" (10-12 cm) long, on one side, parallel with the center front.

PATTERN FOR PANTS
USE BASIC PATTERN A, STRAIGHT PANTS

Choose a size with about 3" (8 cm) ease. Determine length, for example, mid-calf.

Draw front and back with grain of fabric lines parallel and side seamlines abutting at the hip or laid far enough apart to give the desired hip measurement.

Add 1¼" (3 cm) at center back. Add 1¾" (4½ cm) hem at the waist.

Cut away about 2¼" (6 cm) from each inseam at the bottom of the leg and connect this line to the crotch. (The total width at bottom must be at least 16-18" or 40-46 cm).

Leather Belt★

A shaped belt tapering from 2 to 2¾" (5 to 7 cm), which can be made from any kind of leather the sewing machine can handle. There are 3 layers—the inside or bottom, the interfacing, and the outside or top, plus optional decoration. For this we've used bits of lizard skin on the back and sides. The top and bottom layers are fairly heavy calfskin; the middle layer is a thick, fusible non-woven interfacing designed specifically for leather. You could also use a thin piece of stiff leather. The buckle measures ¾" (1.8 cm) and is attached with rivets.
• The belt is designed to rest on the hips.
• The pattern in the Pattern section is shown in 2 sizes. The size can be further regulated by the placement of the strap and the buckle.

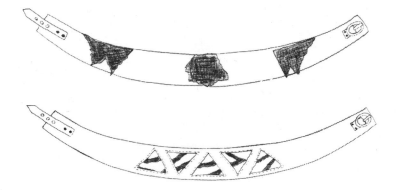

★

MATERIALS
Outer layer, stiffening, and lining:
36 x 8" (90 x 20 cm)
Optional: decorative leather trim
Leather glue • Buckle
4 rivets • 3 eyelets

CONSTRUCTION
1. Cut out 3 layers, adding ¼" (½ cm) seam allowance all the way around. Cut 2 straps, 2¾" and 6¼" (7 and 16 cm) long to fit the buckle. Allow ¼" (½ cm) seam allowance on the shorter strap and omit the interfacing.
2. Optional decoration can be applied 2 ways:
   • *Applique:* Sew on after the layers are joined, or through only the top and interfacing.
   • *Cut-away:* The top layer is cut away in a pattern to reveal the decorative skin. Decide the shape and placement of the decoration. Score the patterns into the outer layer and cut them out. Transfer the pattern to the interfacing, and glue the decorations to the markings, or have a whole layer of decorative leather showing through. Glue the top layer and stitch around the openings.
3. Press or glue the layers together.
4. Stitch around the edge, using the presser foot as a gauge, so the stitching is ¼" (¾ cm) from the edge. Sew a pointed tip on the longer strap. Trim the edge about 1/16" (2 mm) from the stitching.
5. Put the belt around the hips at the desired height and mark strap and buckle placement (for example 1½-2¼" (4-6 cm) from the ends and exactly centered).
   • Set 3 or 4 grommets in the long strap and attach the strap to the belt with 2 rivets. Cut a hole for the tongue of the buckle in the middle of the shorter strap, and attach it with 2 rivets placed side by side.

Beret*

A beret is a versatile addition to your wardrobe. It can be worn in many ways and looks quite different depending on the material used. The design here was made of leather, but knits, tweed, heavy silk and soft plastic fabrics are all good choices. It can also be made with one part in a contrasting color, with "confetti" on it or with piping at the seams. It can be made in sections or of 2 whole discs and with a narrow band, and it can be lined, depending on how you feel and what it's made of.

• The beret pattern is included in the pattern section and is given in 3 sizes.

• In leather, it can also be made of tiny irregular scraps, laid over each other, starting in the middle and working outward. You could instead cut a piece of fusible interfacing and iron the scraps onto it, so the surface would be completely smooth (see the section on Working with Leather, p. 128).

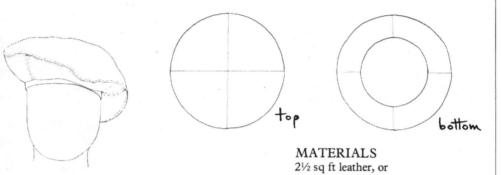

MATERIALS
2½ sq ft leather, or
12" (30 cm) fabric
Optional: 12" (30 cm) lining fabric

CONSTRUCTION

1. Cut 4 top and 4 bottom quarters, or 1 whole top and 1 whole bottom. If using woven fabric, cut the band on the bias, 2" (5 cm) wide and to the head measurement + seam allowance. For a lining, cut whole discs rather than quarters, and omit the band.
   • If the fabric needs stiffening, cut interfacing in whole circles and without seam allowance.
2. Pin/clip and sew the quarters together in pairs, right sides together. Press the seams open. Pin/clip and sew the halves together, with right sides together, and press the seam allowances. Press on fusible interfacing and stitch the seam allowances down from the right side, about 1/16" (2 mm) on each side of the seamline. Pin/clip and sew the pieces of the bottom portion together the same way.
3. Pin/clip upper to lower section, with right sides together, matching seams, and sew. Use the edge of a sleeve board or a tightly wound ball of yarn to press the seams. Stitch the seam allowances open.
4. Sew the optional lining like the outer beret, and pin/clip to the edge of the beret with wrong sides together.
5. Notch the lower, inner seam allowance at 1½-2" (4-5 cm) intervals. Join the ends of the band, with right sides together. Mark it in 4 equal sections. Pinning/clipping right sides together, matching marks to seams/markings, apply like bias edging (p. 152, or if leather, p. 153). Topstitch the edges if desired.

Cap with Visor*

This cap has an oversized crown, with 6 identical gores, a choice of visors, and a firm band. Patterns are provided for head sizes 22, 23, or 24" (55, 58, or 61 cm). Almost any fabric or leather could be used, and it can be made with or without a lining.

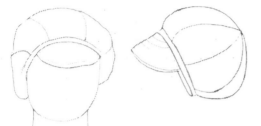

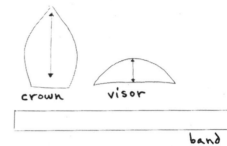

crown   visor

band

MATERIALS
12" (30 cm) fabric, 50" (130 cm) wide, or
3 sq ft soft leather

CONSTRUCTION

1. Adding ⅜" (1 cm) seam allowance to all pieces, cut the visor from doubled fabric. Cut 6 identical gores for the crown. Cut the band 1" (2½ cm) wide in the head measurement x 2 from doubled fabric. Cut a lining for the crown, if desired.
2. Zigzag the curved edges of crown sections, unless it is to be lined.
3. Sew the pieces of the crown together 3 at a time. Stitch the seam allowances down and sew the halves together. Make lining the same way and zigzag it to the crown at the bottom edge.
4. Press optional interfacing on one or both visor pieces, depending on the fabric and how stiff you want the visor. Sew the 2 visor sections, with right sides together, along the curved edge. Trim the edge closely, turn, and topstitch ¼-⅜" (½-1 cm) from the edge. If you wish, sew another 4-8 lines of stitching, equally spaced, following the curve of the edge.
5. Join each of the 2 band strips at the ends, with right sides together. Mark center front on the bands (the seam = center back) and visor. Pin a band on each side of the visor, right sides toward the visor, matching center fronts and center backs, and stitch the layers together all the way around. Press under the seam allowance of the inner band ⅜" (1 cm).
6. Sew the outer band and visor to the crown, with right sides together, so that 1 crown section is centered on the center front of the visor. Sew on the inner band like a waistband (p. 154).

Helmet★

Very practical and warm, a helmet is more or less an unattached hood. In woven fabrics and leather, it's made with an opening in front; with knits, it's simply pulled on over the head. It can be made as a rain hood in plastic fabrics or oilcloth. The edge can be finished with a facing, a trim, or a ribbing, if it is to fit closely.

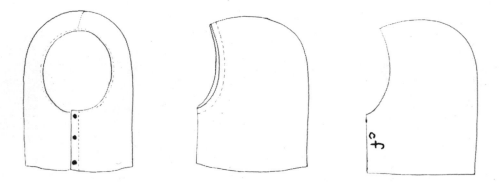

CONSTRUCTION

1. Cut 2 pieces adding ⅜" (1 cm) seam allowance. If there is an opening in front, mark center front.
2. Sew the curved seam, with right sides together, and stitch down the seam allowances if desired.
3. If there is an opening in front, turn and stitch the front edges in. Otherwise sew them together, with right sides together.
4. Finish the front edge with facing (p. 150), trim (p. 152), or ribbing (p. 127).
5. Hem the bottom and set optional snaps in the front edge, or make buttonholes and sew buttons on the center front.

MATERIALS

Fabric width 35" (90cm)
Height of helmet x 1
3 buttons or snaps (optional)

USING
THE
PATTERNS

"From the practical viewpoint, what can an object be used for? Is it a matter of indifference what script is used as long as it is legible? But from the aesthetic viewpoint—what impression does it make on me?—it is the writing itself that one looks at. Style is the handwriting of the period and the people. When one can interpret it, things speak."

—From *Everyday Art — World Art* by R. Broby-Johansen

Patterns

All the clothing in this book is developed from basic patterns found in the pattern section in the back of the book.

• To make one of the examples shown, you must first find the relevant basic pattern, choose the right size, and enlarge the pattern, drawing it on pattern tissue or muslin, and perhaps adjusting it somewhat. The block of text describing each pattern indicates how much has been added to the pattern for the amount of ease seen in the photographed garment. Following that is a description of the additions, panel cuts, etc., shown in the *pattern drafting diagram*. When the pattern has been drawn, it can be checked by comparing it with the *cutting layout*, where the individual pieces, with markings, are shown laid out on fabric. This process is described in more detail on p. 113.

• Examples marked * are fairly easy to make and require no significant changes to the basic pattern. Examples with ** require a little more sewing experience or a little more effort. There are directions for all examples at both these levels.

• Suggestions marked *** are intended to inspire your own original ideas. If you wonder how to translate a drawing into a pattern, read the section on p. 116, and page through the book to find examples with similar changes which are already drawn up.

THE PATTERNS

The basic patterns to all the new clothes are found in the Pattern section, beginning on page 178.

Basic patterns for tops: A — dropped shoulders
B — set-in sleeves
C — kimono cut
D — raglan

Basic pants patterns: A — straight pants
B — full pants

Basic skirt patterns: C — straight skirt
D — full skirt

Collar patterns I, II, & III
Pockets
Hats

All the basic patterns are drawn as simply as possible on the sheets without any additions or changes shown.
• Tops have round necks and are knee length.
• Pants are full length; skirts are mid-calf length.

SIZES

Tops are in 6 sizes, so they can be used for both outer and inner wear.

• Pants and skirts are in 4 sizes.

• Take body measurements shown in the Table of Measurements II and III. The measurements are taken as shown in figs. A, B, and C, close to the body but without binding.

• Because the looseness or tightness of tops depends on individual preferences, there are no hard and fast sizes given for tops. Measurement Table I is a guide, corresponding to the lines used for the examples in the book. If the hip measurement is more than 4" (10 cm) larger than the bust measurement, some attention should be paid to this fact when choosing sizes for tops that go down over the hips.

• For pants and skirts, size is based on the hip measurement. If your measurements don't match those in the Table of Measurements, then choose the nearest larger size and adjust with a lengthwise tuck (p. 97), or draft the pattern between 2 sizes if this works for your measurements. The hip measurement of the patterns (the measurement across the hips) should not be smaller than the actual hip measurement of the body except when making stretch pants (p. 37). Basic Pants Pattern A and the Basic Straight Skirt Pattern C include 1½" (4 cm) extra width over the hips, allowing them to lie smoothly without strain.

• Back length and crotch length should not be changed, but sleeve and pants leg length and the length of the entire garment can of course be changed as you like.

• If there is a difference between the length measurements of the body and those of the basic pattern, adjust the basic pattern before making alterations outlined in the pattern drafting text for specific patterns (p. 97). The same holds true for waist measurements of pants and skirts.

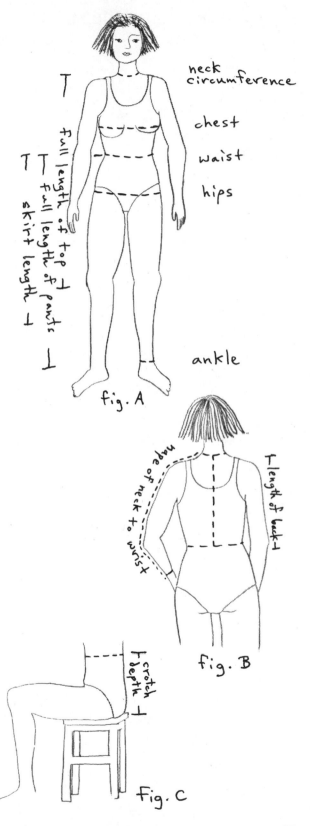

neck circumference

chest

waist

hips

full length of top
full length of pants
skirt length

ankle

fig. A

nape of neck to waist

length of back

fig. B

crotch depth

Fig. C

95

TABLE OF MEASUREMENTS I
GUIDING MEASUREMENTS FOR TOPS

Pattern size	I	II	III	IV	V	VI
	in/cm	in/cm	in/cm	in/cm	in/cm	in/cm
Bust measurement of pattern: 1/1	39½/100	43½/110	47/120	51/130	55/140	59/150
Bust measurement of pattern: 1/4	9¾/25	10¾/27½	11¾/30	12¾/32½	13¾/35	14¾/37½

Actual bust measurement: in/cm

	I	II	III	IV	V	VI
Blouses Small jackets Jumpsuits	31½-33½/ 80-85	35½-37½/ 90-95	39½-41½/ 100-105	43½-45½/ 110-115	—	—
Large sweaters Jackets and coats (of moderate fullness)	—	31½-33½/ 80-85	35½-37½/ 90-95	39½-41½/ 100-105	43½-45½/ 110-115	—
Larger outerclothes Loose capes	—	—	31½-33½/ 80-85	35½-37½/ 90-95	39½-41½/ 100-105	43½-45½/ 110-115

Choose size according to the desired width and adjust for length if necessary. Remember to pay attention to the hip measurement if this is more than 4" (10cm) greater than the bust measurement.

TABLE OF MEASUREMENTS II
MEASUREMENTS FOR USE WITH TOPS

Pattern size	I	II	III	IV	V	VI
	in/cm	in/cm	in/cm	in/cm	in/cm	in/cm
Bust measurement of pattern	39½/100	43½/110	47/120	51/130	55/140	59/150
Back length	15¾/40	16½/42	17¼/44	18/46	19/48	19¾/50
Entire length (to knee)	37¾/96	39½/100	41/104	42½/108	44/112	45¾/116
Nape of neck to wrist	30¾/78	31½/80	32¼/82	33/84	33¾/86	34½/88
Shoulder width	5¼/13½	5½/14	5¾/14½	6/15	6⅛/15½	6¼/16
Circumference of neck	14½/37	15/38	15¼/39	15¾/40	16⅛/41	16½/42

TABLE OF MEASUREMENTS III
MEASUREMENTS FOR USE WITH PANTS AND SKIRTS

Pattern size	I	II	III	IV
	inches/cm	in/cm	in/cm	in/cm
Waist	26/66	28½/72	30¾/78	33/84
Hips	35½/90	38½/98	41¾/106	45/114
Crotch (from chair seat to waist)	10½/27	11/28	11½/29	11¾/30
Full length—skirt (to mid-calf)	30/76	31/79	32¼/82	33½/85
Full length—pants	40/102	41¾/106	43¼/110	45/114

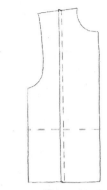

fig. A
taking in
with a tuck

ALTERATION OF SIZES

Choose a size according to the body measurements and/or the desired fullness, and correct the length if there's a difference between the body and pattern measurement. Generally, fullness is always added where it is needed and taken in if it is excessive.

• To *reduce fullness* in a pattern, fold a tuck ¼ the width of the desired alteration on each front and back piece, as each piece represents ¼ of the total measurement (fig. A). (Remember that a tuck ½" deep takes up 1".) A tuck is made in the center of the pattern piece, parallel with the grain of fabric line.

• To *shorten* by, say, 1", fold a tuck ½" deep, at right angles to the grain of the fabric. If the side seam slants, correct for this (fig. B).

• To *widen* a pattern, cut through the pattern piece lengthwise, parallel with the grain of fabric line, and move the pieces apart by ¼ of the desired alteration. Pin the pieces onto a new piece of paper the length of the first, and redraft the piece (fig. C).

• To *lengthen* a pattern, cut through the pattern horizontally, at right angles to the grain of fabric line, roughly in the middle of the part to be lengthened, and move the pieces apart to the desired length (fig. D).

• Shortening and lengthening of straight vertical lines can be done directly, at the bottom of the line (fig. E). Small adjustments in length can also be made directly to the end of the piece.

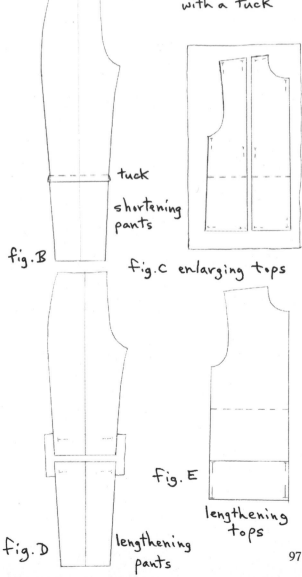

fig. B

tuck
shortening
pants

fig. C enlarging tops

fig. D

fig. E

lengthening
pants

lengthening
tops

97

LENGTHENING OR SHORTENING SLEEVES AND PANTS LEGS

If a sleeve or a pants leg must be lengthened, one must carry the wrist/foot measurement down, or the opening will become narrower unless the two sides are straight. Extend the centerline the necessary amount. Mark the width out to the sides, at right angles to this line (fig. F). Connect these points to the side/inseam, letting the new line merge with the original line. If a sleeve or pants leg must be shortened, the width at the bottom would become correspondingly wider. In this case, shorten the centerline, mark the width of the bottom higher up the center line and connect the points with the side/inseam lines as above (fig. G).

fig. F

fig. G

CORRECTING THE WAIST MEASUREMENT

If the waist measurements of the pattern and the body differ, correct this at the side seams.

• To alter the waist measurement for Basic Pants Pattern A and for Basic Straight Skirt C, figure the difference between body measurement and pattern measurement, divide it by 4, and add or take away at the side seams. If the waist must be taken in by more than 2¼" (6 cm), it may be necessary to make one or more darts, or the side seams would become too rounded (fig. H).

• Swaybacked persons may also need additional darts in back. These can be positioned during fitting, following the grain of the fabric. You can also take in a little—at most ½" (1½ cm)—at the center back seam (fig. I): more may cause folds to occur further down the back.

• On Basic Pants Pattern B, the waist can be altered up to 1½" (4 cm) by adjusting the pleats. If more is needed, ¼ of the difference can be added to (or subtracted from) the back at the side seams; a greater alteration would move the seams too far back (or forward). The front pieces are altered with pleats.

fig. H

fig. I

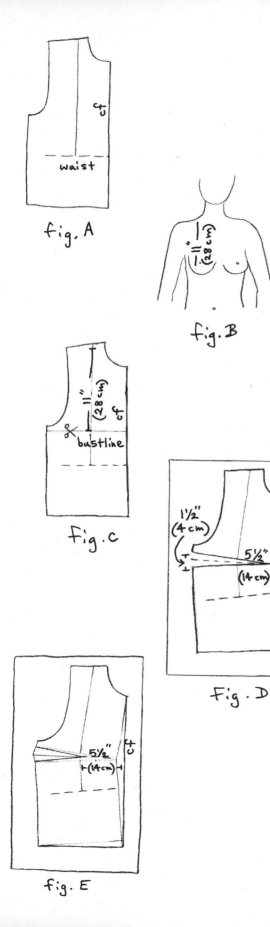

fig. A

fig. B

fig. c

Fig. D

fig. E

INCREASING BUST FULLNESS WITH DARTS

If the difference between the bust measurement (measured at the point of greatest fullness) and chest measurement (taken under the arms and above the bosom) is greater than 4-5" (10-12 cm), you can increase bust fullness by adding a dart. Darts are used in straight garments with neither pleats nor gathers, where ease is 4½" (12 cm) or less, and only in garments made of woven, not knit, fabric.

• Size of the dart is determined by the chest measurement:

1. On tissue, draft the pattern for the front with basic neckline, and cut out. Draw in a "bust depth line" down the middle, parallel with grain of the fabric (fig. A).
2. Measure depth of the bust from shoulder midpoint to nipple (fig. B). Mark the measurement on the bust depth line and draw a line (the bust line) at a right angle to it across the whole front (fig. C).
3. On a new piece of tissue, draw a vertical line toward the right side.
4. Cut the pattern at the bustline from side seam to center front. Lay the pattern pieces on the new piece of tissue with the front point of the neckline touching the vertical line, and spread the top and bottom parts of the pattern about 1½" (4 cm) apart at the side seam. Glue the pieces in place (fig. D).
5. Draw a line through the center of the cut at a right angle to the vertical line which is now center front. Mark a point 5½" (14 cm) from the center front on this horizontal line, and draft in the stitching lines of the dart with 2 slanting lines by connecting this point with the points of the cut at the side seam. Now extend the side seam out at an angle coming out to a point about ⅝" (1½ cm) beyond the side seam—otherwise the dart won't extend to the seam when sewn. Redraw the bottom edge at a right angle to center front (fig. E).
6. Cut out the pattern.

When you cut and sew a pattern with darts, mark the 2 lines at the side seam with notches in the seam allowance and the point of the dart with a pin or a chalk mark. Sew the dart from the side seam toward the point and press the seam allowance downward.

Basic Patterns for Tops

BASIC PATTERN A — DROPPED SHOULDERS

The shape is completely simple. The sleeves can be cut as part of the front and back pieces, or by themselves with the same inset front and back. In principal, this top can be divided up any way you like.

• Some examples are shown below:

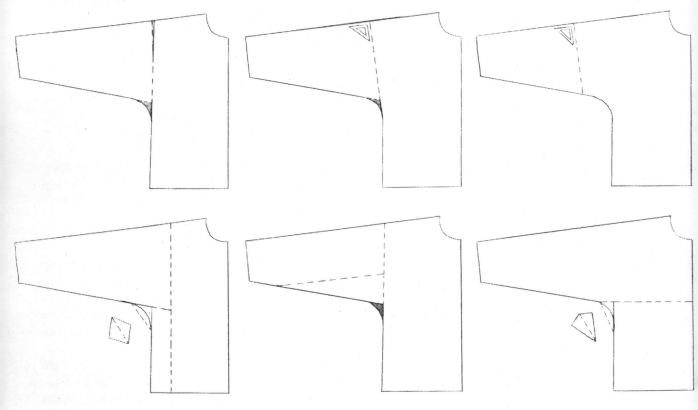

The fullness of the sleeve can also be altered as you wish, as long as you are careful that fitted sleeves allow enough room for elbow movement, and that fullness of the upper sleeve is not less than ½ the circumference of the upper arm + 1½" (4 cm).

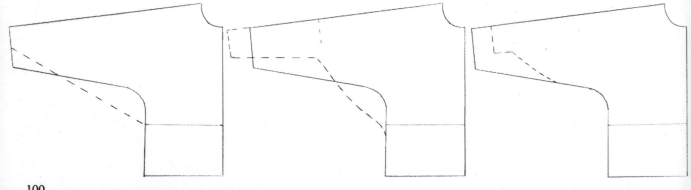

BASIC PATTERN B — SET-IN SLEEVES

This basic pattern has set-in sleeves with fairly flat sleeve caps and has an inset both in front and in back. The sleeve is drawn in two pieces, as the front of the sleeve is drawn with the front and the back of the sleeve with the back. Draw up the two sections and tape or pin them together (fig. A).

fig. A

If you want pleats or gathers in the sleeve cap, expand the width as shown in fig. B or C.

fig. B

fig. C

fig. D

The depth of the armhole can be raised or lowered with tucks or by cutting horizontally from center front/center back to armhole. The sleeve must be adjusted accordingly (fig. D). Be sure the front and back are precisely the same depth, and remember to make sure the armhole and the sleeve cap fit together. The cap can be about ⅜" (1 cm) larger than the armhole, but it can't be smaller.

See suggestions for *panel cuts*, p. 22, 60, and 62.

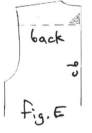

back

fig. E

Yokes
Figure out the depth of the yoke by measuring down from the shoulder both in front and in back. Transfer the measurement to the pattern. On the back, draw in at a right angle from the center back line (fig. E), unless the yoke is to be shaped. In that case, draft the line for one half and transfer it to the other side, so that both sides are symmetrical.
• In front, you may choose to let the yoke line be parallel with the shoulder line, or at right angles to the center front (fig. F).
• Yokes can be made with or without shoulder seams (fig. G).
• If you want pleats in the main pieces, cut these and expand them (see fig. C, p. 97), and pleat (p. 138) to the desired width.
• For pleats at center back, the pattern can be placed a distance (corresponding to the depth of the pleat x 2) from the folded edge of the fabric.

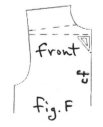

front

fig. F

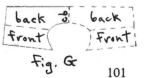

back | back
front | front

fig. G

BASIC PATTERN C — KIMONO CUT

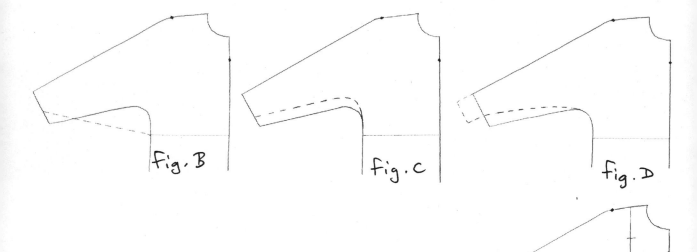

The sleeves in the kimono-cut pattern are drawn in one piece with the front and the back, which means that there will always be a seam from the neckline to the sleeve end. There is not as much room for movement in this cut as in the other three, but ease can be added with a gusset under the arm, as shown in the coat on p. 63 and the shirt on p. 14. For placement of such a gusset, draw a line on the pattern, 4" (10 cm) long, from a point under the arm up toward the shoulder (fig. A). A diagram for the gusset and sewing instructions can be found on p. 141
• The sleeve fullness can of course be changed. There are no limited to the amount of fullness that can be added, (fig. B), but the sleeve should not be narrowed more than about 2" (5 cm) at the underarm. In knits, the wrist/underarm fullness can be changed to make the sleeve fit quite closely (fig. C). In woven fabrics, the sleeve can't be made much tighter than shown in the basic pattern, unless it is also lengthened by about 3" (8 cm) to allow room for movement (fig. D).

• The basic pattern can be drawn with panel cuts made either diagonally, or vertically from shoulder to the bottom edge. Straight panel cuts are drawn in parallel with the center front, and for shorter tops these can be combined with darts, as on the leather jacket, p. 69. See also the various suggestions in the section called Easy Style. Make matching points on the panel cut lines before the pattern is cut apart and use these when assembling the pieces for sewing (fig. E).
• Should you wish to make the shoulders higher to allow for shoulder pads, do this by raising the shoulder line as described under Basic Pattern D — Raglan, which follows.

BASIC PATTERN D — RAGLAN

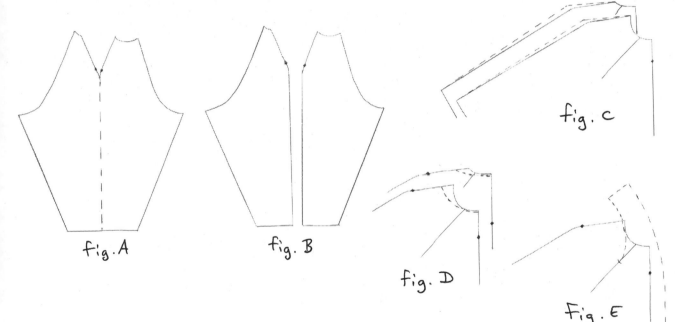

This basic pattern has raglan sleeves, and can be made with a shoulder dart or with an upper seam extending down the arm.
• For a shoulder dart, trace the front and back sleeve pieces, lay the upper straight edges together, and sew the open angle together as a dart (fig. A).
• For an upper sleeve seam, cut out the sleeve pieces separately and sew them together (fig. B).
• If the shoulder is to be raised to make room for a shoulder pad, do this by raising the shoulder line on both front and back pieces (fig. C).
• The sleeve width can also be altered at the wrist. See Basic Pattern C — Kimono (p. 102).

fig. A

fig. B

fig. c

fig. D

Fig. E

Collars

It is suggested that you read the section on Collars (p. 104).
• As the raglan sleeve seam enters the neckline, the top of the sleeve/neckline must be adjusted whenever the neckline is changed. To get the neckline drawn properly on all four pieces, hold front/sleeve and back/sleeve together when the neck/collar is drafted.
• The collar is drafted this way:
• Draw the shoulder line and the whole neck on both front and back (fig. D). Trace the sleeve pieces separately and lay them aside. Place this basic pattern over Collar Pattern I, II, or III, and trace the neckline or front edge/collar.
• If using Collar Pattern III, the front corner of the neckline on the front sleeve piece is rounded off, as in fig. E. Either the neckline or the rounded shape is matched to the sleeve pattern by markings on both pieces (figs. F & G). If using Collar Pattern I, the collar is traced directly in the correct size (see Collars, p. 104).

Fig. F

Fig. G

Collars

There are 3 basic collar patterns in the back of the book, for a total of 24 different collar styles in 6 sizes.

COLLAR PATTERN I: Separate collars for round necklines.
COLLAR PATTERN II: Separate collars for shaped necklines.
COLLAR PATTERN III: Collars cut as a part of the garment front.

As the 4 basic patterns all have the same basic neckline and shoulder slope, all the collars will fit all the basic patterns and can be used as desired. On both tops and collars there are matching points ◇ on the shoulders and at center front and back.
• The basic patterns are drawn so that the shoulder line is different for each size (fig. A). The collar patterns are drawn with a single shoulder line used for all sizes (fig. B). And the fronts and backs of the collars are drawn over each other, while the front and back pieces of the tops are drawn separately (figs. A and C).

• When the basic top pattern is transferred to tissue paper, the matching points and the neckline are drawn in, regardless of what collar is to be used. Then the collar is added by placing the front and back pieces for the top over Collar Pattern I, II, or III, matching diamonds and tracing:

I: Neckline, in the desired size (neck measurement and corresponding collar size of the desired shape).
II: Neckline, in the desired shape, and the corresponding collar.
III: Collar and front edge in the desired shape.

Remember to draw in the back part of the neckline on the back, as the shoulder line for the front and back will otherwise not be the same length. If the neck measurement is too large or too small on the basic pattern you've chosen, adjust it by choosing a neckline and collar that do fit.
• The numbers on the collars refer to the page on which they are shown. That is, the shawl collar for the coat on p. 69 is so labeled, and on the page where the pattern is given, an alphabetical legend directs you to the correct collar for specific garments.

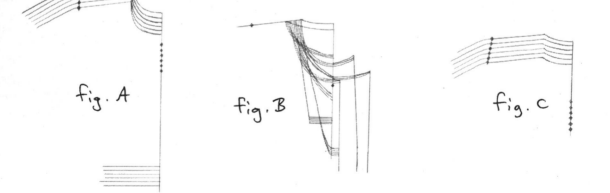

fig. A   fig. B   fig. c

ALTERATION OF NECKLINES AND COLLARS

A neckline can never be made smaller once it has been cut out of fabric, but can always be enlarged, by trimming. If you are in doubt, always choose the smaller neckline.
• A neckline is usually trimmed at the sides and in front. Try on the garment after the shoulder seams are sewn. Draw the trimming line with chalk on one half. Remember that the seam allowance for the collar/facing seam is ⅜" (1 cm). The back neckline is usually not trimmed, as the garment is carried there. It should only be trimmed a little in cases where this edge actually strains against the back of the neck, because of body shape. Fold the garment at center front and center back, matching shoulder seams. Pin together,

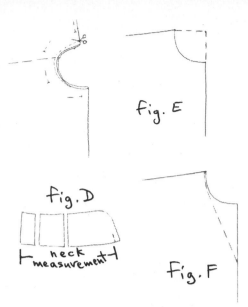

fig. E

fig. D

neck measurement

Fig. F

fig. G

Fig. I

fig. H

fig. J

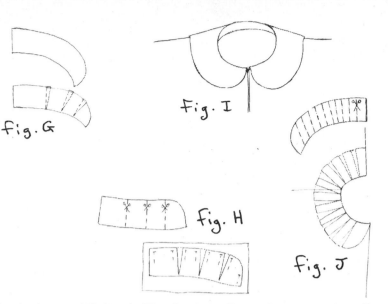

and trim, with ⅜" (1 cm) seam allowance, so that both sides are identical (fig. D). Transfer this correction to the pattern as well. Measure the neck and choose the collar size to fit, or correct the collar pattern by trimming and expanding until the neckline and the neck side of the collar match.

• If you prefer a completely straight neck opening, don't use the round neckline in front, but cut straight across to the center front (fig. E).

• If you want a V-neck, decide where the point of the V should be. Lay a ruler from the outer edge of the printed neckline and across the point of the V: mark, connecting the points (fig. F).

• In other cases where a direct cutting of the neckline seems desirable, it is easiest and safest to cut a regular round neck opening and draw the desired neckline on the garment when it can be tried on, transferring the neckline markings to the pattern for later use.

• The outer edge of the collar shape can be changed as desired. If you want the collar to lean in toward the neck, it must have a slight upward curve in the neck edge from center back to center front, so that the outer edge is slightly smaller than the neck edge. Or the collar can be made to slant away from the neck if the collar neck edge is made ⅜" (1 cm) smaller than the neckline measurement.

• The outer edge of the collar can be brought in closer by setting a few wedge-shaped pleats from the outer edge in toward the neck until the collar has the desired shape (fig. G).

• If you want a collar that falls away or flares out from the neck, it must have a downward curve from center back to center front, making the outer edge larger than the neck edge. The collar can be eased in by, at most,

⅜" (1 cm). That is, the collar neck edge can be ⅜" (1 cm) greater than the neckline.

• The outer edge of the collar can be made larger by cutting across the collar and spreading the outside edge. The resulting pattern must be pinned to a new sheet of paper and recut (fig. H).

• If you wish an entirely flat collar, as shown in fig. I, the pattern is spread as in fig. J, so that the collar pattern will lie completely flat on the patterns for the front and back assembled at the shoulder seam.

• In any case, it's important not to alter the neck edge of the collar, as it must match the neck opening. If the collar is cut as one piece with the front, the back section of the collar's neck edge must match the back edge of the neck opening. If you're using a collar on raglan neckline, see p. 103.

• Straight collars are cut with the back point of the neck at a right angle to the center back and with a downward curve toward the front. The collar should be neither held back nor stretched during assembly in order to retain the exact neck measurement. A straight collar can also be simpler—a straight strip, but this style works best with knit fabrics.

As mentioned above, it's very important that the neck opening and the neck edge of the collar match. If the front edge of the collar is at a right angle to the neck edge for about ¾" (2 cm), the collar will be easier to sew on.

• If you change the shape of the collar, it's a good idea to try it by making the top—front, back, and the collar itself—of tissue paper. Pin or tape the pieces together. Try the collar on another person or a mannequin and make any corrections to the paper pattern.

Pants

The basic pants pattern, like the patterns for tops, is drawn very simply, without fly, pockets, pleat markings, or other details.

- There are 2 basic patterns, each in 4 sizes which correspond to Measurement Table III.
- Basic Pattern A is for close-fitting pants.
- Basic Pattern B is for looser pants with a deep crotch curve and pleats. The pattern allows 7¾"/ 8"/8¼"/8½" (20/20½/21/21½ cm), respectively, for pleats in the front pieces. First compare your measurements with the Measurement Table and choose the size nearest your hip measurement. If your measurements fall between 2 sizes, the pattern can be made by drawing between these 2 sizes.

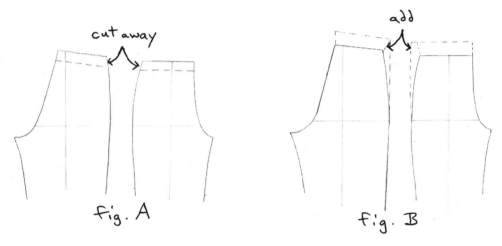

The crotch depth of Basic Pattern A is meant to correspond to the body measurement (as shown in the Measurement Table), without additions or subtractions for hems or waistbands. This means that any waistband width must be subtracted from the crotch depth (fig. A) and any hem at the top (for an elastic casing) must be added (fig. B).

- The crotch depth as it is would only be used for waist-high pants with no waistband and no channel for elastic (in which case a facing would be added).
- If the waistband is to be quite low, subtract more from the printed crotch depth and measure the length of the waistband according to the new line. Check the width of the pattern at the waist against body measurements.

The crotch depth of Basic Pattern B allows for construction with a facing and buckles or belt tabs, thus includes the height of the waistband. If the waistband will be sewn on, its width should be subtracted from the crotch depth.

- If the pants are to be high-waisted, the extra height must be added on.
- If you are in doubt whether the crotch depth is correct, you can compare the measurements of the pattern with your body measurements. The crotch of the pattern is measured along center front and center back, with the measuring tape on edge. Measure your body by holding the measuring tape at the waist at center back, running it between the legs and to the waist in front. Any excess/lack is adjusted with half the difference on the front and half on the back crotch line.

The amount of width to be added depends primarily on the garment and the material. With the straight pants pattern (A), there should be at least 2¼" (6 cm) and at most 7" (18 cm) on each side of the front for the pants to drape well. If more fullness is desired, use Basic Pattern B, which can be widened up to 12" (30 cm), including about 8" (20 cm) already allowed. The more tightly woven and stiffer the fabric, the less fullness it can accommodate. For a tightly woven duck, 4¾" (12 cm) will do nicely for pants of medium fullness.

Draw the pattern front in the desired size on tissue, and draw in the grain of fabric and center lines. Cut out the piece.
• According to the rule that all fullness is added or taken away where it is needed or excessive, extra fullness should be added at the middle of the front, and that is just about where the pleats are placed.
• Make a vertical line down the center of a fresh piece of tissue paper as long as and 8-12" (20-30 cm) wider than the pants pattern. Cut the pants pattern up the center line in one of the ways listed below:
    1) to 2" (5 cm) below the knee and then slanting to the sides if you wish the pants to have the original width from the knee down (fig. C);
    2) to ⅜" (1 cm) from the bottom edge, if you want fullness all the way down but wish to retain the original width at the ankle (fig. D);
    3) all the way down, if you also wish to increase the width of the leg at the bottom. It's important for the 2 pieces to be placed at exactly the same height. Draw a vertical line across the bottom of the new paper to help align the bottoms (fig. E).

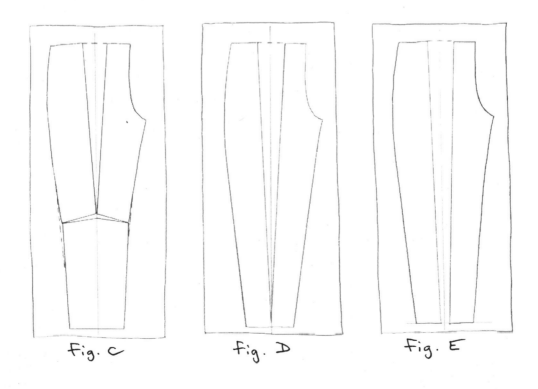

Fig. C   Fig. D   Fig. E

Lay the pieces of the pants pattern on the new paper. Pin at the bottom, matching centers.
• Decide how much extra fullness there should be.
• Spread the front pieces with half the desired additional fullness on each side of the centerline and pin. Trace around the edge to make a new pattern. If the width is added only to just below the knee, ease the side and seamline if there are sharp angles there.
• Straighten the bottom edge to a right angle with the centerline and connect the new waistline in a gentle curve.
• Cut out the new pattern and save the old. For later use, write on the pattern how much was allowed for pleats.
• You can also cut a strip of paper corresponding to the additional fullness and paste it onto the original split pattern.

The back pattern can be altered in the same way.

If you want less fullness for pleats on Basic Pattern B, trace the pattern and cut it out. Fold the pattern at the centerline (the grain of fabric line) and make a wedge-shaped pleat to bring the waist to the desired measurement. This pattern is not recommended for making straight pants, however; leave at least 2½" (6 cm) for pleats (fig. F).

fig. F

ALTERING THE FULLNESS ON PANTS LEGS

To alter the fullness of pants legs, add or subtract equally from the front and back and on both sides of the centerline in order to preserve the balance. That is to say, the difference between the original and the desired measurements must be divided equally by 4, and the amounts distributed at the four edges. Draw the lines so that they blend evenly into the original side seams and inseams (fig. G). If the legs are to be narrowed, be sure to leave enough fullness around the thigh (fig. H).

↳ add ↲
fig. G

↳ cut away ↲
fig. H

Panel cuts can be added, either crosswise or lengthwise. Remember in each case to keep and transfer the grain of fabric line as it is on the original.

It is helpful to mark matching points on the panel lines before the pattern is cut to use in re-assembling the pieces.

Close-fitting yokes at the hips are drawn following Basic Pattern A and can go all the way around (fig. A), be added only in back (fig. B) or only in front (fig. C), or can be tied into a pocket structure (figs. D & E).

When cutting across a pants leg (for example, for leather pants), pay attention to the location of the knee, so that the seam is either above or below it.

Lengthwise panel cuts can be made like those in the pants on p. 48, where the panel line is drawn on the basic pattern.

fig. A

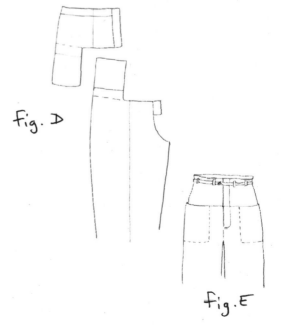

fig. D

Fig. B

fig. C

fig. E

Jumpsuits

Always use Basic Pattern B, for full pants. You can use basic top pattern A, B, or D, but not C (kimono), which has too little ease.

ALL-IN-ONE JUMPSUIT

The top pattern and the pants pattern must fit together.
• *Width.* If the hip measurement is greater than the bust measurement, choose a top size that will correspond to the hip measurement + the desired ease. If the bust measurement is greater, choose the pants size according to the bust measurement + desired ease.
• *Length.* Measure the length, from nape of the neck, under the crotch, and up to the throat. The jumpsuit should be 2½-5" (6-12 cm) longer at the centerline than this measurement, to allow free movement and belting.
• Choose correct size, and trace the back of the top pattern to the waist. Trace the front in the same length, and cut it out, leaving room for possible additions at the front edge and center back.
• Draw the front and back of Basic Pattern B, full pants (remember the grain of the fabric), in the correct size. Cut out the front, leaving room for additions at center front. Measure the top and pants front sections across the waist, and take a tuck corresponding to the difference on the centerline of the pants front, so both pieces are the same width. Draw in a new grain-of-fabric/centerline, down the middle of the leg. Pin the pants and top together at the waist (fig. A).
• Subtract ⅝" (1½ cm) from the width of the top back at the waist, taking out a wedge-shaped section starting about 8" (20 cm) below the neck edge, as shown in fig. B. As with the front, the waist measurement of the pants back must match the waist measurement of the top back. Measure the difference. Cut the pants back up the centerline and spread the pattern according to the instructions on p. 107, so that the pants waist measurement equals the top waist measurement. If the difference is 1½" (4 cm) or less, you can simply place the top pattern so that it extends ¾" (2 cm) over the pants at each side, then ease the side seamline and the center back seamlines with the top. Lay the top and the pants together at the waist, so that the sides meet and the top overlaps the pants waistline at center back by ¾" (2 cm), which is subtracted to allow for the natural inward curve of the spine there.

• Measure center front and center back from neckline to crotch. Add the two measurements and compare with the measurement taken on the body. The 2½-5" (6-12 cm) ease is determined by how loose you want the jumpsuit to be and whether it is to be worn with a belt. If you want it very baggy, you can add up to 6" (15 cm) or 3" (7½ cm) on each piece. Any difference between the 2 measurements (the pattern's and the body's + ease) is divided equally between the front and back pieces and is added or subtracted at the waist (see p. 97). Check the side lengths on the front and back; they should be equal. Trace the sleeves, and draw the front edge, pockets, etc.

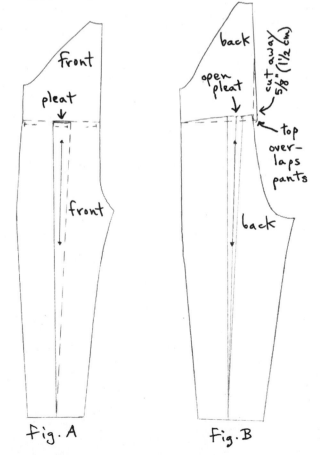

Fig. A   Fig. B

Width. The width of the top and the pants is chosen according to the body measurements, and independent of each other; differences are controlled with pleats, gathers, or darts at the waistline.

• *Length.* Measure as for the All-in-One Jumpsuit. The length of the suit should also be 2½-6" (6-15 cm) greater than the body measurement.

• Trace the back and front of the top in the desired size, to the waist + ¾" (2 cm). Measure from nape of neck to the edge, and from the throat to the edge, and write in the measurement.

• Trace the front and back of the pants in the desired size. Take a tuck in the pants front, if you want less fullness for pleats. Measure center front and center back, and write down the measurement. Add the four measurements together and compare with the body measurement + ease.

• The placement of the waistband is determined after the top and pants have been sewn together. As it's best located at the waist height you yourself find most comfortable, there will probably be a slight adjustment. Optionally allow for this in your pattern.

Skirts

The basic skirt patterns, like the pants patterns, are in 4 sizes, which correspond to Measurement Table III.

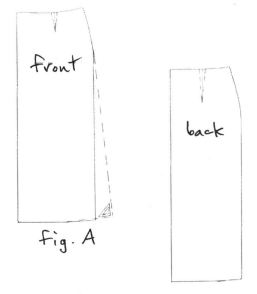

fig. A

BASIC PATTERN C
STRAIGHT SKIRT

This pattern has darts marked in front and in back. The height of the waist allows for a sewn-on waistband. The length is to mid-calf, which means that the skirt must have some kind of slit or kick pleat, unless extra fullness is added at the waist. In that case, the pattern should be expanded as described on p. 97. See also pleats, p. 138.

• The side seams can also slant outward as you wish, but must always be the same length as the center front and center back, so that the sides don't droop (fig. A).

BASIC PATTERN D — FULL SKIRT

The pattern is for a skirt that is closely pleated at the waist. The body's waist measurement is multiplied by 3 to get the fullness of the pattern at the waist. The side seams slant outward, and the width at the bottom is 102-110" (260-280 cm), depending on size.

• If you are wide in the hips, the skirt will be more flattering if the pleats are set apart somewhat. In that case, multiply the waist measurement times 2 or 2½, and reduce the pattern accordingly (p. 97).

• The length here is also figured for mid-calf, but can of course be varied according to your preference.

The two basic skirt patterns can be combined. The upper portion of the straight skirt can be used as a yoke, as shown in fig. A, with the full skirt pattern used as the lower portion, either pleated or gathered.

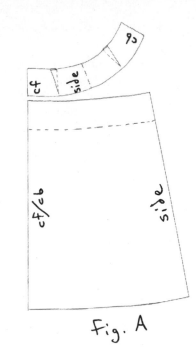

Fig. A

Pockets

The rectangular patch pockets are drawn from the construction diagrams using the measurements given. Use a ruler and a square to make them perfectly rectangular.

• The other pockets used are included in the Patterns section, beginning on p. 178.

• Inset pockets are drawn by laying the waist and side lines of the pattern on the corresponding lines of the pocket pattern. In some cases there will be irregularities, but they are unimportant, as long as the pocket opening is at least 1½" (4 cm) larger than the hand and the pattern for the outer fabric that goes down into the pocket is drawn using the corrected pattern.

Hats

Patterns for berets, caps and helmets are in the Patterns section. Three sizes are included, corresponding to head circumferences of 22", 23", and 24" (55, 58, and 61 cm).

• If the head size is between two pattern sizes, draw between the sizes.

Drafting Patterns

TOOLS

LONG RULER or STRAIGHT EDGE to draw and extend lines.

A SQUARE to draw right angles.

A SOFT LEAD PENCIL.

A good, soft ERASER.

TISSUE or TRACING PAPER in roll or sheets (rolls are more economical). Draw on the rough side.

PAPER SHEARS

TAPE or GLUE STICK

One of the most convenient ways to preserve your patterns is in plastic envelopes. Label each one and record what's inside (it's a good idea to date each one, too). Keep them in a ring binder, a magazine binder, or in file folders.

• When drawing patterns or cutting them out, many people find adequate lighting and space a problem. A kitchen counter or table, or the floor are often good choices, although these have certain drawbacks.

• A light-colored, completely smooth surface makes the most pleasant work space. Get one or two large, heavy pieces of cardboard (available at graphic arts supply stores and sometimes at stationers) that fit the table top. This will protect the surface of the table when you cut and use a tracing wheel, and is absolutely necessary if you work on a rug. (The cardboard is easily stored behind a bookcase or the like).

• A folding cutting board of heavy cardboard and printed with a grid in square inches can be found at most fabric and notions stores. It is very helpful when enlarging patterns to scale.

• To improve the lighting, use a light bulb stronger than that normally used, and keep it specifically for a work light (75-100 watts is minimal). A hanging lamp can usually be raised, by making a loop in the overhead cord and securing it with a rubber band, so you don't bump it while you're working.

DRAWING THE PATTERNS

1. Decide what you're going to make.
2. Find the relevant pattern in the correct size. Enlarge it and make necessary alterations.
3. Trace the corrected pattern onto tissue paper, with room enough for additions called for in the instructions. Remember to mark matching points on tops at the shoulders, center front and center back for adding the collar. Also remember to mark matching points if there are any panel cuts. For raglan, see p. 103.

   DON'T CUT YET . . .
4. Following the pattern drafting diagrams and accompanying text for the specific garment you're making, draw in all panel cuts, additions, extensions, etc., on the pattern. Side and sleeve edges and the like should match exactly for fronts and backs: draw them first on the front and transfer them to the back.
5. Draw the collar and neckline by placing the traced pattern over the enlargement of the collar pattern you want, following the correct letter for the size you're making. Draw in the collar. Measure and draw any necessary facings. Enlarge the appropriate pocket pattern.
6. Make separate patterns for facings from your tracing. Cut out the pieces, and identify each piece, including the size. Check the pattern layout diagram to be sure you have everything.

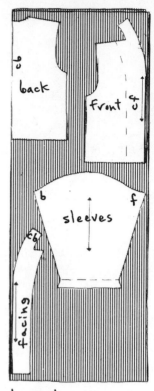

layout

There are a few simple rules that you must follow when you make additions, extensions, and draw in lines on patterns:

Additions to center front/center back. Measure and mark the width of the extension at the top, the bottom, and in the middle before drawing in the line (fig. A).

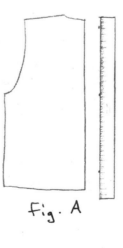

Fig. A

Lengthening side seamlines and center front/center back. Extend long lines only by about half your ruler's length at a time to be sure you get a STRAIGHT extension and not one that bows part way up (fig. B).

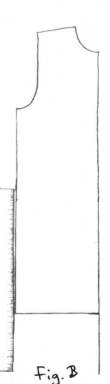

Fig. B

Lengthening the bottom edge. Measure and mark the length on the centerline, the side seamline, and in the middle. Draw the line at a right angle to the center front/center back and to the side seamline, so that the lower edge curves, as otherwise the sides will droop. Draw in a soft curve (fig. C).

fig. C

If there will be a *cuff or hem*, it's easiest to fold the pattern at the lower edge as it will be folded on the finished garment, then draw the cuff or hem following the side seamlines. When the pattern is unfolded, it will have the correct slants (fig. D).

1

2

Fig. D

1½" (4 cm)
1½" (4 cm)
¾" (2 cm)

3

fig. F

Rounded corners are drawn by measuring out from the corner as in fig. E, or by tracing around something that's the right size (fig. F)—a plate, a jar, or the like.

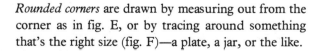

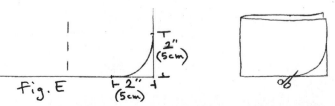

Fig. E

2"
(5cm)

2"
(5cm)

ALTERATION AND COMBINATIONS OF PATTERNS

In principle, every pattern can be cut up any which way then be reassembled. Practically speaking, though, some cuts are more successful than others, since any seam creates a line of doubled fabric which will be heavier and stiffer than the rest of the garment.

• Every panel cut is an opportunity to make the garment tighter or looser by adding or reducing fullness. When choosing where to put such a cut, try to think if and where more fullness is needed or if and where there will be too much fullness when the garment is worn: that is probably the best place for a panel cut.

• It's equally important to preserve the original balance of the basic pattern by respecting and maintaining the indicated grain of fabric, even when expanding or reducing dimensions, as the garment will hang best when you follow the indicated grain lines.

• When making panel cuts, draw in the matching points before cutting the pattern. These are especially important on curved lines.

• The garments in this book show different methods of alteration. These can be transferred and combined to create many more styles, limited only by your desires and imagination.

DRAFTING PATTERNS FROM THE IDEA SKETCHES

Some of the sketches (marked ***) in this book are suggestions, intended as inspiration for your own designs. It doesn't matter whether you use one of these ideas, one of your own drawings, or a combination of different garments illustrated, you will still be drafting your very own pattern.

1. Draw a sketch of the garment, from the front and from the back. If you wish, use one of the idea sketches in the book for proportions: they're drawn on a scale of 1:20.
2. Trace the desired basic pattern onto semi-transparent paper from one of the pattern drafting drawings in the book.
3. Draw in the necessary changes. For this you must use imagination and your ability to visualize. For tips, look at other garments in the book that have similar lines or details. At the same time, measure on the person where it will be best to place the various lines. If you're measuring yourself, do it in front of a full-length mirror, if possible, so you can keep an eye on proportions. Measurements of, for example, bias openings, should be made from the centerline. Remember to stand up straight when you're measuring lengths on yourself.

4. Draw the alterations and measurements you have developed onto your basic pattern sketch, using a scale of 1:10, so you have a complete pattern diagram. This step can be omitted if you wish to draw directly on your actual pattern enlargement, but you will find it a big help with later projects to be able to look at your handy little sketch before spreading the pattern out.
5. Continue, following the instructions for pattern drafting, p. 114, steps 2-6.

CONSTRUCTION

Before you begin to sew, think through the steps involved in your project and determine the sewing sequence that will be most efficient. Many different techniques are used in this book for jackets, shirts, and pants, and they differ according to the garment style and materials used.

• Look through the construction directions that apply to the kind of garment and materials you're using, and decide on the order of doing things that best suits your project.

SEWING TECHNIQUES

"If you're going to repair a motorcycle, an adequate supply of gumption is the first and most important tool. If you haven't got that you might as well gather up all the other tools and put them away, because they won't do you any good.

Gumption is the psychic gasoline that keeps the whole thing going. If you haven't got it, there's no way the motorcycle can possibly be fixed. But if you *have* got it and know how to keep it, there's absolutely no way in this whole world that motorcycle can *keep* from getting fixed. It's bound to happen. Therefore the thing that must be monitored at all times and preserved before anything else is the gumption."

—*Zen and the Art of Motorcycle Maintenance, by Robert M. Pirsig*

Sewing Tools

SHEARS

Choose a pair of good quality shears with long blades. They should fit your hand comfortably and not be too heavy. Use them only for fabric, or they will quickly become dull.

EMBROIDERY SCISSORS

For thread, small notches, and seam ripping.

THREAD SCISSORS

Use only for threads and ripping out seams. Very handy.

SEAM RIPPER/ BUTTONHOLE CUTTER

Be careful when you rip out a seam: cut only a few threads at a time to avoid tearing the cloth. Cut buttonholes from each end to the middle

CHISEL AND BLOCK

To cut buttonholes. Preferable to a seam ripper.

BODKIN

Use it to pull elastic, etc., through sewn channels.

NEEDLE THREADER

Used to thread both hand sewing and machine needles. May be necessary, for example, with very heavy threads, like button/ carpet thread.

STRAIGHT PINS

Buy long, thin dressmaker's pins, which do not mark the fabric. For thick, soft fabrics, colored heads can prevent the pins from disappearing in the fabric.

MEASURING TAPE

Buy a good quality. Handiest is one worked in inches on one side and centimeters on the other.

SEAM GAUGE

To measure seam allowances.

TRACING WHEEL AND PAPER

To transfer markings for seams, pockets, etc.

TAILOR'S CHALK

For marking. Available in several colors, in pencils and squares.

PINNING CARD

A piece of stiff cardboard or shirt board to lay between two thicknesses of cloth when only the top one is to be pinned, as for example, if pinning pockets onto a garment already sewn together.

HAND SEWING NEEDLES AND THIMBLE

Choose the best quality needles, and try to have a variety of sizes and lengths. A thimble is helpful for sewing through firm fabrics.

SPRAY BOTTLE

To dampen cotton and other fabrics that can tolerate direct pressing. Available in hardware stores and gardening supply stores.

PRESSING CLOTH

A well-washed piece of cotton cloth (a dish towel, for example).

SLEEVE BOARD AND TAILOR'S HAM

Helpful, but not necessary. A tightly wound ball of yarn substitutes nicely for the tailor's ham in some cases.

IRON AND IRONING BOARD

SEWING MACHINE

If you are buying a new sewing machine, you should require that it at least can zigzag and that it has special stretch stitches for knit fabrics.

• If you often make buttonholes, a buttonhole attachment will make life easier for you. Additional capabilities of some machines include reinforced seams, embroidery stitches, double fabric advancers, basting stitches, and more. Most of the newer machines have a free arm, which is very helpful for sewing ribbing onto sleeves, or for darning. These machines generally have an extension table, which provides a larger work surface for sewing when the free arm isn't needed.

• As every brand and model has its own special characteristics, try to find one you feel at ease with so you can utilize your machine to the fullest extent. Buying a machine with greater capabilities and more gadgets than you can handle is not a good investment. On the other hand, getting a machine that can only manage part of your real needs is a little shortsighted. It often makes better sense to buy a good, used sewing machine of a known brand than a new, cheaper one that can do everything under the sun.

• When you shop for a machine take samples of various kinds of fabric, and give yourself enough time to try different models in the store, so you get a machine that meets your needs and that you really like.

• If the machine has to be moved every time you use it, think also about weight and how easy it is to pack and unpack and set up. If the machine is going to stand open, it should be covered when not in use, to keep it from collecting dust.

• An older machine that no longer sews well may only need to be cleaned and adjusted. Follow the recommendations in the instruction book about cleaning and lubricating.

• If you have a box of presser feet and other attachments lying around, and have no idea how to use them, take a little time to read the instruction book and try these things out. The least that can come of this is that you may find better ways to do some things and that you'll be able to glimpse future possibilities.

• The presser feet you will need most, besides the standard one used for ordinary sewing, will be the:

zipper foot: a one-sided presser foot, for sewing in zippers and piping.
buttonhole foot: with 2 grooves in the bottom.
teflon or roller foot: see the section on Working with Leather, p. 128.
applique foot: with a wide groove on the underside, for sewing broad, tightly spaced zigzag and embroidery stitches.
quilting gauge: mounts on the presser foot or shaft to measure the distance between lines of quilting.

SEWING THREAD

Choose thread that corresponds to the weight of the fabric, with the same characteristics and ability to withstand the same kind of cleaning and pressing. In synthetic garments, cotton thread may shrink in the wash and make the seam pucker. It will also seem to lie on top of the fabric. On the other hand, synthetic thread used on cotton garments may melt when pressed at the correct temperature for cotton.

• Light wools and silks can be sewn with silk or cotton thread.

• Use strong synthetic threads for leather, or special thread for leather. Use ordinary synthetic thread for knits. (See also the sections on Working with Leather, p. 128, and Working with Knits, p. 125).

• Thread should be strong and smooth, so that it doesn't break during sewing and so the stitching will be durable.

• Choose a color just a bit darker than the fabric, as a lighter shade will show up. For patterned fabric, choose the most dominant color or the one you wish to emphasize.

• For decorative stitching, use a heavier top thread and an ordinary thread in the bobbin. Not all heavy thread can be used in all sewing machines. If it's difficult to thread the needle, use a needle threader or a heavier needle.

SEWING MACHINE NEEDLES

Needle size and type should correspond to the fabric and the thread.

• For light fabrics use needle no. 70, for medium weight, no. 80, and for heavy fabrics, nos. 90-100. A fine needle used in a heavy fabric may break, while a heavy needle will make holes in a light fabric and pull the stitches out of the fabric. There are fine needles with large eyes, intended for sewing with heavy thread in thinner fabrics.

• For knit fabrics, use a ball point needle, available in sizes 75-90.

• For very firm fabrics, use a jeans or denim needle. This has a flattened tip, and is available in sizes 90-100.

• For fine garment skins, use an ordinary size 90 needle. For somewhat heavier skins, use a size 100 needle or a leather needle (with a sharp angular cross-section), available in sizes 80-110. If the machine skips stitches, try a ball-point needle.

• There are also double needles, used for sewing flat pintucks and certain stitches on knits. They're available in several sizes and with varying amounts of space between needles.

• If the needle is bent, or the point is damaged, it should be thrown away, as it will cause wear on the machine and break the thread. It's well worth the money to buy the best quality needles, as they last longer.

WASHING AND CLEANING

The quality of a particular piece of fabric determines whether it should be washed or dry-cleaned. If you are in doubt, ask for the washing/cleaning instructions where you purchased the fabric.

• Fabrics that shrink (as cotton most often does) should as a rule be washed before you cut and make up the garment. As some fabrics lose part of their finish, and many collect dirt more easily after the first wash, it's not always an advantage to wash first—for example, on outer clothes. On the other hand, fabric which contains a great deal of sizing becomes softer, especially if rinsed with fabric softener or in a vinegar solution. One should always wash all-cotton knits and sweatshirt fabric before it's sewn, as these can shrink up to 10%.

• Always remember to turn the fabric wrong side out when washing, especially in a machine, as creases become worn and the color can lose its richness. If you plan to dry the garment in a clothes dryer, the fabric should probably also be dried in it before cutting and sewing.

• If you're combining fabrics or colors in a garment, the fabrics should be laundered separately beforehand, both to keep colors from running together and because of differing rates of shrinkage. When the garment is made up, it should be treated as its most delicate fabric. Most fabrics shrink only the first couple of times they're washed, and mostly in the length. An option with pants is to baste in the hems, and remove them before the first laundering. If you don't want to wash the fabric before making the garment, make a laundry sample of the fabric.

• Clothing worn directly against the skin, especially tops, should probably be made only of washable fabric, while outer clothes and clothes not used on a daily basis can certainly be made of fabrics that must be dry-cleaned.

• Quilted clothing should be washed, unless the dry-cleaner is certain that the filling can tolerate the cleaning process.

• Most woolens should be dry-cleaned, but some (usually those blended with 20% polyester) can be hand washed.

• Leather must be dry-cleaned through a special process. A garment trimmed with small pieces of leather can probably be hand washed, then worked between the hands as it dries to soften it.

Fabrics

Choose fabric according to the garment's purpose and the demands you will make of it. The most important thing is that you like the color and structure of the fabric.

• There are many exciting fabrics in shops, in many different weights, styles, and price ranges.

• Natural fibers are, in my opinion, absolutely the most comfortable, both to wear and to work with. But one shouldn't overlook the advantages of various blends: 20% polyester, for example, can strengthen a natural fiber, and when mixed with cotton it gives a good wind/moisture-proof fabric. Cellulose fibers (as in viscose rayon) often lend a lovely soft drape to a fabric, and there are many interesting patterns and textures in viscose and synthetic fibers.

• Below is a short summary of the characteristics and possible uses of various fabrics. The qualities (durability, warmth, structure, surface, bulkiness) of a piece of cloth depend upon what raw materials are used to make the threads, how they are spun, woven and finished (shiny, furry, water repellent, etc.). As a rule, firmly woven fabrics are stronger than loosely woven ones, so one can't assume that a heavy fabric is more durable than a thinner one.

Fabrics made of natural fibers (wool, silk, cotton, linen, etc.) are comfortable to wear, as they absorb perspiration and allow the skin to breathe freely through the fibers. Furthermore, natural fibers age gracefully, unlike most synthetics, which generally end up looking a little down-at-the-heels. The durability of linen and cotton is good, but, of course, depends on the threads and the weaving. Wool retains body heat well because of the lofty, fluffy structure of the threads, but unblended wool is not very durable.

• *Fabrics made of cellulose* (rayon, acetate, viscose, etc.) breathe fairly well. They don't wear as well as cotton or linen of comparable weights, but heat retention qualities are roughly the same.

• *Synthetic fibers* (polyester, polyamid, nylon, acrylic, etc.) are manufactured from crude petroleum or coal. The resulting fabric often stores static electricity and many people find it uncomfortable to wear next to their skin. The skin can't breathe, and manmade fibers often work backwards, that is, they chill one in cold weather, and feel warm and sticky against the skin when it's hot, because they can't absorb perspiration. If one wears cotton against the skin, or wool under them, however, their heat retention is improved. Generally, they can't tolerate hot water washing or direct ironing. They are available in all weights, from the thinnest fabrics for evening wear to heavy qualities with great durability.

SURVEY OF DIFFERENT FABRICS AND THEIR USES

PRINTED COTTON

Many different weights designed for both clothing and home furnishings.
- Widths: 35-55" (90-140cm).
- *Blouses, dresses, summer clothing, light jackets, skirts and pants.*

WOVEN PATTERNS:
STRIPES AND CHECKS

Developed by changing the color of either the weft or warp threads, or both.

IKAT

Patterned with some irregularity, which occurs because the threads are dyed before weaving to form a pattern.

JACQUARD, DAMASK

Monotone fabric with a woven pattern of flowers, stripes, or checks, creating a brocade effect. Many weights and qualities, often blended with linen and/or viscose.
- Widths: 43-55" (110-140cm).
- *Light weights can be used as above, the heavier are good for jackets, pants, and light coats.*

ORGANDY, GAUZE

Thin, loosely woven cotton, available with both smooth and crepe surfaces.
- Widths: 35-50" (90-130cm).
- *Good for very lightweight clothing with fullness and gathers.*

WINTER COTTONS:
FLANNEL, COTTON
MELTON, COTTON
CHAMOIS

Patterned or plain and/or brushed cotton fabric. Soft and warm.
- Widths: 27-60" (70-150cm).
- *Night clothes and shirts, as well as linings for pants, jumpsuits, and short jackets.*

HEAVY COTTON

Twill, herringbone, cambric, cotton gabardine, denim and canvas.
- Widths: 50-60" (130-150cm).
- *Jackets, coats, pants, and skirts.*

CORDUROY

Available with both wide and narrow wales in many weights from pinwale, which is light, soft, and very narrow-waled in 100% cotton, to heavy pants-weight corduroy with wide wales and containing some polyester. To bring out the dark, deep sheen, cut so that the nap feels rough from top to bottom. The other way around, the fabric has a lighter, polished sheen, which disappears, however, after a few washings.
- Widths: 35-60" (90-150cm).
- *Pinwale corduroy: shirts, dresses, full skirts, and full pants.*
- *Heavy corduroy: pants and outer clothes.*

TERRY CLOTH

Cotton with small loops on one side or both sides (see also knit fabrics, p. 125).
- Widths: 46-60" (120-150cm).
- *Bathrobes and linings for short, lightweight jackets.*

DOWNPROOF TICKING

Windproof, 100% cotton.

POPLIN

Windproof cotton/polyester. Silicon-treated varieties are moistureproof as well.
- Width: about 55" (140cm).
- *Jackets, light coats, and pants.*

CHINTZ

Cotton or cotton/polyester with a wax-treated surface. Lighter weights are designed for clothing, heavier ones for home furnishings.
- Widths: 35-50" (90-130cm).
- *Jackets, pants, skirts, as well as linings.*

SATIN, SATEEN

100% cotton with a lustrous surface. Acetate with a rough cotton reverse side. Pure acetate with a shiny surface, which can get blotchy from washing: should be dry-cleaned.
- Widths: 35-55" (90-140cm).
- *Shirts, dressier pants, skirts, linings, and trims.*

RAW SILK	Matte, soft silk, available in light and heavy weights.
THAI SILK	Slightly irregular, shifting shiny surface. • Widths: 35-46" (90-120cm). • *Blouses, jackets, pants, and skirts.*
LINEN	Sometimes blended with cotton, viscose, or polyester. Available in canvas and herringbone weaves. • Widths: 50-55" (130-140cm). • *Jackets, coats, pants, and skirts.*
WOOL	100% wool or wool/polyester blends. • Available in monotone, striped, checked, plaid, nubby, or tweed weaves. • Some kinds are washable. • Widths: 35-60" (90-150cm). • *Available in thick, soft blanketing or coating weights for jackets and coats.* • *In medium weights for pants, skirts, jackets, and coats.* • *In lighter weights for dresses, full skirts, indoor jackets, and full pants.*
NYLON	Parachute nylon is smooth; crinkle has a bumpy finish. Can be quilted with polyester filling or lined with a brushed cotton flannel, plush, or terry cloth. • Widths: 55-60" (140-150cm). • *Warm-up pants, jackets, jumpsuits, short coats, and vests.*
POLYAMIDE	Moistureproof "oilskin." Available in waffled, waled, or smooth finishes. • Width: 60" (150cm). • *For coats, jackets, and coveralls.*
POLYESTER ACETATE	Many silk imitations are made of 100% polyester or acetate. Available as light, heavy, or soft fabric, generally with a very handsome drape difficult to obtain in cotton.
VIYELLA	One of several brand names for a lightweight 50% cotton and 50% wool blend. Soft and warm. • Widths: 35-45" (90-120cm). • *Shirts and dresses.*
QUILTED FABRICS	Polyester filling with cotton or satin on one or both surfaces. • Widths: 35-55" (90-140cm). • *Jumpsuits, jackets, pants, vests, and linings.*
BACKED NYLON	Nylon, backed with cotton or cotton blend. Windproof, water resistant, and durable. The right side is shiny, the wrong side, a soft, napped finish. • Width: 55" (140cm). • *Coveralls, etc.*
KNITS	See the section on p. 125.
LEATHER	See the section on p. 128.

INTERFACING AND LINING FABRICS

Interfacing is used between the outer fabric and the lining, or in facings, collars, and edges, either to reinforce, stiffen, or to add thickness or warmth.

FOR STIFFENING AND REINFORCEMENT OF COLLARS, FRONT EDGES, WAISTBANDS, ETC.

PELLON	Made of pressed fibers. It has no grain and can be used in any direction. Available in many weights in white, gray and black. • Widths: 24-27" (60-90cm).
IRON-ON PELLON	The same, with heat-activated glue on one side. • Available in various weights, in tape for waistbands, and in a special weight designed for leather. • Width: 35" (90cm).
ARMO-WEFT	A soft or stiff canvas with heat-activated glue on one side. Cut it with the grain and iron on. • Width: 45" (120cm).
STITCH-WITCHERY	An iron-on surface with supporting paper for ironing two surfaces together. To be used, for example, for applique. • Available by the roll, in a narrow strip, or in 22" (56cm) width.
SEAM TAPE	A thin, soft twill tape with selvages, sewn up close to a seamline to reinforce an edge that might otherwise stretch out of shape. • You can also use a narrow strip (3/8" or 1 cm) of the fabric's own selvage (the outer, firmly woven edges), which are ordinarily discarded.

INTERLININGS AND LININGS

LAMB'S WOOL	Loosely woven, with a fuzzy surface. • Most often used doubled and lightly quilted, to keep it from losing its shape. • A synthetic substitute is also available, in white, gray and black. • Full width 55" (140cm).
POLYESTER FILLING, FIBERFILL, SYN-THETIC SHEET BATTS	Available in various weights and degrees of softness. Some varieties can be divided into 2 thin layers. Quilted with lining, outer fabric, or both.
DOWNPROOF TICKING	Can be used as a windproof interlining or lining. • Width: 55" (140cm).
COTTON FLANNEL	Can be used as a light interlining. • Available in several widths.
QUILTED COTTON SATEEN OR NYLON	Very warm lining or interlining. • Widths: 35-55" (90-140cm).
PLUSH	100% polyester. Also available in cotton/polyester in off-white.
LINING SATIN	Shiny, slick acetate.
PONGEE, LINING SILK	Very light silk.
TAFFETA	Lightweight acetate or polyester, with slightly lustrous quality. • Widths: 50-60" (130-150cm).

See also the section on lining fabrics (p. 159), to learn the use for each kind.

Working with Knits

Clothing made of knit fabric is comfortable to wear, and often feels warm because of its softness. Knits are well suited to almost any kind of garment, but one should be aware that they don't have much body of their own, unlike many woven fabrics. If you like to have your clothing fit snugly, choose a size smaller than you would use for woven fabrics, as the softer drape of the knit fabric around the body gives it a larger look.

The most usable kinds of knit fabrics for the examples in this book are:

SWEATSHIRT FABRIC — most often used for warm-up suits and sweatshirts, but can also be used for light jackets, coats, and skirts. Smooth knit upper surface with a waffled reverse, usually brushed and fuzzy.
• Available in light and heavy weights, in 100% cotton or blended with polyester or acrylic. Widths: 50-72" (130-180 cm).

INTERLOCK — used for underwear, T-shirts, night clothes, etc. A tightly ribbed knit with a smooth appearance on both surfaces.
• Available in 100% cotton and cotton blends. Widths: 35-55" (90-140 cm).

JERSEY — a lighter stockinette knit with a smooth upper surface and a purl undersurface. Available in many weights and fibers: cotton, rayon, polyester, and wool/mohair. Used mostly for dresses and tops, but can also be used for all lighter garments. Widths: 55-63" (140-160 cm).

SILK JERSEY — as above, but knit with a lustrous thread.
• Available in a cotton/acetate blend.

STRETCH VELOUR, STRETCH TERRY — two fabrics with loops knit into the top surface. In velour the loops have been cheared to create a soft, lustrous surface. In terry, the loops are left and the fabric has a shaggier look.
• Used for the same kind of garments as sweatshirt fabric.

QUILTED JERSEY — a double layer of jersey, often with a crinkly appearance. Width: about 60" (150 cm).
• Used like sweatshirt fabric.

RIBBING — circular knit bands, 32-35" (80-90 cm) wide, for edging. Purchase a good quality, cotton with some lycra, which stretches widthwise. Avoid cheaper varieties which tend to stretch out of shape.

In addition, there are many fashion knits and many other weights and fiber blends. It's impossible to give an accurate summary of them, as knit fabrics are developing rapidly, with new types and combinations appearing on the market constantly.

NEEDLES

Always use a stretch/jersey sewing machine needle to sew knit fabrics. This has a ball-point tip which slips between threads without damaging them as an ordinary needle would.
• For double-needle work (a substitute for overlock), use a double needle, no. 80-90, with 2-4mm spacing. This can be used to sew channels for elastic and the like, and produces 2 parallel lines of stitching on the right side and a zigzag on the reverse.

THREAD

As synthetic thread is stronger than cotton thread, it can be a great advantage to use it on knit fabrics, especially if your machine cannot sew the stretch stitches.

SEWING MACHINE

You need not use a machine with special stretch stitches for sewing knits, even though this is an advantage in most cases. If your machine can zigzag, it can sew knits. If the presser foot can be set, it should be loosened to keep the fabric from bulging or ripping along the seam. Thread tension should not be too tight, or the thread may break when the garment is worn.
• If there is a special presser foot for sewing elastic fabrics, use it. If the machine has stretch stitches, read carefully through the instructions for them. These stitches vary somewhat from manufacturer to manufacturer. Try out the possibilities on more and less elastic fabrics, so that you can utilize your machine to its best advantage.
• The seams called for here are based on an ordinary zigzag stitch and can be replaced with special stitches to the degree they are suggested in the manufacturer's instruction book.

ABOUT CUTTING

As tubular knit fabrics "turn" slightly, it's almost impossible to lay them out perfectly once they've been cut. You must simply accept the fact that the edges will never be exact. If the fabric is forced to lie straight, there is the risk that it will pull itself back the way it wants to be after the garment is made. When cutting striped fabrics, pin the 2 thicknesses together at the stripes so that these at least will match on both side seams.
• Very lightweight knit fabrics can often be hard to cut, as they give way and the edges roll during cutting. Always pin with the pin at right angles to the seamline when you sew: this will help to keep the edge flat. Allow ⅜" (1 cm) seam allowance.

SEWING

Ordinary seam. Sew together ⅜" (1 cm) from the edge with a zigzag (stitch width 1/2-1; length 1/2-1). Trim the seam allowances to 3/16" (½ cm). Zigzag the edge with a stitch width of 4 and a length of about 2, so that on the left the needle comes very close to the seamline and on the right just barely drops over the fabric edge so the stitches "lock" around the edge. If too tight a zigzag is used, the edge will be hard and wavy.

• In firmer qualities of sweatshirt fabric, stitching down the seam allowances works well. The seam allowances are not trimmed off then, but are zigzagged together. Sew from the right side, 3/16" (½ cm) from the seamline using a very narrow zigzag stitch.

• If you want to press the seam open, zigzag the edges first, sew the seam with a zigzag stitch as above, then press.

As most knit fabrics stretch most in the crosswise direction, seams in this direction are often the most difficult to sew neatly. At the neck and shoulder seams, place a seam tape in the seam so these seams won't stretch when worn. For kimono and raglan sleeves, the seam tape is sewn from the neckline to the rounding of the shoulder.

• Before hemming the bottom edges, always make a little test hem. If the fabric becomes very wavy when sewn, it sometimes helps to pin the hem up with a strip of tissue paper on the wrong side and sew through it. Press the seam lightly, if desired. After sewing, the paper can be ripped off easily. (Sew with a stitch width of 1/2-1; and a length of 1-2.)

CUTTING AND SEWING RIBBING AND RIBBED TRIMS

Ribbing. The stretchability of the ribbing can be determined by holding the ribbed fabric around the relevant body part and estimating the length. It will most often be 15-20% shorter than the edge to which it is to be attached, depending on the quality of the ribbing and the fullness of the garment, but it must in any case be large enough to match the edge when it is fully stretched out.

• The usual width for a ribbed trim is between 1½-2¾" (4 and 7 cm), but remember that it becomes narrower when stretched. Cut the measured length (which becomes the width), and the width x 2 + ¾" (2 cm) seam allowance (allow only 3/16" or ½ cm at the ends).

• Zigzag the ends together to form a tube (fig. A). Fold in half, with wrong sides together. Divide the edge into 4 equal parts and mark with pins (fig. B). Do the same with the garment edge. Pin the ribbing to the right side of the garment, matching pins. Stretch the rib if necessary and pin in place. Sew the layers together with ⅜" (1 cm) seam allowance. Trim the seam allowances and zigzag with stitch width 4 and length 2 (a tighter zigzag than this will cause the edge to be hard and wavy).

fig. A

fig. B

For *trim,* cut a strip of fabric in the direction with the greatest stretch. Cut the edging 15-20% shorter than the actual measurement of the edge to be trimmed, and in the finished length x 4 (in heavier fabrics cut it only x 3, as the inner edge won't be turned under but will be zigzagged and sewn on). Always mark the strip and the garment edge in 4 equal sections for pinning. Sew as described on p. 152.

• *Note:* cut it 15-20% less than the edge *only* if the edge is to be pulled up. For a smooth edge in firmer fabrics, the strip should be cut to the same measurement as the edge, as in the short dress (p. 24).

Working with Leather

In addition to the standard sewing equipment, you will need:

BROWN WRAPPING PAPER FOR PATTERNS
STONES OR OTHER HEAVY ARTICLES to hold the patterns to the leather
LETTER OPENER OR KNITTING NEEDLE to mark on leather
SPRING CLIPS to hold pieces together for sewing
TAPE to hold pieces together
A LEATHER NEEDLE (optional) • LEATHER GLUE

Leather clothing has many advantages. It retains the body's heat and is windproof, but also lets the skin breathe freely. It is relatively durable and pleasant to wear. And the lighter skins, at least, produce a garment that hangs softly and attractively.

• Leather isn't hard to work with if you know what you're doing and use the right techniques, but it is an expensive material to buy. As it's almost impossible to make a seam look right again once it's been taken out and resewn, you must be sure to do it right the first time—therefore practice a little beforehand.

• This means too that you should be sure that the pattern will fit, as it is usually impossible to make corrections in the middle of a project. Make a muslin version first, or sew the lining first and make necessary corrections, which can then be made to the pattern before cutting the leather. You must be painstaking with the pattern and with marking the leather, as this forms the groundwork that prevents having to make corrections during the assembly process. If you have never before made anything of leather, try something small first, like a belt, a beret, or a bag.

Most leather clothing is lined, both to keep its shape and because it is more comfortable. A satin lining fabric or a light, smooth cotton is best. On shorter jackets, the fronts and the back can be lined with wool, and the sleeves, with a smooth light fabric. For pants and skirts, which are worn next to the skin, it's advantageous if the lining can be removed and washed separately, as the leather can't be washed but must be specially cleaned. In skirts and pants it's not necessary for the lining to be full-length, but all other clothes are lined throughout. (See, in addition, the section on Linings, p. 159).

Calf is the most commonly used leather for clothing. It is available in many weights: heavier weights for outer clothes, straight pants, and skirts, and very thin skins which drape handsomely in full skirts, pleated pants, shirts, and very light (perhaps quilted) jackets.

• The skins vary from 20-35 square feet (a square foot is 30 x 30 cm), but one can usually buy half a skin.

• Another delightful skin is sheep or lambskin. This is a little thicker than calf but very soft. The skins are quite small, 6-8 feet, and it takes 4-5 skins for a pair of pants or a short jacket.

• Deerskin, pigskin, and goatskin are also available.

• Most of the designs in this book can be made of leather. However, skin footage is given only for those designs sewn specifically in leather. It takes about 25-27 sq ft for a pair of pleated pants, 15-20 sq ft for a straight skirt (depending on the length), 30-35 sq ft for a jacket, 55-60 for a coat, and 12-15 for a vest. To take the best advantage of the footage, try to choose garments made up of smaller pieces and avoid those with large flat pieces.

• For the greatest economy, it's a good idea to take all the pattern pieces with you when you buy skins, to avoid getting too much or too little.

Most garment skins are aniline-dyed with stain, which is quite durable and helps preserve the skin's natural surface.

PATTERNS

When working with leather, you must draw a pattern for EACH piece, both right and left sides, as leather, unlike fabric, always must be cut in a single layer. Mark an X on the wrong side of each pattern piece. This will show when laid on the wrong side of the skin and assure you that there are 2 opposite fronts, sleeves, etc. If you are making clothing with diagonal closings or other asymmetrical lines, remember to check that these lines will occur on the correct side. Don't forget the facings, belt tabs, pocket flaps, etc.

• It's easiest to work with rather heavy paper, like brown wrapping paper, as the pattern pieces are not pinned, but are laid in place then outlined with scratch marks on the skin itself.

• Enlarge the pattern from the basic pattern onto tissue paper, one of each piece. Transfer these to heavier paper, making two of each, adding seam allowances to the pattern if you wish. Mark right and left sides on the pattern pieces as well as the X for the wrong side, and any other markings. If the paper is creased or wrinkled, press it first.

LAYOUTS ON SKINS, MARKING AND CUTTING

If the leather is wrinkled, it can be pressed lightly on the smooth side with a dry iron on a low setting, using brown wrapping paper as a "pressing cloth" (woven fabric can mark the skin's surface). Leather must NOT be ironed directly or steam-ironed!

• If the leather has holes or rough places in it, mark these on the back side, so the less visible pieces can be put there. As this is a natural material, there will be irregularities in almost all cases, but these also give leather its handsome, alive look.

• Spread the skin out with its rough side up (the back, even if you're working with suede). Place all pieces on the skin and smooth them out. Leather has no real grain and can be used in any direction, although there's a little more stretch crosswise than lengthwise. If you are using suede, lay the pieces as much in the same direction as possible relative to the nap. Don't forget to allow for seam allowances at all edges, if you haven't already added them to the pattern. You may have to move the pattern pieces around quite a bit before they're settled into the best positions.

• On large dyed skins there is often a color difference between one end and the other. If this is so, try to keep adjacent pattern pieces in the same area of the skin. Try to confine the color shifts to the side seam areas on upper garments, and to the inseams of pants, where they will show less.

• When all pieces are in place, mark them on the leather. Start at one end. Place a stone or other heavy object in each corner, as leather shouldn't be pinned. Mark around all the pieces with a knitting needle, or with a pair of round-tipped scissors, scratching in markings and, if you wish, the seam allowances. Cut out all pieces.

leather jacket
layout

SEWING

Very light skin can be sewn with an ordinary no. 90 needle, heavier skin with a no. 90 leather needle. If the machine skips stitches, which can happen when sewing through more than two layers, use a no. 90 jersey needle.

• Use a synthetic thread designed for leather, or a carpet thread.

• Sew with a stitch length of 2.5-3.5, as smaller stitches will perforate the leather. Don't backstitch at the ends of seams, but fasten threads by knotting them. If a seam doesn't begin at the edge, pull the top thread through to the bottom and knot it there. If you don't like knots, you can use a fine canvas needle and backstitch over the machine stitches.

With the rough side of the leather upward, an ordinary presser foot will work, but with the smooth side up, the leather will drag to the point that the feed dogs won't be able to advance the leather, and the stitches will become irregular and too small. Use instead a teflon or roller presser foot. Adhesive-backed teflon tape is also available, which can be used to wrap a standard presser foot and will last through one or two projects. This is an inexpensive solution, and, if you don't plan to do a lot of sewing of leather, can save you the expense of buying a special presser foot for your machine. You can also lay a strip of tissue paper over the seamline when sewing on the smooth side of leather, then pull it off when the seam is sewn. But you'll have more control with a teflon coating on the presser foot. In any case, make a sample to be sure the needle and thread work correctly and that the stitches lie nicely.

Straight pins don't pierce leather readily, and when they do, they leave marks. They should be used only in the seam allowances. Clip the leather together with small spring clips instead. These are available in stationery stores; 8-10 will be enough. In the middle of wide surfaces, fasten pieces together with tape. If you use tape on the smooth side of the leather, test a scrap first to see if the tape marks the surface. On the wrong side this is not a problem. Patch pockets, belt tabs, etc., can be glued at the seamline before stitching.

For longer, free-hanging seams (pants and skirts) and seams that need extra strength (front edge, pocket edges, center back seam of pants, etc.), press a strip of iron-on woven or felt interfacing on the seamline, or sew a narrow seam tape into the seam. As leather can't tolerate high heat, use a special interfacing available at leather shops. This can also be used as ordinary interfacing, where necessary or desirable.

• As the seams can't be pressed out, the seam allowances can either be stitched open (in very light leather, they can both be stitched to one side) or glued down with leather glue, which is also available in leather shops. The seams should be pounded or flattened well after gluing.

The fact that leather doesn't fray makes many seams easy, as they can be stitched with wrong sides together and without turning under one or both seam allowances. After sewing, the excess is cut away very close to the stitching with embroidery scissors, as described in Trimming with Leather Strips (p. 153). This method also can be used for waistbands, cuffs and sewn-on collars.

• Otherwise, most seam treatments used with fabric will work with leather, with the difference that the seam allowances are glued down, not pressed. As mentioned above, leather can stand pressing with a dry iron on a low setting, using paper as a press cloth. This method can also be used carefully during construction.

• Glue is used for hemming. On a full skirt, the edge might instead be left unhemmed.

• Snaps, applied with a hammer or clamp, work well in leather garments (p. 167). If buttons and buttonholes are preferred, the buttonholes should be bound (p. 165).

See also construction steps for pants (p. 43) and jackets (p. 66).

Patterns and Fabrics

The individual pattern pieces are enlarged and drawn on tissue paper, with markings for the grain of fabric lines, matching points, center fronts, center backs, pockets, fasteners, etc. (fig. A).

• The *cutting layout* given with each garment project shows how the pattern is laid out on fabric of the indicated width. If the fabric is of a different width, the pattern layout will have to be adjusted.

• The pants and top patterns consist of a front and a back piece, unless panel cuts are made, in which case there will also be side pieces and 1 or 2 sleeve pieces for the tops. All pieces are cut from doubled fabric, folded with right sides together so that you get two opposite pieces from each half, or one whole piece if the pattern piece is laid on a fold. (Asymmetrical closures and facings are exceptions to this rule).

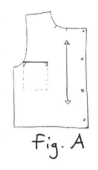

Fig. A

As the amount of fabric required depends on size and especially on the length of the garment, each design is accompanied by an explanation of which measurements are used to determine the fabric needed. Remember always to allow extra for seam allowances, cuffs, and sometimes for shrinkage, just as you must often allow extra for collars, facings, pockets, waistbands, etc., if these can't be worked in between the larger pieces.

• Fabric width can vary from 27-63" (70-160 cm), but the most common widths are 45" (110 cm) and 55-60" (140-150 cm).

• For tops, a length equals the measurement from the shoulder to the bottom edge of the garment. The length of the sleeve depends on the cut. For example, for raglan it's measured from the neckline to the wrist. With smaller sizes it is sometimes possible to get both fronts and backs on one length if the fabric is wider, but more often—especially when there is an overlap in front and a pleat in back—the front and the back must be laid one beneath the other. It may be possible then to put the sleeves alongside. For Basic Pattern A with dropped shoulders, and C, kimono, where the sleeves are cut as part of the front/back, the fabric requirement is based on length but depends on the fabric width relative to the measurement from the garment centerline to the wrist. It would only be possible to avoid a center back seam if the fabric were wider than 55" (140 cm).

• For pants, a length equals the measurement from the waist to the bottom edge. For fabric 35" (90 cm) wide, 2 lengths are needed. If the fabric width is 50" (130 cm) or more, 1 length is required for fitted pants and 1½ for full pants.

• For straight skirts, allow 1 length for fabric 50" (130 cm) wide and 2 lengths for 35" (90 cm) wide fabric, while the full skirt requires 2 lengths in 55" (140 cm) wide fabric. For each example, a cutting layout is illustrated, which can be used to make sure all pieces are accounted for, and also to show how the pattern can be laid out on fabric of the width indicated.

FABRIC REQUIREMENTS

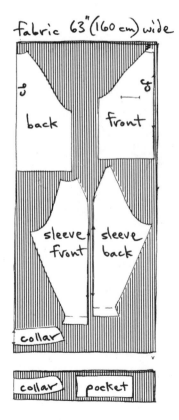

fabric 63" (160 cm) wide

back   front

sleeve front   sleeve back

collar

collar   pocket

FABRIC

fig. B

fig. c

The fabric must be completely smooth. If it's wrinkled or has creases in it, it should be pressed or smoothed out first. Fold the fabric with right sides together and the selvages parallel, either directly over each other, or folded in to the centerline, or off center if this works better with the pattern (figs. B and C). If the fabric is to be used full width, fold it crosswise or cut into 2 pieces which are laid on top of each other, depending on the nap. For fabrics with a true nap (corduroy, velour) and fabrics with a one-way print, all pattern pieces must be laid out in the same direction if you want the same pattern or tone throughout. Most other fabrics can be turned—that is, it's all right to turn the pattern pieces one way or the other lengthwise to make best use of the fabric. With stripes or plaids, be careful to place the pattern on the fabric in such a way that the stripes or checks meet at the side seams and in center front and center back, depending on the example. This often takes a little more fabric, depending on the size of the stripes or checks. A plaid can only be turned around if the stripes that make up the plaid are the same on both sides of the center of each square. This is easiest to see if you turn a part of the fabric around and compare the stripes/squares.

• Even-weave (canvas weave) fabrics are usually equally strong in both directions. Most other fabrics are strongest in the lengthwise direction, and using them lengthwise usually gives the best result, as the fabric will drape best that way.

• On some fabrics, it is difficult to tell the right side from the wrong side. There may be no difference, but if you are in doubt when you remove the pattern, make a chalk mark cross on all the pieces on the side you decide is the wrong side. In this way you will also avoid finding yourself with two left sleeves or two right pants legs.

PATTERNS ON FABRIC

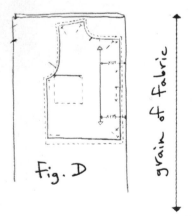

Fig. D

grain of fabric

When the smooth fabric has been folded with the right sides together, the pattern (which must also be perfectly smooth) is laid on it. The pattern pieces are laid out so that the grain of fabric lines are parallel with the selvage (fig. D). On the basic patterns for tops and skirts, center front and center back lines are the grain of fabric lines. These must be respected or the finished garment will pull, or won't hang evenly.

• The cutting layouts are drawn for the medium size: they will not always work for another size.

• Lay the pattern pieces out on the fabric, leaving room for the seam allowances. Lay out the largest pieces first, then the smaller ones. Remember which pieces must be placed on the foldline. If they don't fit immediately, try moving them around a little or folding the fabric differently to utilize it more effectively.

• Lay out all pattern pieces before you cut, so you're sure there is enough fabric for all of them.

• Pin the pattern pieces at all corners and in the middle of long, straight edges.

The patterns are given without seam allowances (the part between the outermost cut edge of the fabric and the sewn seam/pattern edge). This is measured with a seam gauge or measuring tape and drawn onto the fabric with tailor's chalk.

• At the shoulder, sleeve, and side seams, allow ⅜-¾" (1-2cm) seam allowance. If you allow only ⅜" (1 cm), be sure the pattern is large enough, as there will be no room to let out seams later. In heavy, thick fabrics, allow ⅝-¾" (1½-2cm).

• At the neckline, armholes, center back seam of pants and other curved seams, allow ⅜" (1cm) seam allowance.

• At the wrists, pants legs, and other bottom edges, allow a 1¼-1½" (3-4cm) hem. Allow 2¼" (6cm) if you expect to lengthen the pants a little after laundering.

• No seam allowance is necessary on edges to be finished with bias tape or trim.

• Mark a ⅜" (1cm) seam allowance on edges to be faced, and on the facings themselves.

SEAM ALLOWANCES

Cut out along your chalk marks. Hold the fabric with the left hand and let the scissors glide on the table, which provides a firm surface during cutting. Mark matching points, center back, center front, pocket placement, etc., with tailor's chalk, basting, or by cutting little notches in the seam allowances. Pocket and fastener placement can also be measured in the course of construction.

• Many find it helpful to mark all seamlines. Lay a piece of tracing carbon on the table and draw these in, going around the edge of the pattern with a piece of chalk or a chalk pencil. The seamlines can also be transferred to the opposite side by using a tracing wheel and tracing carbon. The markings can be transferred the same way, or by putting two pins in a cross and chalking on the wrong side.

• Remove the pattern from the fabric when you are finished marking.

CUTTING AND MARKINGS

Pinning, Basting, Pressing and Fitting

How much you pin and how much you baste depends on how much experience you have, what you're making, and how precise you wish your work to be. On curved lines— necklines, armholes, etc.,—and on fabrics that have a tendency to give or slip, it always pays to baste, as basting is easier to remove than a seam.

• Following the construction directions that say to baste or pin will pay off in both quality and efficiency of work.

PINNING Place the pins in at a right angle to the seam for sewing, with the pinheads on the right side, so they can easily be pulled out while sewing. Smooth out both thicknesses and place a pin in each end of the seam, one in the center, one in each new center, and so forth (fig. A). If there are matching points, match and pin these first of all. When pinning two opposite curving edges (collars, for example), it will be necessary to notch the inward curving edge (fig. B). In checks or plaids, the pins are set exactly in the same stripe of both thicknesses. Pinning of collars, pleats, zippers, etc., is described in those sections.

Fig. A

Fig. B

MACHINE BASTING Some machines have special stitches for basting. Without a special basting stitch, set the stitch length as long as possible and loosen the top thread tension a little, so the bottom thread will pull out easily afterward.

HAND BASTING Use thread in a contrasting color. If you must press over basting, use a fine thread, preferably silk, or the fabric may be marked. Start with a knot and baste just to one side of the seamline with small, regular stitches of about 3/16-3/8" (1/2-1 cm), so the layers won't pull apart. When you sew by machine, sew exactly on the seamline and not over the basting thread, or the basting may be difficult to remove afterward.

• When you use basting for markings in one thickness of fabric, use a contrasting thread color, but the stitches can be larger.

FITTING THE PATTERN In some cases it can be helpful to "try on" the paper pattern before cutting it out in fabric to see whether the closure, the pocket placement, etc., seem right. For fitting, cut out the pattern with ⅜" (1 cm) seam allowance, fasten it together with pins or tape, and try on one half by pinning or taping it onto your clothing at the center front and center back lines. It's easier if you have someone help you, but it can be done alone in most cases, even though it takes a little more time.

• If you're working with leather or another very expensive or special fabric and you want to be sure the design will look good on you, it is a good idea to make it up in muslin first and make any necessary corrections on this.

DRESSMAKER'S MANNEQUINS

If you do a lot of sewing, it's nice to have a mannequin, but it is absolutely not necessary. To be most useful, a mannequin should be as close to your own measurements as possible.
• Mannequins are fairly easy to make (although you'll need a helper). You may be able to find an adult education course, or a class through your local fabric store, where you can make your own mannequin.

TRYING ON

For fitting, put the garment together with pins, or baste the seams.

TOPS

Try on before sewing in the sleeves to check the width across the shoulders.
• Try on before sewing the sleeve/side seams to be sure there is enough fullness.
• Try on before finishing the neckline, to see that it fits correctly (remember there is a ⅜" or 1cm seam allowance).
• Try on when you mark hems at the bottom edge and sleeves.

PANTS AND SKIRTS

Try on before sewing the side seams to be sure of the proper fit.
• Try before sewing on the waistband; make the waist large enough and at the right height.
• Try on before hemming the bottom edges.

PRESSING

Press as you go; it makes sewing easier and gives better results. Press only after fitting at each step as it is difficult to remove a crease from some fabrics.
• To press, use a steam iron and a dry pressing cloth, or a dry iron and a damp pressing cloth laid over the fabric.
• For more stubborn fabrics, use a spray bottle to dampen the fabric. If ironing directly on the right side, lay a piece of tissue paper over it, as some kinds and colors of linen and cotton become shiny when ironed directly.
• Avoid pressing over pins in the fabric: this leaves marks, just as the basting thread should be very fine for the same reason. If the seam allowances leave marks on the right side, press these out by running the iron under the seam allowances.
• Press a sample of the fabric if you don't know how much heat it can stand.
• A sleeve board can be very helpful in pressing sleeve seams and other difficult-to-get-at places, just as a tailor's ham and a point presser/clapper will facilitate pressing curved seams, sleeve caps, etc. A tightly wound ball of yarn can take the place of a tailor's ham in some cases.
• Pants can be pressed and smoothed along the center back seam before the inseams are sewn (fig. A).
• Facings, collars, etc., that must be turned and folded exactly on the seamline will look best if the seam is pressed open before the facing is turned right side out.
• Seam allowances that are to be stitched down (for example, on a waistband where the inside seam allowance is stitched down from the right side) will also look best if it is pressed in first, and the bottom hems on coats, skirts, pants, etc., are easier to sew if pressed before hemming.

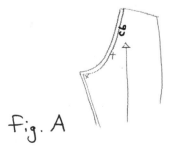

Fig. A

Stitches

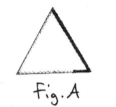

Fig. A

APPLIQUE STITCH. Change to the applique presser foot. Set the stitch length between 0 and 0.5 mm and the width to 2-4 mm (the more loosely woven the fabric, the wider the stitch). The top thread tension should be loosened slightly so that it can barely be seen from the reverse side. For flat, even stitches, you can sew with a piece of writing paper between the fabric and the machine's stitching plate. The paper can be removed easily after sewing. Applique is easiest if the motif has first been zigzagged to the background fabric with a narrow, open stitch (fig. A).

fig. B

BACKSTITCH is a hand sewing stitch. Bring the needle up, then down behind the thread, then up again a short distance from the point where the needle originally came up. Stitch length can be varied according to how visible and how durable a seam you want (figs. B, C, and D).

BASTING. See basting, p. 134.

fig. C

almost invisible seam

fig. D

visible dense stitches

CURVED SEAMS. Notches must be cut in the seam allowance to allow curved seams to be pressed out.

GATHERS are sewn with a long stitch length and loose upper thread tension. Sew a line of stitching on each side of the seamline, ¼" (½ cm) apart. Pull the bobbin thread to gather the fabric to the desired length. Distribute the gathers evenly across the work and secure the ends. Sew along the seamline at the normal stitch length and remove the gathering threads (fig. G).

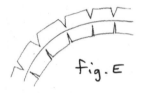

fig. E

HEMMING BY MACHINE. In lighter fabrics, turn under the edge, first by ¼" (½ cm), then ½-¾" (1-2 cm), so the raw edge is concealed. If the hem needs more body, you can turn it up double by, say, ¾" and ¾" (2 and 2 cm). You may wish to press the folded edge first, then stitch by machine. In heavier fabric a double turn-up is too bulky. Zigzag the raw edge instead and turn up a single thickness.

SEAM ALLOWANCES STITCHED DOWN. Zigzag or overcast both seam allowances together, if the edges weren't zigzagged beforehand. Press the seam allowances to one side and stitch in place with 1 or 2 lines of stitching, sewn from the right side of the work.

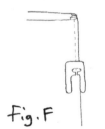

Fig. F

SEAMS, STANDARD. For sewing sections of fabric together, use a stitch length of 2-3 mm. At the beginning and end of each seam, backstitch (run the machine back and forth along the seamline) to fasten the ends, except when using a leather needle on leather.
• Turn corners with the needle in the fabric but the presser foot lifted. Whenever possible, sew lengthwise seams from top to bottom and horizontal seams outward from the midpoint.

SLIP STITCH is used for hemming and hand sewing in general (fig. H).

STRETCH SEAMS. See Working with Knits (p. 127).

TACKING is a hand stitch used to blind-hem pants, dresses, skirts and other clothing where the stitching shouldn't be visible from the right side. Tacking is quicker and easier than an overhand stitch, but isn't as durable, as the looser sewing makes it easier to pull a thread.
• The zigzagged or overcast edge is folded over twice. Stretch the fabric between the little finger and thumb of the left hand (fig. I). The stitches are sewn from side to side over the folded edge. Pick up only one thread of the fabric with the needle, so the stitches will be invisible from the right side, and avoid pulling the stitches taut. Push the needle into the fabric toward you, and sew the stitches away from you.
• When pressing the hem, don't press over the sewn edge, as this may cause press marks on the right side.
• If your machine has a blind hem stitch, this can be used instead.

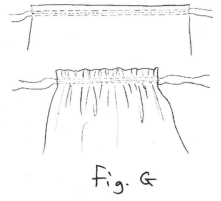

fig. G

TOPSTITCHING is a line of stitching often sewn very close to the garment edges. It is used to hold a double thickness of fabric in place and as decorative stitching, and is sometimes done with a heavier upper thread. To get the stitching line precisely even, you can guide the edge of the fabric, for example, along the inner edge of the presser foot. Use stitch length 3-4. Some machines have extra-long stitches designed for decorative topstitching (fig. F).

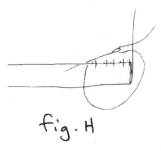

fig. H

ZIGZAG, OVER RAW EDGES. To prevent raw edges from fraying, zigzag on the very edge, so that the needle goes over the right edge of the fabric. Use stitch width 3-4 and length 2-3 mm. For firmer fabrics, zigzag only the edges that will not be enclosed—that is, not hidden by facings or other coverings. If a seam is to be pressed open, zigzag it first; if the seam allowances will be sewn down, zigzag the edges together when the seams are sewn.
• If the fabric is loosely woven, zigzag all raw edges of each piece before sewing to prevent them from raveling during construction. In such cases, allow ⅛" (½cm) extra seam allowance when cutting.
• For very loosely woven fabrics, the seam allowance will often ravel so much that you may have to edge it, so it won't "dissolve" in use. If this seems too bulky, you may have to stitch down all the seam allowances. The loose structure of such a fabric will usually make these stitches almost invisible.

ZIGZAG STITCH is also used for a reinforced seam at center back and other places that must endure great strain—unless your sewing machine has a "reinforced straight stitch" or something similar. Use a stitch length and width of 1 mm.

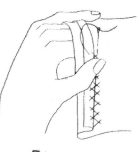

fig. I

Pleats and Tucks

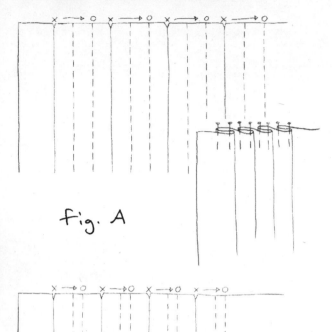

fig. A

The purpose of pleats and tucks is to give a garment extra fullness or to gather fullness in attractively.

• The depth, number and closeness of pleats, and the way they are folded and sewn creates their effect. For example, if 8" is allowed for pleats, a single pleat 4" deep will give an entirely different from 8 narrow pleats ½" deep

• Whether you want pleats from the shoulder, neckline, waist, or sleeves, you must add extra fullness to the pattern. Decide first how many pleats you want and where you want them, for example, 5 pleats 1" deep. As a pleat, or a tuck, is a double layer of cloth, multiply by 2. That is, 1 x 2 = 2" for one pleat x 5 = 10". Add the measurement you get to the pattern as described under Expanding Patterns (p. 97).

• For pants, see p. 107.

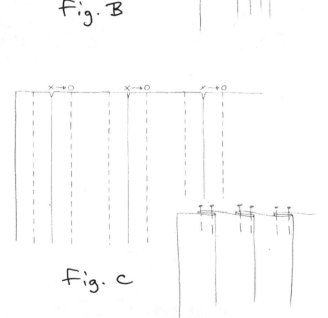

Fig. B

Fig. c

The foldlines of the pleats are marked first, with notches in the seam allowance. Look at figs. A, B, and C, to see markings for very close pleats (A), overlapping pleats (B), and pleats set apart (C).

• Whenever possible, fold pleats with the grain of the fabric.

• They can be folded (for soft pleats), pressed, or stitched down.

• They can be laid simply from the center and out to the sides or from the sides in toward the center, and they can be paired, like a double pleat or a box pleat (fig. D).

• For soft pleats, fold them at the edge, pin and secure them with machine basting. Make sure none of the pleats "droop"—that is, all folded edges must be flush with the top edge, or the pleats will hang unevenly.

• For pressed and stitched pleats, it's often necessary to mark the folds with chalk (on the wrong side), pins, or basting.

• With pleats that go from one edge to another (for example, pleats in the back of a jacket), cut notches in the seam allowances of both edges and press the pleats by folding from notch to notch.

• For pleats to be stitched, say 2", down their length, this measurement should be marked on the fabric.

• Fold and pin so the pleat doesn't slip. If the pleats are to be pressed flat, they should be basted first.

• If the pleats are to be visibly stitched down, one or two lines of stitching are sewn and the ends are secured by backstitching or pulling the top thread through to the back and knotting it (fig. E).
• If they are to be stitched down invisibly, sew the pleats like channels on the wrong side and fold them afterward in the desired direction (fig. F).

Double pleats and box pleats are marked and folded as in fig. D. If the pleat is to be stitched down, fold it like a channel (fig. G), sew, then fold with one half on each side of the seam. Press, and finally stitch down as shown in fig. H or I. This method can also be used for kick pleats. See straight skirts, p. 34.

If the purpose of tucks is to gather in fullness, as at the waist, they are folded in the middle of the fabric rather than at the edge. They can then be either single or double tucks. Try on the garment and pin the tucks to the desired width. Then adjust and correct them so they are precisely placed and exactly symmetrical on both ends. Press and stitch (figs. J and K).

Pintucks are narrow "erect" tucks about 1/16" (1/4 cm) deep. They can be sewn with a double needle, but will not have the same effect, as they will then be quite flat.
• To make pintucks, mark the "top" of each tuck with a basting thread or by notching in the seam allowance and folding and pressing them in along the grain of the fabric. If you are going to pintuck a larger area, it can be difficult to figure how much extra fabric you will need. Figure on the generous side and sew the pintucks. Then pin the pattern to the fabric again and trim to size. Remember that the extra fullness you allowed for the pintucks must be taken in on the pattern as well when you re-cut after making them (fig. L).

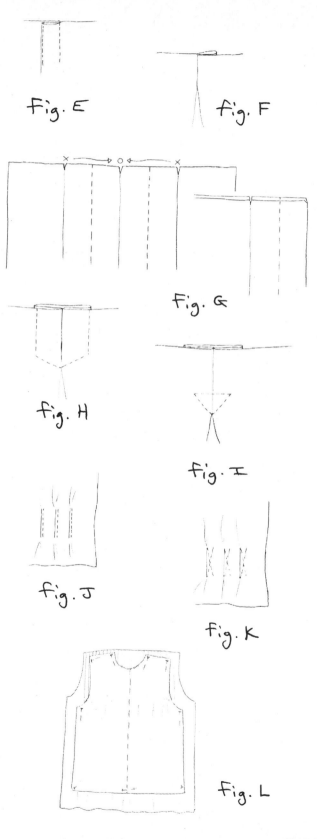

KICK PLEAT OR VENT FOR JACKETS, COATS AND SKIRTS

Fig. M

If the garment will be lined, see Lining Coats and Jackets, p. 162.

Cut the pleat 4" (10 cm) wide + ⅜" (1 cm) seam allowance and the length you prefer (for a coat 14-18" or 35-45 cm is standard).
• Pin and sew the center back seam to ¾" (2 cm) below the base of the pleat (fig. M). On thinner fabrics, hem the bottom edge before making the kick pleat. For heavier fabrics, the pleat is turned; it is sewn at the base with right sides together, before the hem is stitched in.
• First fold in the underlying side ⅜" then 2" (1 cm then 5 cm), and pin. If the fabric is loosely woven and has a tendency to pull apart, you can press on some thin interfacing, or pin seam tape into the fold.
• Make a double fold in the other side, the overlapping side: ¾" then 2⅛" (2 then 5½ cm).
• If you want buttonholes, it is best to add interfacing as reinforcement. Make the buttonholes lengthwise on the centerline about 1⅛" (2¾ cm) from the edge, when the pleat is folded the first time. For a slit 16" (40 cm) long, for example, make 2 buttonholes, 3¼" and 7" (8 and 18 cm) down.
• Fold the pleat double, stitch it down, and topstitch (fig. N).
• Stitch center back seam allowance to the side of the pleat, and stitch across the pleat itself at the base (fig. O). If you made buttonholes, sew buttons on the opposite side.

Fig. N

PLEATED SKIRTS

Fig. O

The number and depth of the pleats depends on the desired fullness. For the skirt on p. 35, the measurement at the waist edge is figured by multiplying the waist measurement x 3, which will result in closely placed pleats all the way around. In heavy fabric, pleats should be at least 1⅛-1½" (3-4 cm) deep. In thinner fabrics, they can be made deep or narrow, as you like.
• Use a measuring tape or a seam gauge when pinning pleats, or mark them as described under single pleats, p. 138, so they are all equally deep, and be sure they lie perfectly vertically, or they will hang unevenly.

PLEATS IN PANTS

The extra width allowed in front on Basic Pants Pattern A can be pleated in various ways, partly dependent upon the fullness. On the full pants pattern, 8-9" (20-23 cm) is allowed for pleats on each front section, but it is fairly easy to increase or decrease the fullness (p. 97).
• If you are in doubt about what will look best for the design, the fabric, and the wearer, you can fold and sew the pleats after the pants are sewn together and pockets and zipper are in place. Pleats made with fold toward the center can be good camouflage for a round tummy. When the pleats are folded and pinned during a fitting, there is likely to be some difference between the right and the left sides, unless you have measured with great care. Choose, therefore, one side and copy the pleats precisely on the other side.

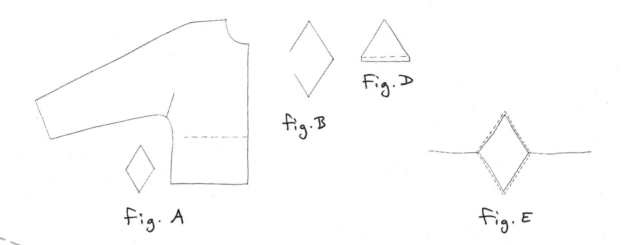

Fig. A

fig. B

Fig. D

Fig. E

The kimono-cut basic pattern can be made with or without gussets. Gussets are unnecessary with knit fabric, unless you wish to add them for effect. In garments of woven fabrics, however, they are a good idea, particularly for active wear.

• On the basic pattern, draw a 4" (10cm) line in from the armhole's deepest point and up, allowing for the addition of a gusset (fig. A).

• The gusset can be sewn in as one piece or as two halves (fig. B). See the pattern on this page (fig. C).

• Cut the gusset with the grain of the fabric as indicated. The seam allowance is also indicated, but if you are making a 2-piece gusset, remember to add a seam allowance where the halves will be sewn together (fig. D).

• It may be easier to sew the gusset in as 2 parts, if you are unfamiliar with the technique. It's a good idea to make a sample first.

• Press a small piece of thin, woven interfacing at the base of each gusset slit, to reinforce it. Then cut open the slit.

• If using half-gussets, sew them in before the sleeve/side seams are sewn.

• If using whole gussets, sew them in after the sleeve/side seams are sewn.

• If you plan to stitch down the seam allowance—which will give a visible seam but which will at the same time reinforce the gusset—it's not necessary to zigzag the edges before they are sewn together. Otherwise, zigzag the edges first.

• Pin the gusset in place, right sides together, matching corner to slit base, corner to seam/edge. A diamond-shaped gusset is sewn in with the sharp corner at the base of the cut, and the obtuse corner at the seam/edge. Sew from the sleeve side. Sew all the way down to the point of the slit before turning your work with the presser foot up and the needle down, then sew the other side. An alternate method is to zigzag the seam allowances together, press and stitch down onto the sleeve (fig. E).

Pockets

Some of the pockets used in the designs are included in the Pattern section, beginning on p. 178. Measurements for the rest are provided in the pattern instructions. Drafting is explained in more detail on p. 112.

• There must be a balance between a pocket's practicality and its decorative effect. Proper placement determines whether the pocket will function as intended. Care should be taken especially in the placement of bound pockets, which can't be moved.

• The pocket opening should be wide enough to get into easily. Place the hand's widest point on a measuring tape, then allow at least 1¼-1½" (3-4cm) additional width for the opening. This of course doesn't apply to breast pockets and other small pockets, where it's not necessary to get the whole hand in. And pockets should be deep enough that things don't fall out of them—7-8" (18-20cm) should be enough for a coat pocket, for example.

• First decide what kind of pocket you want and where you want it.

• On *coats,* pocket openings should be 1½-4" (4-10cm) below the waist, depending whether the coat will be belted or not, and should end no lower than about 2" (5cm) above the fingertips when the arm is hanging straight down. If the pocket opening is diagonal, count the 1½-4" (4-10cm) from the highest point. Measured from the shoulder on a woman 5'7" (170cm) tall, this would be 19-20½" (48-52cm) down.

• On *jackets,* pocket placement will often depend on garment length. On shorter jackets, pockets will be considerably above the waistline.

• In *pants* and *skirts,* the pockets are perhaps 1" below the waistline, if not actually starting at the waist as inset pockets.

• Light cotton fabric is best used for pocket bags for inside pockets. If the garment is lined, the lining fabric can often be used for the pocket bags.

• It is of course important that pockets on both sides of a coat be at exactly the same height, so be careful when you measure and mark their placement.

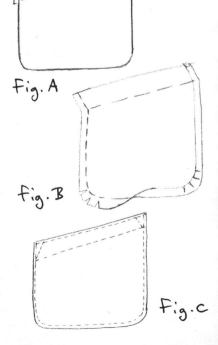

Fig. A

Fig. B

Fig. c

PATCH POCKETS

SINGLE LAYER

Cut the pocket in the desired size and shape, adding ⅜" (1 cm) seam allowance at the sides and bottom and 1¼-1½" (3-4cm) at the upper edge for a hem. If the upper edge is other than a straight horizontal, draw the side edges of the hemmed portion on the pattern by folding the pattern over at the desired slant and cutting the sides to match the rest of the pocket (fig. A).

• Zigzag around the edge. If there are curved edges, notch the seam allowance before turning it in, and press in the sides and bottom (fig. B). Fold the hem, either double or singly, depending on the weight of the fabric; press. If the edge is cut on the bias, or if the fabric is very loosely woven, baste a seam tape up to the foldline. Stitch the hem down, and topstitch if you wish.

• Place and pin the pocket onto the garment. It's a good idea to pin small pieces of fabric to the wrong side of the garment at the top corners, as reinforcement.

• Stitch around the edge, beginning and ending with a cross or a little triangle (fig. C).

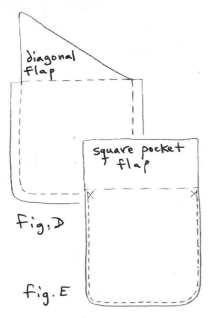

Fig. D

fig. E

DOUBLE-THICKNESS POCKET WITH DECORATIVE FLAP

Adding ⅜" (1 cm) seam allowance, cut the pocket in the desired width and depth + the length/shape of the doubled flap (if the upper edge is straight, cut the doubled flap as part of the pocket). Pin and stitch, with right sides together, leaving an opening of 4" (10 cm) at the bottom. Clip the corners, turn right side out, and press the edges and flap down. If desired, topstitch the flap. If the fabric is very heavy, cut the pocket from a single layer of fabric. Trim the flap along the edge, and make the pocket itself like an ordinary single-thickness pocket (fig. D).

• Place and pin the pocket onto the garment. If desired, reinforce by pinning small pieces of fabric to the wrong side of the garment at the upper corners. Stitch the pocket to the garment around the edges, beginning and ending with a cross or a triangle (fig. E).

LINED PATCH POCKET

Cut the outer fabric as for a single-thickness pocket. Cut the lining with a seam allowance but without a hem (fig. F). Mark the foldline. Sew the outer pocket to the lining, with right sides together, at the upper edge. Press the seam open. Fold right sides together on the foldline. If the outer fabric is loosely woven or cut on the bias, baste a strip of seam tape along the foldline, or press a strip of interfacing onto the edge. Pin and sew together, leaving an opening of about 4" (10 cm) along the lower edge. Clip the corners, turn, and press. Take care that the lining doesn't show along any of the edges. If desired, topstitch the upper edge. Place and sew the pocket to the garment as a single-thickness pocket.

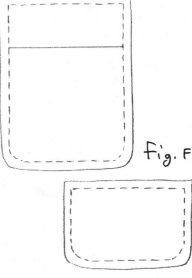

Fig. F

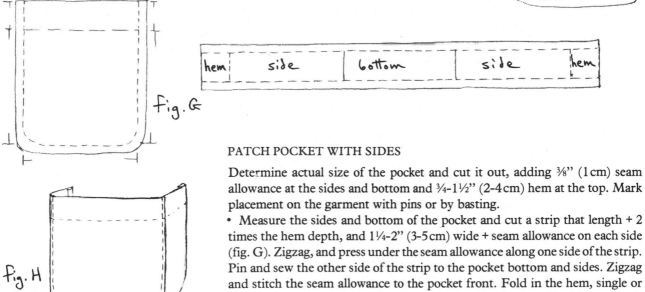

fig. G

| hem | side | bottom | side | hem |

fig. H

PATCH POCKET WITH SIDES

Determine actual size of the pocket and cut it out, adding ⅜" (1 cm) seam allowance at the sides and bottom and ¾-1½" (2-4 cm) hem at the top. Mark placement on the garment with pins or by basting.

• Measure the sides and bottom of the pocket and cut a strip that length + 2 times the hem depth, and 1¼-2" (3-5 cm) wide + seam allowance on each side (fig. G). Zigzag, and press under the seam allowance along one side of the strip. Pin and sew the other side of the strip to the pocket bottom and sides. Zigzag and stitch the seam allowance to the pocket front. Fold in the hem, single or double thickness, and sew (fig. H). Pin and sew in place on garment.

BOUND POCKETS

There are many different kinds of bound pockets. Here we describe six kinds, some with flaps and some without.
• If you have never made a bound pocket before, it's a good idea to make a test one first. They aren't difficult to make, but some mistakes can be complicated to fix.
• These pockets are sewn on a garment before the major pieces are assembled unless you are unsure of the placement on the garment. In that case, make the pocket after trying on the garment.
• If the bound pocket opening is horizontal, the pocket is made square or rectangular (fig. A).
• If the bound pocket opening is slanted, the pocket is rounded (fig. B).

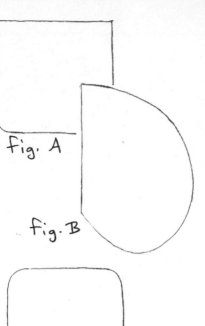

fig. A

fig. B

POCKET BAG AND BINDING IN ONE PIECE (SUITABLE FOR THINNER FABRICS)

Cut the pocket bag 2" (5cm) wider than the opening and 1½" (4cm) longer than twice the depth of the pocket.
• For pockets of sweatshirt fabric, cut the pocket bag only ¾" (2cm) wider and ¾" (2cm) longer than twice the depth.
• Mark the opening on the wrong side, ¾" (2cm) and ⅜" (1cm) respectively from the centerline (fig. C). Mark the pocket opening on the right side of the garment (fig. D).
• *Sewing.* Zigzag the edges of the pocket bag/binding. Pin it to the garment with the right sides together, matching markings for the opening. If desired, baste through both thicknesses and mark the width with chalk or a basting stitch, on each side. Staystitch with small stitches ¼-⅜" (½-1cm) on each side of the opening. Stitch back and forth at both ends and try to make the stitching lines precisely even in length. For sweatshirt material, sew ⅛" (¼cm) from markings, *all the way around*, with a narrow zigzag, about ⅛" (¼-½cm) wide.
• Cut as shown in fig. E, taking care not to cut through the stitches at the corners. For sweatshirt material, zigzag the edges with a fairly tight stitch. Tuck the pocket bag through the opening and pull out to the sides.
• For woven fabrics, fold the fabric so that the edges meet just over the opening and a pleat is created on each side (fig. F). In heavy fabrics, the seam allowances can be pressed apart so that the binding is folded around only one thickness of fabric.
• Sew the side pleats together by hand, and, if desired, sew to these the small triangles that form under the pleats. Press.
• If there is to be a zipper in the pocket, sew it in a hidden zipper (p. 169). Stitch in the lowest seam furrow of the opening. Fold the second part of the pocket bag down, so that the edges match, and stitch the sides and bottom of the bag together. Stitch the sides and the top seam furrow of the opening (fig. G). If the pocket will have a button loop and a button, fold a button loop, about 3" (7-8cm) long, position it at the center under the uppermost seam furrow, and pin it in place. You can also sew on a decorative triangle at both ends of the pocket opening, in fabric or leather, which will function both to secure the stitching and as decoration.
• *Sweatshirt material.* If the pocket is to be closed with a snap, set the inside snap before sewing the pocket bag together.

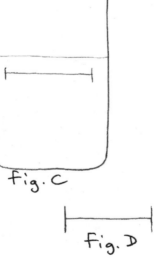

fig. C

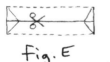

fig. D

fig. E

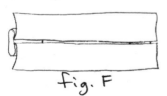

fig. F

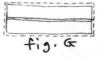

fig. G

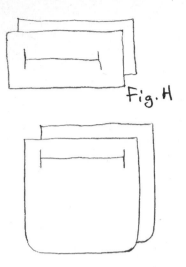

Fig. H

POCKET BAG AND BOUND POCKET OF DIFFERENT FABRICS (ALWAYS USED WITH GARMENTS MADE OF HEAVY FABRIC)

Cut the binding from the outer fabric, or other fabric, 2" (5 cm) longer than the pocket opening and 3¼" (8 cm) wide. Cut a pocket stand of the same fabric and of the same measurements. Cut out two pocket bags from thinner fabric, 2" (5 cm) wider than the pocket opening and ¾" (2 cm) longer than the desired pocket depth. In all cases, cut along the thread of the fabric. Mark the pocket opening on the garment's right side, on the binding's center, and ¾" (2 cm) from the top edge of one of the pocket bag pieces (fig. H).

• *Sewing.* Zigzag the binding and one pocket bag piece. Pin and zigzag the pocket stand at the top of the second pocket bag piece and zigzag. Place the pocket back without stand, wrong side to the garment's wrong side, matching markings, and the binding to the garment with right sides together, again matching markings. Pin/baste on the markings through all three thicknesses, marking the width with chalk or 3-4 basting stitches on each side.

• Using tiny stitches, sew ¼-⅜" (¾-1 cm) on each side of the opening, back-stitching at the ends, and taking care that the stitching lines are precisely even in length.

• Cut as shown in fig. E and take care not to cut through the seam threads in corners. Turn the binding through the pocket, pull out to the sides, and fold the edges so that these meet just over the opening as pleats on each side (fig. F). If desired, press the seam open, so that the binding is folded around only one thickness of fabric. Sew the side pleats in by hand, and if you wish, sew the small triangles under the pleats to them. Press.

• If there is to be a zipper in the pocket, sew it in at this point as an invisible zipper (p. 169).

• If there is to be a buttonhole, make it at the center.

• Stitch in the bottom seam furrow, or just inside of it.

• Pin the second pocket bag piece, with the stand up, to match the edges of the first piece. Pin/baste through all layers in the top seam furrow as well as in the sides of the opening. If using a button loop, fold a loop about 3" (7-8 cm) long, and pin it under the top seam furrow, at the center, before stitching.

• Stitch in sides and the top seam furrow, or just inside it (fig. G). Stitch the pocket bag together.

Fig. I

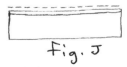

Fig. J

WELT HIP POCKET

The pocket is cut much like the above, with the following differences:
The binding is cut 4" (10 cm) long instead of 3¼" (8 cm), and there is no pocket stand. Mark, sew and cut as above.

• Fold the top seam allowance up and baste from the right side (fig. I). Turn the binding in, pull out to the sides and fold the bottom part around the seam allowance, so that this binding fills the *entire* opening (fig. J).

• Fold the top part back and stitch in the bottom seam furrow or just inside it. If desired, make a buttonhole in the center. Place the inside pocket piece so that the upper edges are flush. Pin the inside and top pieces of the binding together and zigzag the edge to the bag. Pin and sew the pieces of the pocket bag together. Stitch the sides and just above the top seam furrow.

145

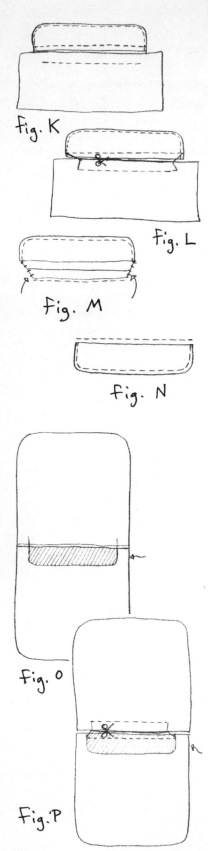

fig. K

Fig. L

Fig. M

Fig. N

Fig. O

Fig. P

FLAP POCKET

Cut the flap from a double thickness of outer fabric in the desired shape (a standard height is 1½-3" or 4-8 cm), as wide as the opening, and with ⅜" (1 cm) seam allowance. Cut one pocket stand 3⅛" (8 cm) long and 1½" (4 cm) wider than the pocket opening, and one binding 1½" (4 cm) long and 1½" (4 cm) wider than the pocket opening, both from the outer fabric. From a thinner fabric, cut 2 pocket bag pieces, 1½" (4 cm) longer and 1½" (4 cm) wider than the actual desired pocket depth and opening.

• Mark the pocket opening on the right side of the garment and on one of the pocket bag pieces, 1⅛" (3 cm) from the top edge and ¾" (2 cm) in from each side (fig. H).

• *Sewing.* Sew the flap sections, with right sides together. Turn and topstitch. Sew the pocket stand to the top of the second pocket bag piece and zigzag both pocket bag pieces. Place the one without the stand on the wrong side of the garment, matching markings, and pin. Place the right sides of the binding and flap on the right side of the garment, one on each side, with the flap at the top and the binding on the bottom. Stitch down the flap, a presser foot width from the mark, and pin at the sides. Stitch down the binding so that the stitches begin and end ¼" (¾ cm) inside the markings (fig. K). Cut as shown in fig. L.

• Turn the binding in through the opening and fold it around the seam allowance. If the fabric is heavy, press the seam open, so the binding is folded over only one thickness. Stitch in the bottom seam furrow from the right side. Fold the pocket piece out of sight and zigzag the lower edge of the binding to the pocket bag. The small triangles at the sides of the opening should be folded between the outer fabric and the pocket bag. Fold in the seam edge of the flap, so that the flap points downward, and pin. Slipstitch the sides down (fig. M). Place the other piece of the pocket bag with the stand up, so that the edges are flush, and pin. Stitch as closely as possible to the top seam furrow, or exactly in it (fig. N). Pin and stitch together the pocket bag sections.

WELT POCKET (POCKET WITH UPTURNED FLAP)

Cut the pocket flap from a double thickness of outer fabric in the desired shape (usually 1⅛-2⅜" or 3-6 cm high) and as wide as the pocket opening + ⅜" (1 cm) seam allowance. If the fabric is very soft, cut interfacing as well.

• From thinner fabric, cut 2 pocket bag pieces 2" (5 cm) wider than the opening and ¾" (2 cm) longer than the depth of the pocket.

• Mark the pocket opening on the right side of the garment.

• *Sewing.* With right sides together, sew the flap sections at the sides and upper edge (including the interfacing). Clip and notch the corners and curves and turn right side out. Press and topstitch. Zigzag the lower edges together and zigzag the pocket bag pieces. Place the flap and one pocket bag just below the marking, and pin. Place the other pocket bag just above the marking, with right sides together (fig. O). Pin, baste if desired, and stitch ⅛" (¾ cm) from the marking and precisely from and to the edges of the flap. Fasten the ends firmly. Sew the top pocket bag piece in the same way, ⅛" (¾ cm) from the marking, but only up to ⅛" (¾ cm) from the end of the opening at each side. Cut as shown in fig. P. Zigzag the cut edges. Fold the bottom pocket bag down into the opening so that the flap turns up. Pin and topstitch about 1/16" (2mm) below the seam furrow. Turn the top bag down. Fold in, pin, and tack down the triangles at the sides of the opening. Pin and stitch the pocket bag sections together. Smooth the pocket and pin the flap down at the sides. Stitch down the sides of the flap, hiding the stitches in the topstitching (fig. Q).

POCKET WITH LOOSE UPTURNED FLAP

This kind of pocket is used on full skirts (p. 35) and is made like a pocket with a down-turned flap turned upside down, which also means that the pocket bags have to go the other way. When the pocket is finished, the flap is secured about ⅜" (1cm) up each side, so that the binding is covered. If buttoned, the buttonhole should be made before the flap is sewn on.

INSET POCKETS

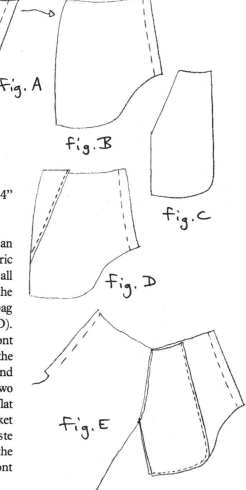

PANTS POCKET SEWN TO PLACKET

This kind of pocket is suitable for close-fitting pants having a maximum of 4" (10cm) extra width for pleats.

Cut a pocket wedge (fig. A) from the pants fabric, with 1½" (4cm) to be an underlap at the inner edge. Cut the two pocket bag pieces from thinner fabric (figs. B and C). Mark center front on the larger pocket bag section. Cut all pieces with ⅜" (1cm) seam allowance. Zigzag the lower and inner edges of the pocket bag section. Pin the pocket wedge, wrong side to the larger pocket bag section right side. Zigzag together at the edge and stitch in the inner edge (fig. D).
• Pin the smaller pocket bag section to the pocket opening on the pants front with right sides together. Place a strip of seam tape along the seamline if the fabric is very stretchy. Stitch together. Press seams open, notch any curves, and turn right side out so that the outer fabric dominates the edge. Sew one or two lines of topstitching. Pin the two pocket bag pieces together so that they lie flat at the side and waist edges. Fold the front piece to the side and sew the pocket bag sections together with 2 rows of stitching (fig. E). Fold back, pin and baste the center front of the pocket bag to the center front of the pants. Zigzag the front and the pocket together at the side and the waist. The pocket center front will be sewn into the placket seam.

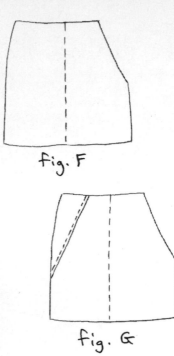

fig. F

fig. G

POCKET WITH A FREE-HANGING BAG

This pocket is suitable for any kind of pants or skirt.

Cut a pocket wedge (fig. A) from the pants fabric, with 1⅛" (3cm) extra on the inner edge. Cut a one-piece pocket bag from thinner fabric (fig. F), or cut as 2 pieces and add ⅜" (1cm) seam allowance. Mark the foldline. Pin the wrong side of the pocket wedge to the right side of the pocket bag at the waist and side seams. Zigzag the edges together, turn under and zigzag the inner edge, and zigzag the lower edge of the open pocket bag (fig. G). Pin the slanted edge of the pocket bag to the pocket opening on the pants, with right sides together. If the fabric is very stretchy, lay a strip of seam tape along the seamline.

• Zigzag together, press the seam open, notch any curves, and turn right side out so that the outer fabric dominates the seam edge. Sew one or two lines of topstitching. Fold the pocket bag so that the side seams match. If more than 4" (10cm) is allowed for pleats in the pants front, make a ⅝" (1½cm) pleat in the waist edge to prevent the pocket opening from straining. With less allowance for pleats, the pocket bag is sewn straight into the waistline. Stitch the pocket bag together at the bottom edge and zigzag it to the sides and waist.

fig. H

fig. I

fig. J

fig. K

POCKET IN SIDE SEAMS OR IN PANEL SEAMS

The seam in which the pocket will be should be cut with 1¼" (3cm) seam allowance the length of the pocket entry, or about 7" (18cm) for a pocket opening 5½" long. The seam allowance should slant at the bottom for about ¾" (2cm) as shown in fig. H. Add the usual ⅜" (1cm) seam allowance as well. Mark the opening ¾" and 6¼" (2 and 16cm) from the top edge. If desired, press a strip of interfacing into the foldline of the opening on the front piece. Cut two pocket bags from thinner fabric. If the pocket begins at the waistline, cut the upper edge straight along it. If it begins in the middle of a seam, the upper edge can be rounded (fig. I). Zigzag the edges. Pin and sew the pocket bags to the pocket edges with right sides together, and stitch down the seam allowances toward the bag. With right sides together, sew the side seam or panel seam, stopping at the pocket opening. Backstitch where you end and restart the seam. Spread the seam, opening the pocket. Press, and stitch the pocket entry to the front with one or two lines of topstitching (fig. J). Pin and sew the pocket bags together. Fold the pockets forward and stitch the seam allowance down back and forth from the opening (fig. K).

These pockets can also be cut as part of the main pieces of the garment, providing the fabric isn't too heavy. See Jogging Pants, p. 21, step 3.

Finishing Edges

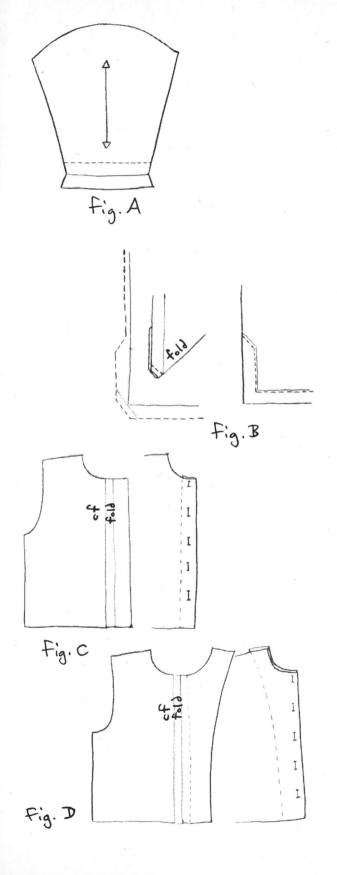

fig. A

Fig. B

Fig. C

Fig. D

A garment edge can be finished with either a single or a double hem, a facing, with tape or strip trims, or with a waistband. Which method is best depends on the fabric and the cut of the garment.

A straight edge at the bottom of the garment and the sleeves is usually cut with a hem allowance of 1¼-1½" (3-4cm) which is then folded under. For a tapered sleeve, the hem allowance is drawn in on the pattern in such a way that the width of the hem corresponds to the width of the sleeve at the point where it will be hemmed, otherwise the edge won't be long enough to go around (fig. A).

• In thinner fabrics, an edge can be folded double, and in heavier fabrics it's turned up once, as a doubled hem would be too bulky. Very loosely woven fabrics that fray badly can be edged with seam tape before hemming. The job is often made easier by pressing the fold in the edge before sewing it.

If there will be a side slit at the lower edge of the garment, it is cut with the same seam allowance as the rest of the edge, then the corner is stitched with right sides together (fig. B), and the corner turned and stitched to the inner edge.

For straight edges on shirts and light, unlined jackets a good method is to cut the front edge with an extension for the row of buttons. On an ordinary button edge, 1¼" (3cm) wide at center front, ⅝" (1½cm) is allowed for overlap, 1¼" (3cm) for the hem, and ⅜" (1cm) more for seam allowance (fig. C). The hem can also be extended up to the shoulder seam, if the collar will be turned down (see the shirt on p. 22 and fig. D).

In lined clothing, the edge can either be sewn to the lining and turned—with the lining extending to the garment edge—or combined with a separate facing cut from the outer fabric. See Linings (p. 163).

For lapels, shawl collars, and other kinds of collars that are turned back, see Collars, p. 175.

FACINGS

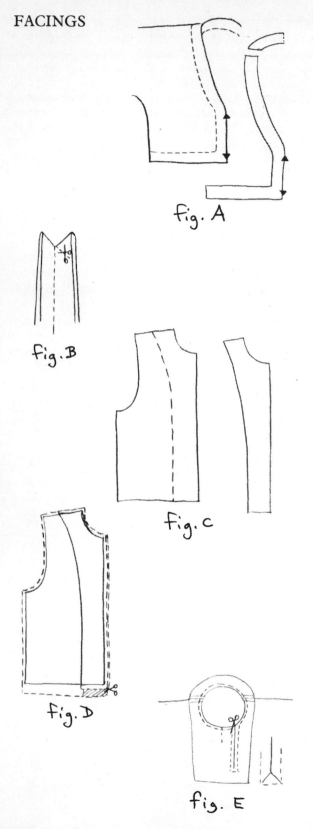

fig. A

fig. B

fig. C

fig. D

fig. E

Shaped edges (edges that aren't cut with the grain of the fabric) should be finished with seam binding or with a shaped facing, cut on the same grainline as the corresponding garment section (fig. A). As a shaped edge will often stretch out of shape, particularly with certain fabrics, it is wise to interface the facing or to sew seam tape into the seam.

• Cut the interfacing without seam allowances, which would make the seam too bulky. You can sometimes get by with using just a thin strip of fusible interfacing, applying it along the seamline, if interfacing the whole surface would make the facing too stiff. If you are making buttonholes, be sure the fabric can support them, otherwise interfacing is necessary for reinforcement.

• For the neatest possible edge on the facing, press open the seams after the facing and edge are sewn together. Trim the seam allowance, if you wish, to 3/16" (1/2 cm) to reduce bulk. At the corners there will be more fabric than can be pressed into the turned corner. Turn the fabric so that the 2 seams lie one above the other (fig. B), then trim the seam allowances. When the facing is turned right side out, it can be topstitched easily.

On the front edges of jackets and coats the facing is drawn in so that it slants up to the shoulder line, which gives the garment firmness (fig. C).

Finishing the lower edge of the facing. Cut the facing with ⅜" (1 cm) seam allowance at the lower edge, unlike the lower edge of the front, which has 1¼-1½" (3-4 cm) hem allowance. Sew the facing to the front edge, with right sides together, and sew across the bottom of the facing. Trim the extra seam allowance from the front (fig. D), press the seam open, and clip the corner. When the facing is turned, the bottom edge will be ready to hem, either singly or doubled (p. 136).

Necklines. If a neckline will be plain, with no collar, cut a shaped facing, 1½-3" (4-8 cm) wide for front and back. If there is a slit opening (there will have to be some sort of opening if the neckline is smaller than the circumference of the head), cut the facing to encompass it, with at least the width of the facing on either side of the slit. Mark the slit, sew on the facing with a line of stitching on each side of the mark, then cut the slit (fig. E).

Unlined garments. With thinner fabrics, turn under the inner edge of the facing ⅛-½' (½-1 cm), press, turn the facing to the inside, and stitch to the front. The stitching line will show on the outside of the garment.

• The edge of the facing can also be zigzagged and lie unattached on the inside of the garment. This works best if there are buttonholes and buttons and possibly a patch pocket to help keep the facing in place.

Start by drawing the facing in on the pattern. The width depends on the design. For an example, see pp. 54 and 79.

• *Cut* the facing from outer fabric, or in a contrasting color or fabric, adding ⅜" (1cm) seam allowance. Decide on interfacing and cut it without a seam allowance. Press or baste it on.

• *Zigzag* the inner edge of the facing, press under the seam allowance, or sew the lining to the facing (see p. 163).

• *Pin* facing to front edge, right sides together (if the facing is to be on the outside, sew it with wrong sides together). If seam tape is needed, place it so that it is just barely included in the seam (tape is pinned best from the facing side, with the garment on a flat surface, so it doesn't bunch up).

• *Sew* on the facing.

• *Press* the seam open. Notch curved lines and trim the corners.

• *Turn* the facing right side out and take care of the inner edge.

• Optionally, *topstitch* the facing in place, using a longer stitch length.

Piping can be used with facings or any place where two pieces of fabric are sewn together, for example, at the join of sleeves to the bodice. Piping is a narrow strip of fabric folded lengthwise to enclose a cord, and stitched to hold the cord in place. Piping is available ready-made (in several colors), and you can make it yourself.

• Cut a strip of fabric 1⅛" (3cm) wide, cutting with the grain if the piping will be sewn into a straight seam, or on the bias if it's for a curved seam. With the fabric wrong side up, lay a cord or heavy thread down the center of the strip, fold the strip lengthwise over the cord. Using a zipper foot, stitch as close to the cord as possible (fig. A). If you want a wide strip of trim, allow 2 x the desired width + ¾" by ⅜" (2 by 1cm) seam allowance. Lay the piping on the right side of one of the pieces to be trimmed, with raw edges of the piping flush with those of the fabric (fig. B). Pin and/or baste, and sew. With right sides together, lay the corresponding garment section on the first, with the piping between the two layers. Pin/baste, turn the work over, and sew by stitching along the first seamline. Zigzag the seam allowances together, if desired.

PIPING

Fig. A   Fig. B

TRIMMING WITH TAPE OR STRIPS

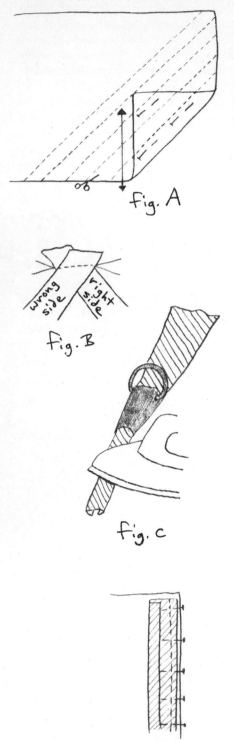

fig. A

fig. B

fig. C

fig. D

In many cases the best and simplest way to finish an edge is with bias tape or bias strips.

• On printed fabrics, a monotone trim can pull together the look of the garment, while a printed trim can liven up a solid-color garment.

• For trim use fabric similar in quality to that used for the rest of the garment, unless you are striving for a special effect by trimming with, say, satin. For heavy fabrics, leather trim can be very effective.

• Cotton and satin bias tape can be purchased in many colors and widths. You can also make bias strips. Cut them on the diagonal of the fabric grain to obtain the greatest amount of stretch (fig. A). Cut strips 1⅛-2" (3-5 cm) wide and sew the ends, with right sides together, until you have a single strip the length you need (fig. B). If you wish, press under the seam allowances on both sides to make your tape the desired width, or use a bias tape folder, available in 7/16, 11/16, and 1" (1.2, 1.7, and 2.5 cm) sizes. For these, cut strips in widths of 1, 1⅜, and 2" (2.5, 3.5, and 5 cm) respectively. Make strips the length you require, and thread them through the folder with the right side out, and press them (fig. C).

• Leather trims (for example, chamois or soft, thin calfskin) are cut about 1½" (4 cm) wide, and as skin has no real grainline, they can be cut whatever way is most economical.

• Edges to be trimmed with bias edging should be cut without seam allowances. Zigzag the edge only if the fabric frays. The edge should be "clean" when the bias is applied. If there are several thicknesses, it will be easier if these are first zigzagged together.

• The edging strip is sewn on in two passes, as this is most durable and gives the best looking results.

FIRST SEAM

Lay the strip with the right edge opened out, so the edge of the strip is flush with the edge of the garment. Place right sides together if you want the stitching line to be invisible on the right side, which looks softer and fuller, or right side to the garment's wrong side if you want the tape visibly sewn down on the outside, which looks more sporty. The distance of the stitching from the edge of the garment will determine the width of the edging. Satin tape 11/16" (1.8 cm) wide gives an edge 3/16-3/8" (1/2-1 cm) wide, while a leather trim 1½" (4 cm) wide makes an edge 3/8" (1 cm) wide. Be sure that the tape is wide enough. If you want a very narrow edge, it will be necessary to trim the seam allowance after sewing the first line of stitching.

• Pin the tape with pins crosswise, heads to the right, so they can be removed as you sew (fig. D). Be sure the tape lies completely smoothly on straight edges. If it's too loose, pleats will form when you sew it; if it's too tight, it will draw up the fabric edge.

• *Edges cut on the bias* of the fabric's grain will usually stretch during sewing. To prevent this, you should staystitch the edge. The trim itself can be measured against the paper pattern before it's pinned on.

- *For outside curves,* ease the tape in slightly, as the outside edge will be longer than the seam (fig. E).
- *For inside curves,* stretch the tape slightly, as the outside edge is shorter than the seam (fig. F).
- *On outside corners,* cut a notch in the seam allowance, and when you sew, turn the corner with the needle down exactly at the corner (fig. G).
- *On slits and inside corners,* turn the corner with the needle at the base of the slit. After the first seam is sewn, cut a notch in the seam allowance all the way to the seam.
- *To start/end on an edge,* the tape should extend 3/16-3/8" (1/2-1cm) beyond the edge. Fold the tape around the edge before sewing the second seam (fig. H).
- *To start/end and join the ends,* begin by folding in 3/16" (1/2cm), and end by laying the end over the folded end and sewing it down (fig. I).

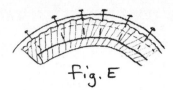

fig. E

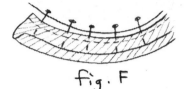

fig. F

fig. H

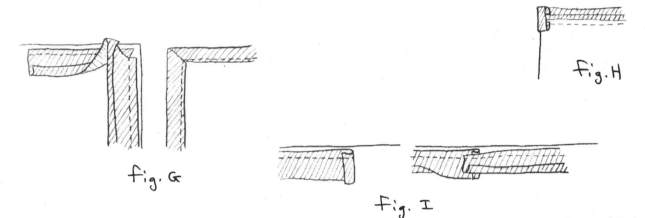

fig. G

fig. I

SECOND SEAM

Fold the tape over to the other side so that the folded edge just covers the first seam. You may have to trim away some of the seam allowance (fig. J). If the right side is to be without visible stitching (that is, the bias strip was sewn on with right sides together), the inside of the tape can be slipstitched in place. On the machine, pin (or baste) the tape—with the pins on the right side and lengthwise, the heads facing you so they can be removed as you sew—then sew from the right side, precisely in the seam furrow (fig. K).

- For trimming with skin strips, fold them so that the edge covers the first stitching by ¼" (¾cm). Sew the second line of stitching from the right side, and trim away the excess with small embroidery scissors about 1/16" (1-2mm) from the stitches (fig. L).
- If the second line of stitching is to be visible on the right side (that is, the trim is sewn with the right side to the garment's wrong side), baste or pin it from this side and sew as above.
- As trim gives the garment its finishing touch, it is important for it to be neatly applied and look smart, so if you're not used to working with trim, it's a good idea to practice a little first.

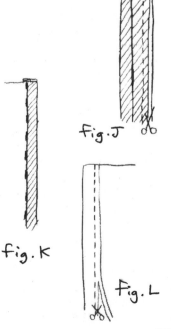

fig. J

fig. K

fig. L

Waistbands

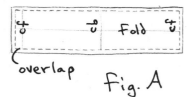

overlap

fig. A

ONE-PIECE WAISTBAND

Measure the length of the waistband, using the body's waist measurement (or the measurement where the waistband will be) + overlaps. Check the waist edge of the pants or skirt and decide on the width—the standard is 1¼-2" (3-5cm). Cut the waistband on either crosswise or lengthwise grain of the fabric, the width x 2 and length + overlaps (the underlying portion of the waistband for a fly is 2½cm). Add ⅜" (1cm) seam allowance all the way around (fig. A). If your fabric isn't long enough, piece the band at center back or at the side seams, adding a seam allowance. Join the sections with right sides together, and press.

underlay

overlap

fig. B

• Cut fusible interfacing without seam allowances and press onto the inside. If you prefer to use waistband stiffening, sew it to the wrong side of the inside, stitching along both edges. (This is available in several sizes, to correspond to the width of the finished waistband.)
• In the following procedure, the waistband closes to the right, that is, the overlap is on the left front.
• Mark center front and center back—remember the underlying extension on the right. Fold the waistband lengthwise, right sides together, turn under the inside seam allowance, and press it. If there is an overlap, cut a vertical notch in the seam allowance at center front and press under the seam allowance just to the notch (fig. B). Sew the ends together. If there is an overlap, sew to the notch. Trim the seam allowance on the ends to 3/16" (1/2cm), turn right side out, and press the waistband. Pin the outside of the waistband to the garment waist with right sides together, placing the pins crosswise, and matching center points (fig. C). Baste if necessary and sew. Turn right side out, bringing the inside folded edge down over the stitching line inside the garment. Pin and baste. Either sew from the right side, in the seam furrow, or slipstitch on the wrong side. If desired, topstitch all the way around. Make a buttonhole and sew on button, or sew on other fasteners.

Fig. C

fig. A

Measure the waistband length as above. The upper edge can be shaped if you wish (and should be drawn out on tissue paper first); look over the suggestions in this book. The waistband can, as called for in the design, open at the side or at center back (it should be marked accordingly). From a double thickness of fabric, cut the waistband in the desired shape and width x length + overlaps with ⅜" (1 cm) seam allowance all the way around. For optional piecing, see One-piece Waistband, p. 154.
• Cut out and press or baste optional interfacing (cut without seam allowance) onto the inside, on one or both pieces.
• If making belt tabs and/or suspenders or the like, sew these as described on p. 168.

• These directions assume the waistband opens at center front toward the right, that is, any overlap is added to the left side.
• Mark center front and center back. Remember the underlying extension on the right.
• Turn under the seam allowance of the inside—if there is an overlap, cut a vertical notch in the seam allowance at center front and press up the seam allowance to this notch (fig. A).
• Pin the two parts with right sides together; if you are adding belt loops, pin these between two thicknesses at center back, at the sides, and on each side of center front, with all edges flush. If there is a strap, pin it to the overlap side. Sew the ends and the upper edge—if there is an overlap, sew to the notch. Backstitch across the strap to strengthen the seam. Trim the seam allowance to ⅛" (½cm). Press the seam open. Turn right side out, press the waistband, and sew on according to the instructions for the one-piece waistband, p. 154. To fasten down the belt loops, turn the loose ends under 3/16" (1/2cm) and pin them just under the waistband. Backstitch with small stitches. If there is a buckle strap, sew on the second part of the buckle (see p. 167).

See also Pants with Facings, p. 45 and 48.

Slits and Cuffs

Cuffs can be added to sleeves and pants legs.
• First make a slit.
• On sleeves, this is placed in the underarm seam, or an inch or so from it on the back half of the sleeve, or in the back seam on 2-seam sleeves.
• On pants, the slit is made in the outside seam or in the outer leg.

SLIT IN A SEAM

fig. A

Add ⅜" (1 cm) extra seam allowance the length of the slit. Fold in the seam allowance double, and stitch around the edge of the slit. Backstitch at the top for reinforcement (fig. A). You can also use a narrow overlap as for the slit in 2-seam sleeves.

SLIT IN A 2-SEAM INSET SLEEVE

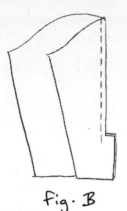

Allow a 1⅜" (3½ cm) seam allowance on the lower 3½-4½" (8-12 cm) of the back seam on both sleeve pieces. Sew the seam, ⅜" (1 cm) into the slit (fig. B). Turn under the side that will lie underneath (the smaller, back sleeve piece) first ¼" (½ cm) then ½" (1½ cm). Pin and stitch the hem in as part of the sleeve seam.

• Turn in the overlapping portion (on the larger, front sleeve section) ⅝" (1¾ cm). Pin and stitch down the inner edge and topstitch (fig. C). Pin the underlying side in place at the base of the slit. Stitch down the sleeve seam allowance on the larger sleeve piece and sew across the overlap with a diagonal line of stitching (fig. D).

fig. B

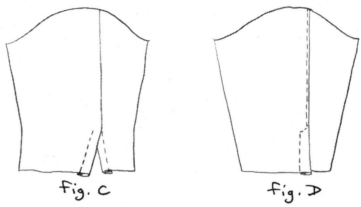

fig. C   fig. D

SLIT WITH A GORE

Mark a 2½" (6 cm) slit straight with the grain, about 3" (8 cm) from the centerline of the back sleeve section. Press a small piece of lightweight fusible interfacing to the base of the slit and cut it open. On the straight grain of the fabric, cut a triangular gore 3½" (8½ cm) including the seam allowance, as shown in the pattern. Turn up a ¾" x ¼" (2 x ½ cm) hem at the bottom, stitch. Trim the corners. Pin the gore into the slit, right sides together, aligning the hemmed edge of the gore with the seamline of the sleeve lower edge (fig. E), and sew from the sleeve side with 3/16" (1/2 cm) seam allowance. At the base of the slit, where the seam allowance is very narrow, turn the corner with the presser foot up and the needle down. Zigzag the seam allowances together and stitch it to the sleeve.

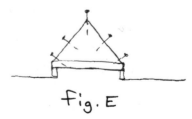

fig. E

BOUND SLIT

Cut a binding strip 4" (10cm) wide and the length of the slit + ¾" (2cm). Zigzag the edges and sew it on as described on p. 145, but with these exceptions: leave one end open, and fold the binding so that it is twice as wide as for a pocket so the binding overlaps instead of meeting in the middle. Turn in the edges of the bindings double when they are stitched at the seamline, so the raw edges are hidden. A small fabric triangle, or perhaps a small leather triangle can be sewn over the base on the right side (fig. F).

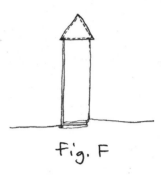

fig. F

- See also Slits in Side Seams under Finishing Edges, p. 149, and Kick Pleats, p. 140.
- See also the shirts on p. 12 and sweatshirt on p. 17, which have sleeves without cuffs.

CUFF WITH BUTTON LOOP

Adding ⅜" (1cm) seam allowance all the way around, cut the cuff the length of the wrist/ankle measurement + ¾" (2cm) ease, and the desired width x 2. Fold and sew a strip of fabric to make a button loop. Fold the cuff, right sides together, lengthwise, and turn under and press the seam allowance of the inside. Lay the button loop between the layers on one side seam (fig. A). Backstitch over the button loop when you sew the ends of the cuff together. Turn right side out and press. The bottom of the sleeve or pants leg can be gathered or drawn up with small pleats, perhaps 4 on each side of the slit, so that the edge fits the cuff. Pin the outer side of the cuff to the sleeve or leg, right sides together, so the button loop will extend toward the body. Baste and sew it on. Turn up the cuff toward the inside of the sleeve or leg so that pressed edge just covers the seam. Pin and baste. Stitch from the right side and, if desired, topstitch all the way around or slipstitch from the wrong side. Sew on the button.

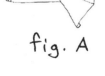

fig. A

PLACKET-OPENING CUFF

Adding ⅜" (1cm) seam allowance all the way around, cut the cuff the length of the wrist or ankle measurement + ¾" (2cm) (for ease) + ¾" (2cm) for overlap and in the desired width x 2. Follow the steps for the cuff with button loop, but don't sew in a button loop. Instead, make a buttonhole horizontally in the overlapping end of the cuff. Sew on a button.

157

Shoulder Pads

There are various kinds of shoulder pads, for both "straight" and "round" shoulders. For washable clothing, shoulder pads are made of foam or other washable materials, or can be attached with snaps, giving the garment the advantage of being wearable with or without shoulder pads. For clothing to be dry cleaned, shoulder pads of batting can also be used.

• Most purchased shoulder pads have no covering. If the garment is lined, the shoulder pads are sewn in between the lining and the outer fabric. If not, cover the shoulder pads with thin fabric before sewing them into the garment.

• It's easy and inexpensive to make your own shoulder pads, and it's especially economical with the "round" shoulder pads. The pads must be precisely identical, or the garment will have a lopsided look. The covering can be thin cotton or lining fabric, and the filling can be foam, polyester batting, lambs wool underlining or old-fashioned cotton batting (for dry-cleanable clothes).

• If the pads need a lot of body, they can be stiffened with a heavier weight interfacing material.

• Straight shoulder pads can be used for set-in sleeves or dropped shoulders. The round ones can be used in all four basic patterns and are always used with the kimono and raglan styles.

large

small

Fold — straight shoulder pad

top & bottom for rounded shoulder pad

STRAIGHT SHOULDER PADS

For 2, cut out 2 pieces of fabric with a fold and with ¼" (½cm) seam allowance, and 2-4 thicknesses of filling with no fold, following either the large or the small pattern on this page. For fairly thick pads, use the larger pattern for the fabric and 1 thickness of filling, and the smaller pattern for 1-3 extra thicknesses of filling. Baste together the layers of filling before the cover is sewn on.

• You can either fold the fabric around the filling, pin and zigzag the edges together, trim the edges and zigzag once more, or you can make the cover, sewing right sides together and leaving an opening to insert the filling. Slipstitch the opening, and topstitch or tack the pads to keep the layers from slipping.

Filling — rounded pad

shoulder line

shoulder line

ROUND SHOULDER PADS

For 2, cut out 4 top and 4 bottom pieces in fabric with ¼" (½cm) seam allowance, and 4 pieces of filling with no seam allowance, all from the boat-shaped pattern. Sew the fabric pieces together in pairs at the shoulder line, and press the seam allowance. Butt and overcast the edges of the filling layers, in pairs, at the shoulder line.

• From the other (rectangular) pattern, cut 1-3 layers of filling, depending on how much thickness you want and the thickness of the filling. Baste all layers together as marked. Pin the fabric, with right sides together, and sew. Leave an opening at one end to insert the filling. Turn the fabric right side out around the filling, pin the opening, and topstitch.

• You can also place all the layers together and zigzag closely around the edges.

• Anchor the filling at the seamline if the layers look like they'll slip.

Linings

The weight of the lining is determined by the outer fabric of the garment. The lining should never be too heavy or thick in relation to the garment itself, whether its purpose is to reinforce the shape of the garment, to give additional warmth, or just to make the garment more comfortable to wear. See Survey of Lining Fabrics, p. 124.

• Many avoid sewing lined clothing because it seems complicated to make it hang well without straining or bagging. But if the pattern drafting, cutting, and marking are carried out with care and the seam allowance is respected, it's really not so difficult.

• If you have trouble achieving a perfectly straight line of stitching, you might try marking the seamlines when cutting the fabric (p. 133). It is equally important to use matching points on all centerlines, and on the facings, etc.

SKIRTS

Straight skirts are lined partly to preserve their shape, and partly because they will hang better and won't creep up. Taffeta, various kinds of polyester, rayon, silk, and lining satin are well suited. If the skirt is made of firm, smooth cotton or the like, there is usually no need for a lining.

• Assemble the skirt except for sewing on the waistband.

• Cut the lining from the same skirt pattern, but 2" (5cm) shorter. Allow ¾" (2cm) seam allowance at the sides, ⅜" (1cm) at the waist, and 1¼" (3cm) at the bottom. Zigzag the edges. If the skirt has no slits or kick pleat, sew the side seams down to about 8" (20cm) above the knee, then hem the remaining seam allowances as for slits. A small reinforcement might be sewn at the top of the slit. If the skirt, for example, has a slit in the back, sew the lining seam with an opening as high as the slit, then sew the lining to the edges of the slit. Turn up a double hem at the bottom. Pin the skirt to the lining at the waist, wrong sides together, matching seams, and sew on the waistband. Slipstitch the lining to the edge of the zipper tape or other closure.

• *Full skirts* of wool, brushed fabrics, and leather should be lined or worn with a slip. For very light cotton fabrics, raw silk, or rayon, a lining is usually superfluous.

• Cut the lining following the pattern for the straight skirt and let it slant outward 3½-4" (8-10cm) at the side seams from the hipline (fig. A). Remember a cut for the seam at center front or center back, depending where the skirt itself opens. Sew the side seams of the lining down far enough to cover the hips, that is, about 12" (30cm) below the waist. Sew the rest as for a straight skirt, above.

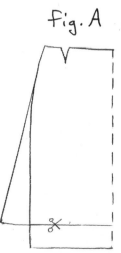

fig. A

PANTS

Leather pants and wool pants are most comfortable when they're lined. For leather pants, which must be dry-cleaned, it's nice if the lining can be taken out and washed. Lightweight synthetic fabrics have the least bulk and feel lightest on. Duck trousers can be lined with brushed cotton to make them warmer.

fig. B

- Make the pants to the point where the waistband is to be put on.
- Cut the lining following the pants pattern, but about 4" (10cm) shorter and without pockets and fly. If there are inset pockets, the pocket wedge should be pinned to the pocket inset before cutting, so that the fronts will be complete (fig. B). For a removable lining, also cut a strip of fabric 1½" (4cm) wide and the length of the waistband + ⅜" (1cm). If there are pleats in the pants, pin and press them in the lining so they have as little bulk as possible. If the fullness for pleats takes up more than 3" (8cm) on each front section, cut the pattern down (p. 108) to that measurement before cutting out the lining.
- Zigzag the edges of the lining. Sew the lining together at the side and center seams and the inseams, leaving the zipper slit open.
- To make a removable lining, fold the waist strip in half lengthwise and press. Turn in the ends ¼" (½cm) and zigzag the raw edges together. Pin the strip to the waist edge of the outer pants on the inside and sew it in when the waistband is sewn on. Then fold over the top edge of the lining twice, ⅛ then ⅜" (½ then 1cm), stitch, and sew by hand to the waist strip.
- To make a permanent lining, join pants and lining at the waist, with wrong sides together, matching seams, and sew on the waistband. Slipstitch the lining around the zipper. French tack the lining at the crotch, if desired.

DOUBLE PANTS

The pants can be sewn as above, optionally with a full length lining, which is hemmed along with the outer pants. Allow extra length for different degrees of shrinkage, or pre-shrink the fabrics.
- A very simple way to make double pants is to underline them, cutting out the lining to match the outer fabric and zigzagging the pants pieces to the lining pieces as you go. Each lined piece is then treated as a single layer. This method can also be used for jumpsuits.

JUMPSUITS

For jumpsuits, brushed or quilted cotton makes a comfortable lining.
- The procedure is roughly the same as that for jackets with turned lining (p. 56), regarding treatment of the front edges and collar.
- For the sleeves and the legs, the two thicknesses are hemmed together, or taken care of with cuffs. Of course, it is important that the fabrics are washed first if they don't have the same degree of shrinkage. If, for example, you combine nylon or polyester as an outer fabric with a flannel lining, the flannel will have to be pre-shrunk.

OUTER CLOTHES

There are many possibilities for lining outer clothes, depending how warm they need to be.

• Brushed cotton, firm knits, and cotton can be used for shorter jackets.

• In all kinds of outer clothes you can use:

• Shiny linings, like lining satin, cotton-rayon satin, or chintz. Smooth cottons, down-proof ticking and poplin (the latter two are windproof); quilted with lambswool underlining or flannel, these make very warm linings (and can also be sewn with shiny lining fabrics).

• Plush, for example, combined with a heavy duck as the outer fabric. The thickest imitation furs can be difficult to use as linings, especially if the outer fabric isn't heavy enough. Wool lining can be combined with smooth linings in the sleeves, perhaps lightly quilted.

• Prequilted lining (a thin layer of polyester batting with nylon, cotton-satin or cotton-rayon satin) can also be used as underlining.

• The garment can be lined with or without facings.

• In coats the lining can hang freely at the lower edge, while linings in jackets are usually sewn in at the bottom.

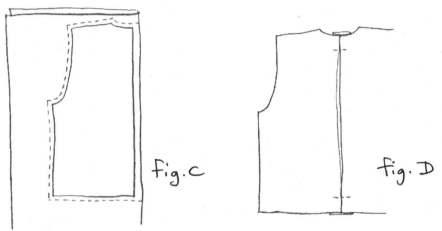

LINING TO THE EDGES ON SHORTER JACKETS

Cut the lining exactly like the outer fabric, even using it as a pattern, so the seam allowances are identical. Notch markings into the seam allowances of the front edges and center back, on the collar, and on the bottom edge.

• For designs made of lighter weight outer fabric and with elastic at the bottom edge, cut the outer fabric with, for example, 1½" (4cm) extra for the hem and channel. The lining can in this case be cut 1⅛" (3cm) shorter than the actual length (1½" minus ⅜" seam allowance, or 4cm minus 1cm seam allowance). With thinner lining fabrics, the center back of the pattern can be moved in ⅝" (1½cm) from the fold of the fabric to make a pleat for ease. Sew the pleat as a box pleat, 2" (5cm) down from the neck and 2" (5cm) up from the lower edge (figs. C and D). Zigzag the edges if the fabric frays. Pin and sew the lining together at the shoulder, sleeve, and side seams. Press or stitch the seam allowances down. Sew the under and upper collars to the outer and inner pieces, adding a hanging loop at the center back on the lining side, if desired. You can also add inside pockets, sewing them as patch pockets or bound pockets (pp. 142 and 144).

• Before sewing the lining and the jacket together, the jacket should be completed with pockets, trim, and straps (unless these are sewn on in the process of sewing the two layers together). You must judge whether buckles and belt tabs, etc., would be better sewn through both layers or only onto the jacket itself. They will hold better if it is sewn through both layers. As an option, straps and button loops at the edges can be pinned onto the outer fabric and sewn into the joining seam.

• Pin the lining to the jacket, with right sides together, at the collar, front edges, and bottom edge (unless you plan a waistband or elastic edge), matching seams and matching points. If the layers tend to slip, it may be necessary to baste through them.

• If you are using an elastic edge or waistband, start stitching at the bottom edge, and sew around the neck and down. If the lining extends to all edges, keep about 10" (25 cm) open at center back to turn the jacket through. If there are tabs in the seams, backstitch over them for reinforcement. Trim corners and notch curves. Turn right side out. Slipstitch the opening in the back. If the whole bottom edge is open, the seam allowances in the front edges can be pressed open to make a neater edge. If not, pin and baste the edges, and topstitch.

• Turn up the sleeve hems of jacket and lining together, baste, and topstitch. Pin and stitch the layers together at the back of the neck.

• If you are using elastic in the bottom edge, turn up ⅜" (1 cm) at the bottom and press. Spread the jacket out and pin the folded edge so that it covers the raw edge of the lining; stitch in place. Pull wide elastic through and sew the ends in place. If you are using a waistband, sew this on following the description on p. 154.

LINING TO THE EDGES ON COATS

Generally, the procedure is the same as for jackets, above, but with the difference that the lining hangs free at the bottom edge. The finished lining should be ⅜-⅝" (1-1½ cm) shorter than the coat. Heavy lining fabrics are turned up once, lighter ones doubled, and both can be sewn by machine.

• Hem the lining before the coat and the lining are sewn together. Pin the front edge, turn up the bottom edge of the coat over the lining so it is ⅜-⅝" (1-1½ cm) longer (fig. E). When the seam is sewn and the coat is turned, the seam allowance will be hidden. Hem the lower edge of the coat before you topstitch the front.

• To make a kick pleat, sew it after the lining and coat are sewn together and turned. Pin, with right sides together, the underlying portion of the coat pleat to that of the lining pleat—which is cut about 1½-2" (4-5 cm) wide and 12" (30 cm) long (fig. F). Turn, then topstitch. On the overlapping side, cut 1½-2" (4-5 cm) off the lining, so the edge is flush with the center back seam (fig. G). Fold the coat fabric around the edge of the lining, topstitch, and hem it to the lining, or baste and stitch down by machine. Pin the underlay in place at the base of the pleat and topstitch to secure it (fig. H). Secure the bottom.

• Make a French tack, ½-¾" (1-2 cm) long at the bottom of each side seam to hold the lining to the coat.

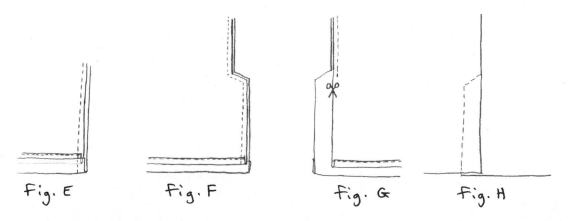

Fig. E   Fig. F   Fig. G   Fig. H

LINING WITH FACINGS

If a garment is to have both lining and front facings, draw up two identical pattern pieces for the garment front. Add a couple of matching points to the front edge of both pieces. Use one pattern for the garment. On the other, draw in the shape of the facing and place one or two matching points along this line. These are particularly important where the line curves. Cut the pattern along the line; use part for lining and the other part for the facing (fig. I).

LINING WITH FACING, SEWN TOGETHER AT THE HEM

Cut the facing and the under collar (or over collar, if the garment has lapels; see p. 177) from the outer garment fabric, with ⅜" (1 cm) seam allowance all the way around (also see Interfacing, p. 124). Cut lining for the sleeves, the back, and the fronts, following the lining pattern and adding ⅜" (1 cm) seam allowance all the way around. Remember to make matching points. Zigzag the edges of the lining pieces.

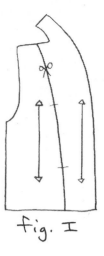

fig. I

- With right sides together, pin the facing to the lining front, matching notches, and sew to 2" (5cm) from the lower edge. Cut a horizontal notch there in the seam allowance of the facing. If desired, sew the seam allowances down on the lining side.
- Sew the shoulder seams. Press, and stitch the seam allowances down.
- Pin and sew the collar, with a hanger loop at center back if you wish.
- Pin and sew the other seams in the same order as for the outer garment, press, and stitch the seam allowances down if desired.
- Turn up the lining ⅜" (1 cm) at the bottom and wrists; press. Assemble the coat completely, with pockets, straps, etc., and turn up and press the hem allowance at the bottom and sleeves.
- Pin the lining to the coat at the collar, front edges and the bottom edge of the facing (where it's ¾" or 2cm shorter than the outer coat). Turn up the seam allowance of the facing's inner edge ⅜" (1 cm) from the notch down. Stitch the layers together. Trim off excess fabric at the bottom of the coat fronts and trim the seam allowances to 3/16" (1/2cm) (fig. J). Press the seam open as well as you can, trimming the corners and notching the curves. Turn right side out; pin and baste the edge. Press, then topstitch if desired. Hem the coat by hand. Pin the folded edge of the lining to the hem, ⅜" (1 cm) from the raw edge, and slipstitch. In this way, you create a horizontal pleat for ease, ⅝" (1½cm) deep. If you wish, make a kick pleat like the one described under Linings to the Edges for Coats (p. 162). Slipstitch the sleeves of the lining to the coat in the same way as the bottom was finished. French tack the lining to the shoulders and to the underarm, if desired. If there's to be a hanger loop at the center back neckline, pin it in place and sew it through all thicknesses.

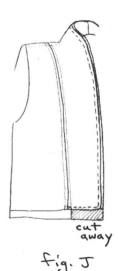

cut away

fig. J

LININGS WITH FACINGS, HANGING FREE AT THE HEM

Cutting and sewing is just as above, with the difference that both the lining and the coat are hemmed before being sewn together as described under Linings to the Edges for Coats.
- If you prefer to slipstitch the lining all the way around, follow the procedure under Coat with Shawl Collar (p. 69).

For *leather coats*, the lining is sewn as above.
- Additionally, the facings on leather jackets are cut at, for example, 1¼" (3cm) + seam allowance to the lower edge. The facings are sewn to the lining, which is cut correspondingly shorter (or with ⅝-¾" or 1½-2cm extra to make a pleat for ease as mentioned above). The lining/facing is sewn, like a lining, to the edge of the garment (p. 161). To put a zipper in the facing, see Zippers (p. 171).

All garments with center front openings must be made with the center front of the overlapping side exactly over the center front of the opposite side. Otherwise, the fit of the garment will be lopsided.

BUTTONHOLES

Buttonholes are always made through two thicknesses of cloth, preferably with supporting interfacing between them. If you wish to make a buttonhole in single-thickness fabric, reinforcing fabric must first be sewn on the right or wrong side, for example, for a buttonhole 1" long, a patch 1½ x ¾" + ⅜" seam allowance could be used. For a line of buttonholes, a strip could be sewn on.

• On an ordinary button front or waistband, the buttonhole is placed just outside the center front point, so that the button will be sewn on at exactly center front (the button will always "rest" in the buttonhole's outer end), or the buttonhole can be placed vertically on the center front line (figs. A and B).

• The size of the buttonhole is regulated by the button and must of course match its diameter—or vice versa. For a button ⅜-1" (1-1.7cm), an overlap of ⅝" (1.5cm) over the centerline is acceptable. If the edge will be hemmed, allow an additional 1⅛" (3cm) + seam allowance; otherwise, cut a separate facing (see p. 150). The buttonhole must be ⅜-¾" (1-2cm) from the edge, depending on the thickness of the fabric. The top button can be placed about ¾" (2cm) below the neckline.

• To mark buttonholes, lay a button on the fabric. Mark on either side with pencil or fabric pen and connect the marks, so the resulting line is perpendicular to the centerline if you want horizontal buttonholes, or on it if you want them to be vertical. If the button is thick, add ⅛" (2mm) extra. Only in corners can buttonholes be made at a slant.

• Measure the distance exactly from the edge. Decide where the top and bottom buttons will be, and space the other buttons evenly in between. For shirts, buttons can be about 4" (10cm) apart, but for coats there might be as much as 6" (15cm) between them.

• Buttonholes can be made with your machine's attachment, with a zigzag, by hand, or they can be bound. Machine-made buttonholes work well in lighter fabrics and in all cottons, but they look a little miserly on thick woolen fabrics. Follow the instructions for buttonholes in the instruction book for your sewing machine. After the buttonhole is sewn, it can either be cut with seam ripper, or with scissors or a razor blade. With a seam ripper, cut from the ends toward the center. This lessens the risk of the cut overshooting the buttonhole (fig. C). To cut with scissors, use sharp embroidery scissors. The most precise way to cut a buttonhole is with a little buttonhole knife, used with a wood block underneath (fig. D).

• *Handsewn buttonholes.* These are used for thick woolen fabrics, among others. They must be sewn rather precisely to look good. If you have never tried them before, practice first on a scrap.

• Mark the buttonhole. Sew a scant ⅛" (2mm) outside the markings with small running stitches or with a machine stitch, using matching thread. Cut on the marking and overcast the raw edges with ordinary thread (fig. E). Then, sew the buttonhole with silk or synthetic buttonhole twist using the buttonhole stitch

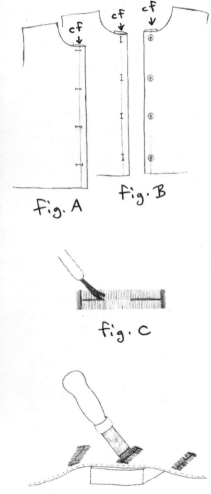

fig. A   fig. B

fig. C

fig. D

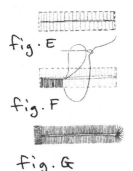

fig. E

fig. F

fig. G

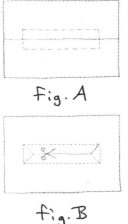

Fig. A

fig. B

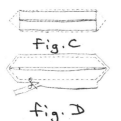

Fig. C

fig. D

Fig. E

(fig. F). Start on the bottom of the inner side and sew closely, to just cover the basic stitches. At the outer end, spread the outer end of the stitches to make a rounded corner; at the inner end, finish by sewing 3 overcast stitches the width of the whole buttonhole, then sew over these with buttonhole stitch at a right angle to the buttonhole (fig. G).

BOUND BUTTONHOLES

Making bound buttonholes is a big job and requires a certain amount of precision, but it's not difficult. First make a test buttonhole, if you haven't made them before, or if the materials are very different from what you're used to.

• Bound buttonholes are often used in tightly woven, heavy fabrics and leather, but they can also be used on lighter fabrics. They look clumsy in very heavy wool unless the binding is made of garment leather. In leather, it's the only possible technique, as machine-made or handsewn buttonholes will perforate and ruin the leather.

• If the bindings are made of leather, the buttonholes can be made without a facing on the back, which would otherwise be necessary to make the inside look neat. The buttonholes are sewn through a single thickness of fabric (preferably interfaced) before the facing is sewn to the inner edge.

• Mark the buttonhole with basting thread or chalk (for placement, see p. 164).

• Cut a piece of binding, either bias or with the grain, 1½" (4cm) wide and ¾" (2cm) longer than the buttonhole. On the wrong side of the binding, mark the centerline of the buttonhole and mark the outer edges about ⅛" (3-4mm) from the center (fig. A).

• Position the binding on the garment, right sides together, matching markings. Baste or clip in place. In leather, you can baste into the marking itself. Sew around the outer edge of the buttonhole with a stitch length of 1½, and turn at the corners with the needle down. Sew exactly the same number of stitches across both ends, so the buttonhole will be even. Secure the ends by sewing ½" (2cm) over the beginning stitches.

• Clip or cut it open as shown in fig. B. Clip all the way to the corners, without cutting the stitches.

• Turn the binding through the opening. Pull the ends out well. Press the seams open. For leather, glue the seam flat. Fold the bindings around the seam allowance so that the two folded edges meet. *If this is a leather binding without a facing*, the whole seam allowance must lie within the fold of the binding. Sew around the edge of the binding, from the right side and in the triangle at each end as in fig. C. Carefully cut off the excess leather on the wrong side (fig. D). *If using fabric and interfacing*, baste the binding around the edges. Press.

• Clip or pin, baste, or stitch down the inner edge of the facing. For leather, glue the corners of the binding, so that the facing doesn't move.

• For fabric, secure it with one or two pins around the buttonhole. Cut the facing through the opening, from the right side of the garment. Notch the corners about ⅛" (3mm), as in fig. B. Fold the raw edges under, so that the folds just cover the stitching on the binding, and baste. Now stitch from the outside exactly in the seam furrow, or just outside it, so that the facing is included in the seam (fig. E). For leather, stitch around the buttonhole before cutting into the facing. Cut the buttonhole from the outside, and cut with small sharp scissors, very close to the stitching, on the inside.

BUTTON LOOPS

A button loop can be made of fabric or tape, folded and sewn together either by machine or hand. Button loops should be just big enough for the button to pass through. Choose a button loop compatible with your fabric and the other sewing techniques you're using.

• A folded and sewn button loop looks robust and sporty. It can be sewn into a seam (fig. A), it can be sewn directly onto the fabric, first one way, then the other, so that the raw ends are hidden (fig. B), or it can be secured by sewing on a decorative triangle or the like (fig. C).

A *turned button loop* should be sewn into a seam, for example, the seam between the front edge and the facing. Cut it on the straight of the fabric, about ¾" (2cm) wide and in the desired length. Should you need many, they can be made as one long strip and cut after the strip is turned. Fold the strip, wrong side out, around a string or heavy thread with a knot in one end. Sew with small stitches, avoiding the string, except to anchor it at one end. Trim the seam allowance fairly closely, and turn by pulling the anchored end gently through (fig E.)

A *handsewn button loop* is very thin and consequently, almost invisible. It is made like a French tack, and is used, for example, for inside buttons. Determine the length according to the size of the button. Make 4 loops with strong thread, corresponding to the size of half a button. Sew tight buttonhole stitches, bundling the loops together, with the knots of the stitches to the outside (fig. F).

Finally, one can use a tab with a buttonhole in it (p. 168).

BUTTONS

When a button is sewn onto a single thickness of cloth, some sort of reinforcement is often necessary on the wrong side. A button can be reinforced by a small, flat button which is sewn on the wrong side at the same time the button is sewn to the right side (fig. A).

• Buttons can be sewn on with a zigzag machine stitch, but this is only recommended for thinner fabrics, as the button will be sewn on very tightly. Place the button on the fabric and under the presser foot (some machines have a special button foot). Set the stitch length at 0, and the width according to the distance between holes in the button. Test by first turning the machine by hand. Sew 5-6 stitches, and fasten the ends by setting the width to 0 and sewing a few more stitches.

• For heavier fabrics and for buttons that absolutely must stay on, use a button thread or other strong thread and sew the button on by hand, with a shank. First sew on the button very loosely, perhaps using a darning needle or a matchstick to regulate spacing (fig. B). When you've finished sewing, pull out the needle or matchstick, wind the thread around the "neck" under the button, and secure the end on the back side of the fabric.

HOOK AND LOOP TAPE

This consists of 2 tapes which adhere to each other. Best known is Velcro®, which is available in different widths and colors. It is good for pockets of active sports clothes. Sew the strip with the hooks onto the pocket, and the soft, fuzzy side onto the flap. It can also be used for inside closures like waistbands.

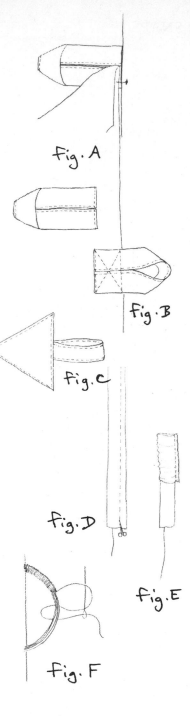

fig. A

fig. B

fig. C

fig. D

fig. E

fig. F

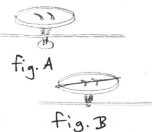

fig. A

fig. B

SNAPS

Heavy, press on snaps are used for medium-weight fabrics and jogging clothes and consist of a ring with small teeth which is pressed through the cloth to hold the actual snap. They are also available with decorative tops. They can be set with a hammer and a spool, or with special pliers. If you sew a lot, it's worth buying the tools, and buying snaps in bulk.

• For heavier fabrics and leather, more solid snaps are used, consisting of four parts and for which a little hole must be punched in the fabric. It is very important not to get that hole too big, or the snap can gradually work itself loose.

• For loosely woven fabrics, press a little piece of interfacing onto the wrong side as support.

• Smaller sew-on snaps are available in several colors and can be purchased in small quantities. Snap tape is also available.

BUCKLES, D-RINGS, AND SO FORTH

All these fasteners must be sewn to the garment with some kind of tab. Tabs can be riveted on, but this works best and is most durable on leather garments. The tab can be made of fabric, of leather, or can be a heavy tape, which fits either full width or folded through the buckle or ring (p. 168).

• Decide which size buckle or ring will look best with the style of the garment, the fabric, and the sewing techniques used.

• Measure the width of the tab to fit the buckles. Determine length by the function and the placement. For a buckle with a tongue, cut a hole in the tab where the tongue will go, and zigzag the edges of the hole with wide, tightly placed stitches. Then set eyelets in the opposing tab.

• A tab to hold only a ring or buckle should be about 4-5" (10-12cm) long and folded as shown in fig. A. It can be difficult to get close to the buckle with the presser foot, so you may need to sew two lines of stitches.

• Always sew the heavier part, the buckle, on the underlying side (or toward the back if the fasteners are on the sides), and the belt strap end onto the overlapping side, whether it is a waistband or the front edge of an upper garment. Belt tabs can be sewn on several ways:

1. Sew the tab into a seam, the seam of a pocket, or in the front edge between the lining and the outer fabric. REMEMBER TO PLAN your work to include sewing in the tabs at the correct point (fig. B).
2. Sew it on with a cross, square or the like, and with the raw end tucked under (fig. C).
3. Sew it on in two steps, so that the raw end is hidden (fig. D).
4. Sew a decorative triangle or other shape over the end, optionally in leather (fig. E).

A few fasteners made for purses can be used to advantage with garments. Check to be sure they can be set into fabric, as they are designed for leather. Get them in leather or sewing shops, or in shoe/luggage repair shops.

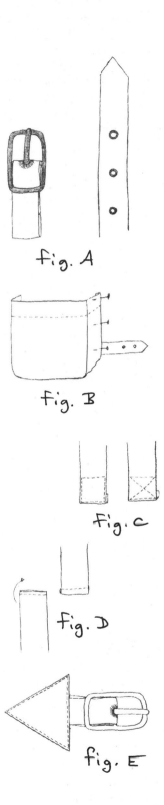

fig. A

fig. B

Fig. C

Fig. D

fig. E

Straps and Tabs

Machine-sewn straps and tabs can either be folded or turned. If you need a number of straps the same width, it's often easiest to make them in one long piece and cut them into smaller pieces. This can't be done with folded straps, however, if the ends have to be hemmed.

• Turned straps are a little more work than folded ones. Which technique you choose will depend in large part on how the garment is made and what material is used. Folded straps look better with active sports clothes and sportswear in general. For wool and other finer fabrics, turned straps add an appearance of good workmanship.

• Straps with eyelets must be reinforced with interfacing (cut without seam allowance), as the rings will otherwise quickly work their way out. Straps to be used with D-rings or buckles must be measured to fit them.

TURNED STRAP WITH FOLD

Cut the strap the desired length x double the width + ⅜" (1 cm) seam allowance all the way around. Cut out and press on fusible interfacing if desired.

• Fold lengthwise, with right sides together, and stitch along the open side (fig. F). Turn right side out and press the seam open (fig. G). The seam allowance can be trimmed to ⅛" (½ cm). Cut the strap into pieces of the correct length if necessary. The strap can be folded so that the seam lies either on the side or at the center of the back. If the outer end is to be closed, draw, cut, and sew a slanted, rounded, pointed or straight end as in fig. H. Trim the excess closely and turn right side out over a rounded stick or a knitting needle. If the strap will be sewn directly onto the garment and not sewn into a seam, turn under ⅛" (½ cm) at the bottom. Topstitch all the way around.

• If the strap is quite long, as for a half belt, it can be turned more easily using a safety pin (fig. I).

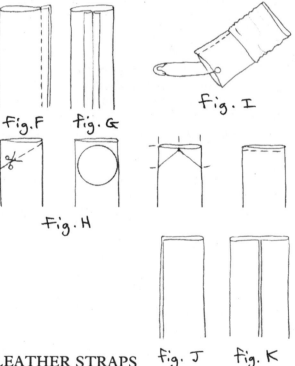

FOLDED STRAPS/ WIDE BUTTON LOOPS

Determine the length and width. Cut the width x 4, for thin fabric, otherwise x 2, + seam allowance. Cut the length + seam allowance. Cut fusible interfacing, if desired, and press it on. Fold the edges in toward the centerline (fig. A), and fold in the seam allowance (fig. B). Then fold double and press the strap (fig. C). Cut one end at a slant, for a pointed strap. Fold out, trim the seam allowance, and turn under the little point. Then turn down the slanted edges by about ⅛" (¼-½ cm) (fig. D). If the strap will be sewn directly onto the garment instead of being sewn into a seam, turn under the lower edge in ⅛" (½ cm) as well. Fold it back together and press again. Topstitch all the way around (fig. E).

LEATHER STRAPS

Cut the strap double width, adding ⅜" (1 cm) seam allowance across the width, if it will be sewn into a seam.

• Cut and press on fusible interfacing, unless the leather is very heavy. Fold the strap once (fig. J) or double (fig. K) and glue. Cut the tip to the desired shape, and topstitch.

Zippers and Plackets

Zippers are available in separating or non-separating styles.
• Non-separating zippers are made of nylon or metal, in both heavy and fine weights, and are used in flies, plackets and pockets. For a fly closure, choose the kind that locks when the tab is pressed down, as these are the most durable and don't slip down. Otherwise choose the zipper according to the weight of the fabric. A zipper that is too long can be cut off (using old scissors) at the bottom. Be sure to overcast the bottom teeth, so the slide doesn't slip off. The length of the zipper is designated according to the length of the zipper teeth, not by the tape, which is about ¾" longer at each end.
• Separating zippers are used at the center front of garments that must open completely. They're available in different weights, in nylon, plastic, and metal. Zipper lengths increase in increments of 2" (5cm), so be sure the front edge allows for this. Never pull the fabric tight or stretch it when sewing in a zipper as this will make the zipper bulge.
• Always use a zipper foot to install zippers by machine. It's easier, and it gives a better result.

HIDDEN ZIPPERS

Allow ¾" (2cm) seam allowance where the zipper will be placed. Leave the seam open as long as the zipper + ⅜" (1cm). Allow extra room above the zipper if you will be adding trim or button loop there.
• Turn under the seam allowances and press. Open the zipper and lay one side so that the edge of the teeth are right on the pressed edge of the fabric, with the outer side of the zipper against the wrong side of the fabric. Pin, then baste in place. Butt the folded edges together and baste with a catch stitch from the right side, so that the folded edges butt up tightly (fig. A). Close the zipper and baste the other side in place.
• On the machine, sew the zipper from the wrong side. If sewing by hand, sew with a backstitch from the right side of the garment. Start in the upper left corner and sew around ⅛" (½cm) outside the teeth. Sew an extra line of machine stitching around the outer edge of the tape (figs. B and C), or slipstitch it by hand.

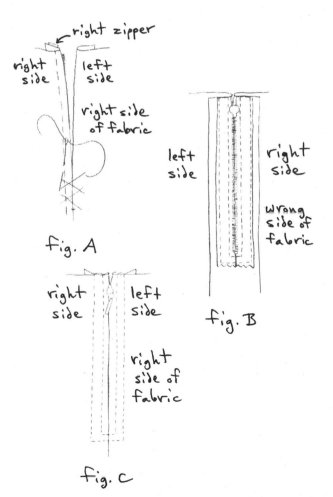

169

FLY ZIPPER

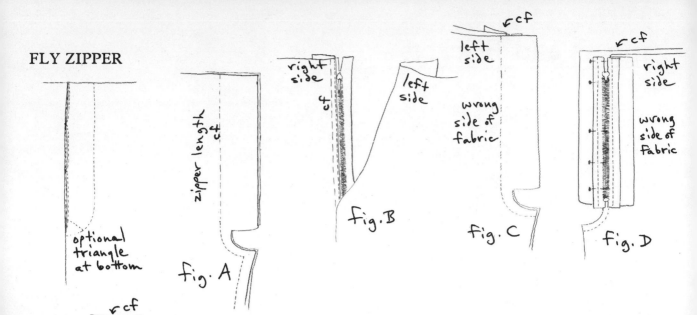

fig. A

fig. B

fig. C

fig. D

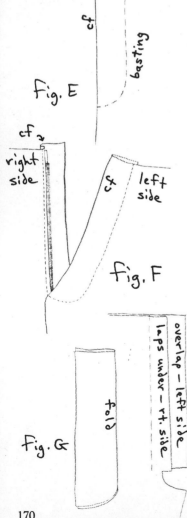

Fig. E

fig. F

Fig. G

These instructions result in a zipper that opens to the right (traditionally the male side), with the overlap on the left side.

• Cut the fly the length of the zipper + 1⅛" (3cm) and with 1½" (4cm) seam allowance (fig. A). Mark the center front. Sew the front, leaving the seam open the length of the zipper + ⅜" (1cm). Allow extra room for any borders or trim above the fly.

• Fold the right front ⅜" (1cm) outside the center front line, and press the seam allowance to the inside of the garment. Lay the right side of the zipper face down against the wrong side of garment, under the fold, with the row of teeth extending beyond the folded edge (fig. B). Pin, baste, and sew the zipper, 1/16" (1/4cm) from the edge.

• Lay the left front garment section over the right, with right sides together, and pin so that the center front lies directly over the opposite center front (fig. C). Place your work so that the wrong side of the zipper is up. Pin, baste and sew the left side of the zipper to the seam allowance, about ⅛" (½cm) from the teeth (fig. D). Open the fronts so that the outside is up. Pin once more, matching center fronts (fig. E). Baste and sew the fly from the right side with one or two lines of stitching, as wide as you wish (up to about 1¼" or 3½cm, as the seam allowance is only 1½"/4cm). Open the zipper and fold the seam allowance of the right side (plus a little of the zipper tape) forward toward the opposite side, and sew into the first seam, stitching very close to the edge (fig. F). Close the zipper, and, from the wrong side, handstitch the underlying extension down.

A fly can also be made with a separate inside extension. This is cut out 1½" (4cm) wide and as long as the fly, including the fold and the rounded end (fig. G). The right side (the underside) is cut with only ¾" (2cm) seam allowance the length of the fly, and the left side is cut with 1½" (4cm) added on as above. Follow the instructions for Zipper in a Fly above, but with the difference that the separate extension is sewn together (with right sides together) at the rounded edge, and is turned or zigzagged together.

• Fold in the right front ⅜" (1cm), and pin the zipper in place under the fold with the extension, so that the extension and the raw edge of the seam allowance are flush. Zigzag the edges together, and sew as described above.

BUTTON FLY

Snaps can also be used.

Cut both front pieces with an extension 1½" (4cm) wide for a fly width, 1¼" + ¼" seam allowance (3½cm + ½cm), and to the desired length + ⅜" (1cm), rounding the bottom edge (fig. A). Mark the center front. Cut a buttonhole strip (double thickness, folded lengthwise) in the same shape and size as the extension (fig. B).

• Zigzag the edges of the buttonhole strip together. Mark the locations of the buttonholes. For example, for a fly 6" (15cm) long and with ⅝" (1.5cm) buttons, mark them 1-1/16 and 4-3/4" (2.7 and 12cm) down and 3/8" (1cm) in from the edge. Make the buttonholes, pin and sew the front sections together up to ⅜" (1cm) above the beginning of the extension. Fold the left side at the center front line and topstitch to the bottom of the opening. (If the fabric is very loosely woven, lay seam tape in the fold.)

• Turn the right side under, first ⅜" (1cm) then 1⅛" (3cm), and stitch down the center front line (fig. C).
• Place the separate buttonhole strip under the fold of the left side so the edges are flush, and pin together. Baste through all thicknesses 3/16" (½cm) from the raw edge and along the rounded edge (fig. D). Pin center front to center front, so that the inside extension is correctly placed, and sew alongside the basting. If desired, sew a small triangle at the bottom for reinforcement. Remove the basting thread (fig. E). Sew buttons (or set snaps) on the inside strip, and handstitch the buttonhole strip and front together between the buttonholes.

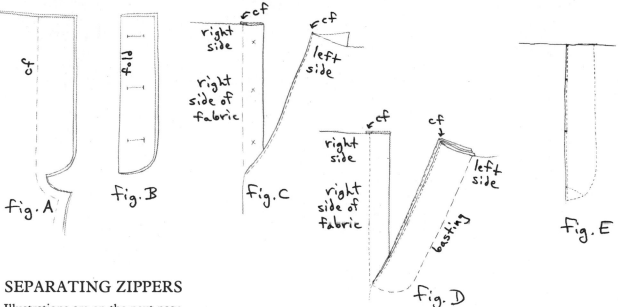

fig. A fig. B fig. C fig. D fig. E

SEPARATING ZIPPERS

Illustrations are on the next page.

IN A GARMENT LINED TO THE EDGES, WITH AN OVERLAP

Cut the lining of the overlap and the outer fabric of the underlying side with a ¾" (2cm) extension at the front edge, to make a pleat. (If the front edge is slanted, cut the pattern up the center front line and expand it for a pleat by laying the pattern pieces ¾" or 2cm apart at this line.) Mark center front.

• With wrong sides together, fold and press the center front lines of the 2 pieces (fig. A). Pin the open zipper to the lining of the overlap side, so that the teeth just show (fig. B). Fold the edge forward so that a pleat is formed in which the zipper tape lies hidden, and stitch the pleat and the zipper into it (fig. C).

• Repeat this process in the outer fabric of the other front section, and assemble the jacket as described on p. 52.

• After the jacket is turned and topstitched, you may wish to sew a line of stitching through all thicknesses along the zipper, to keep it in place.

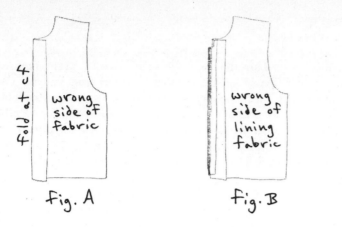

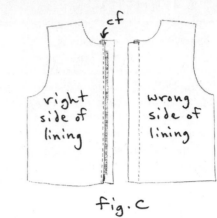

fig. A   fig. B   fig. C

IN JACKETS WITH LININGS AND/OR FACINGS

Adding ⅜" (1 cm) seam allowance, cut out the facing for the overlying side as an inside facing extending to the centerline, and cut an extension that extends from the centerline to the front edge (fig. A, below). Cut the front for the underlying side at the centerline, and the inside extension from the centerline to the edge, for example 1½" (4 cm) wide (fig. B).

The facing of the underlying side can be cut like the front, to the centerline and with a separate extension in the same pattern (fig. C), or it can be cut as one piece (fig. D).

Lay the half of the zipper without the slide on the overlap side (the outer side), so that the edges are flush and the teeth turn in toward the facing. If desired, zigzag together at the edges. Lay the overlapping extension over it, so that the zipper lies between the 2 thicknesses, and stitch as closely to the teeth as possible. Stitch the

seam allowances down on the inside facing (fig. E).

• If the facing and extension for the underlying side were cut out separately, sew the separate inside extension together at the ends and outside edge, with right sides together (fig. F). Trim the seam allowances closely, turn and topstitch. Pin the other half of the zipper onto it, so that the raw edge and the zipper tape edge are flush. Be sure its placement corresponds to that of the other half, and zigzag in place (fig. G). Pin the jacket front (the underlying side), right side to zipper side, and the facing to the other side of the separate inner extension, with the edges still flush. Stitch through all thicknesses (this can be done at the same time the lining/facing is sewn on). Smooth the front and facing and topstitch down center front.

• If the facing and extension were cut as one piece, sew the second half of the zipper as the first. Remember that placement of the halves must be exactly even. Sew on facings as described on p. 150.

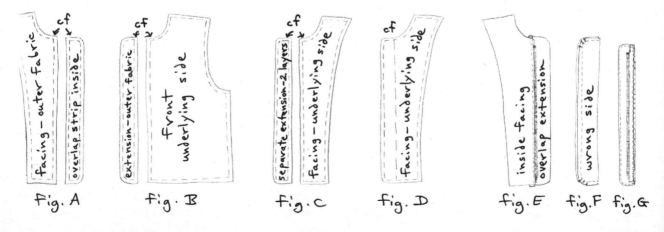

fig. A   fig. B   fig. C   fig. D   fig. E   fig. F fig. G

172

Neck Openings

A neckline opening can be finished in different ways. It can be made with a facing as described on p. 150, as a bound slit, as described under Slits and Cuffs, p. 155, as a fly with a button strip (p. 171), or as a placket opening or inset as described below.

PLACKET OPENING

Decide how long and how wide you want the slit and the placket. Cut the placket from a double thickness of cloth, the width x 2 and the length + 1⅛" (3cm). Add 3/16" (1/2cm) seam allowance all the way around.

• Mark the length and width of the slit on the wrong side of the front piece with chalk and cut to within 3/16" (1/2cm), the seam allowance, of the bottom (fig. A).

• Be sure that the facing opens on the correct side. If it will open toward the right (traditional for men), sew the placket overlap to the left. If toward the left (traditional for women), sew the overlap to the right.

Fold the overlapping placket piece, with right sides together, and sew across the bottom and 1" (2½cm) up the side, or sew a curve (fig. B). Cut a small notch at the top of the side to be sewn to the front (fig. C), and turn

right side out. Sew it to one side of the opening, and the other placket section (the underlay) to the opposite side, with right sides together. Cut a small horizontal notch in each side of the seam allowance of the front, at the bottom corners of the slit (fig. D). Fold the placket underlay section in half lengthwise toward the inside of the garment. Turn under and press the seam allowance, baste from the wrong side so that the seam is hidden, and sew together from the right side (fig. E). Fold the overlap in half lengthwise around toward the inside of the garment, pin and sew in the same way. Topstitch around the outer edge. Sew the bottom of the overlap to the front, optionally with a cross at the bottom (fig. F). Make buttonholes in the overlap and sew buttons on the underlay. Sew on a collar, or finish the neckline.

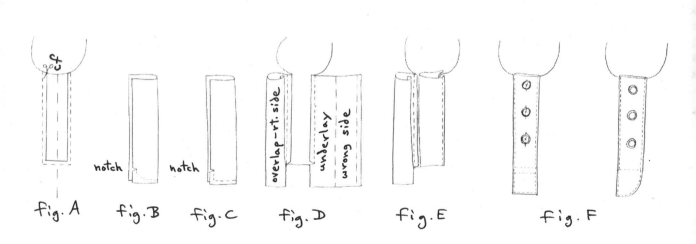

fig. A   fig. B   fig. C   fig. D   fig. E   fig. F

INSETS

For neck openings that are wider or are shaped, use an inset. The inset can open in front or at the side; it can be made with a collar or with an open neckline, or can be combined with the collars from Collar Pattern III. See the examples on the next page.

• Decide the shape of the inset, draw it on the pattern of the front and cut out (fig. G).

• Decide where the inset should close and determine the shape of the collar, if you will add one. Draft a pattern for the inset (fig. H).

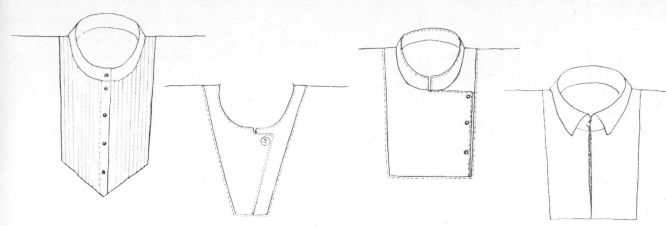

- Cut out from a double thickness of fabric, adding ⅜" (1 cm) seam allowance on the inset and at the corresponding seamlines of the front/back. Mark center front on the top and bottom edge of the inset and on the front.
- Sew the inset sections, with right sides together, and turn the inset at the front edge. If there will be a collar stand or collar, the neckline will be finished by the collar.
- If the inset has an overlap and the collar is to reach only to the front centerline, cut a notch at center front in each side, and make the two pieces, sewing each (right sides together) from the front edge to the centerline (fig. I). Sew on the collar between the notches.
- If you are not adding a collar, sew the inset, with right sides together, at the neck and outer edges, and turn. Sew the inset to the front before sewing the shoulder seams.

- Sew together the front edges of the inset, with right sides together, turn, press, topstitch and make any buttonholes.
- Pin the overlapping side of the inset to the underlying side (making sure that it closes on the correct side), so center fronts match. Cut a notch at each corner or point of the front (fig. J). Pin the inset and the front together at the vertical/slanted sides and stitch. Pin and then sew the horizontal seam across the bottom. Be careful to avoid wrinkles in the corners. Topstitch the seam allowances down onto the front from the right side of the garment.
- After sewing the shoulder seams, the ⅜" (1 cm) seam allowance will remain at the back neckline. It can be hemmed, trimmed or finished with the collar (p. 175).

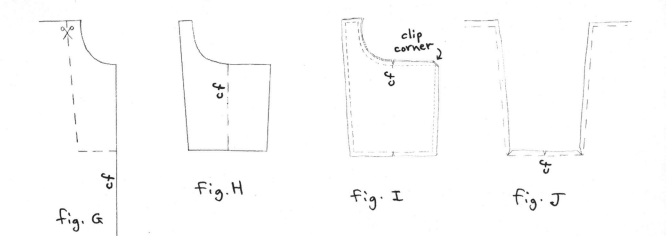

fig. G

fig. H

clip corner

fig. I

fig. J

Collars

There are patterns for 24 different collars in the pattern section in the back of the book. They are described in more detail on p. 104.
• All the collars made with basic Collar Patterns I and II are made using one of the methods below (lapels are described on p. 177).
• All the collars made with Collar Pattern III are drawn as part of the garment front. The technique for making these is described on p. 176.

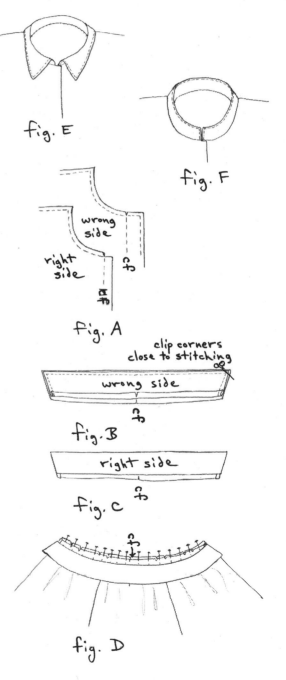

fig. E

fig. F

fig. A

clip corners close to stitching

wrong side

fig. B

right side

fig. c

fig. D

TURNED COLLAR OR COLLAR STAND

Cut the collar from a double thickness of fabric, with ⅜" (1 cm) seam allowance. Decide on interfacing according to your fabric and your preference, cut it with no seam allowances, and iron or baste it on. Mark center back on both pieces and at the back of the neck. If the collar has an overlap, mark the center front on both collar pieces and on the fronts. If there's no overlap, the ends of the collar will correspond to the center front. If there is an overlap on the fronts and the collar reaches only to the center front, mark the center front with a notch in the seam allowance, fold the front/facing with right sides together, at the foldline and stitch from the front edge to the centerline, and turn it (fig. A).

• Press under the seam allowance of the neck edge of the outer collar/inner stand and sew the sections together, with right sides together, at the ends and outer edge (fig. B). Remember to include any tabs or button loops. Trim the seam allowance to 3/16" (1/2 cm) and notch/trim all curves/corners. Press the seam allowances open as well as possible, and turn right side out. Baste the edge, if necessary, and press (fig. C). Pin the undercollar/outer stand to the neck edge, matching center backs and fronts. Clip the curve of the neck edge, cutting in 3/16", to make pinning easier, placing the pins at a right angle to the seamline about ¾" (2cm) apart (fig. D). Now is the time to put in a hanger loop in the back of the neck, if desired. Baste, then stitch. Turn the over collar/inner stand toward the wrong side, so the pressed edge just covers the seam. Pin, baste, and sew or slipstitch along the edge. For a collar, topstitch on the over collar (fig. E). For a stand, topstitch from the outer stand (fig. F).

SEWN-ON COLLARS WITH LINED GARMENTS

They can be sewn on as described above, or they can be attached by sewing the under/outer collar to the jacket, and the over/inner collar to the lining or facing. The collar sections then are assembled at the same time the lining is sewn to the jacket. The latter is an easy method, and always produces a neat front edge, if you are careful that the seamlines of both layers are exactly matched during assembly. After the collar is turned, stitch both thicknesses together at the neck edge to give stability.

A third method is to sew and topstitch the collar as a collar with stand (below). Pin it to the neck edge of the outer jacket, pin lining and jacket together with the collar between the layers and all raw edges flush. Stitch the front edges and the neck, and turn the garment right side out. Stitch along the seamline of the neck opening.
• See also Linings, p. 159.

COLLAR WITH STAND

Cut the collar and stand from doubled fabric, with ⅜" (1cm) seam allowance. Mark center back on all 4 pieces and the back (fig. G). Cut interfacing, if any, without seam allowance, and iron or baste it to one collar piece and one stand piece. Sew the collar sections together, with right sides together, at the ends and outer edge. Trim the seam allowance to 3/16" (1/2cm) and notch/trim corners and curves. Press the seam open, turn, and topstitch. Turn under and press the neck edge seam allowance of the inner stand section. Place a stand section on each side of the collar, with right sides together, and matching center backs. Sew through all layers (fig. H). Turn the stand down and sew it to the neck edge as a turned collar, and topstitch.

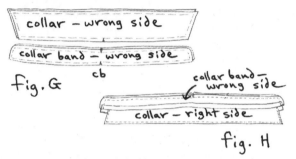

fig. G

fig. H

COLLARS CUT AS PART OF THE FRONT (SHAWL COLLARS)

Usually this kind of collar is made with a facing, but can, if the material is suitable, be made in a single layer, with the edge hemmed or bound with leather, tape, or fabric.
• For facings, add ⅜" (1cm) seam allowance at all edges. Cut a facing for the collar and the front edge (see p. 150). Cut interfacing (without seam allowance), depending on the fabric and your preferences.
• If the collar will be a single layer with a hemmed edge, allow ¾" (2cm) hem allowance at the outer edge. If the edge will be trimmed instead, don't add a seam allowance at the outer edge.
• Cut a notch ⅜" (1cm) deep at each inside corner (fig. A).
• Sew the center back seam on the garment and facings, and press the seams open. For a single layer, turn under the seam allowances neatly and hem or cover with trim. Press or baste in interfacing at this point. Pin and baste the front and back shoulder and neck seams (fig. B). For raglan garments, sew the front and back sleeve sections together, sew the sleeves to the back, and pin the front to it at the raglan and neckline (be careful at the rounding of the sleeves) (p. 103).

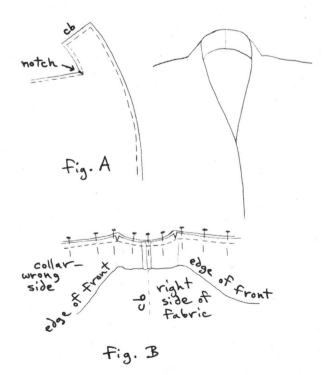

Fig. A

Fig. B

• Sew from the front. Just before the notch, you may have to lift the presser foot with the needle in the fabric, and push the top thickness through to avoid a pleat in the seam.
• Press the shoulder seams open and press the seam allowances of the neck edge upward.
• If there is no lining, turn under and press the seam allowances of the inner edge of the facing.
• For a lining, see p. 161.
• Pin, baste, and sew the facing to the collar/front edge, with right sides together. Trim seam allowances to 3/16" (1/2 cm), and/or notch curves. Press the seam

LAPELS

The patterns include a version with narrow, single-breasted lapels and one with wider, double-breasted lapels. Either can certainly be altered.
• A lapel is always made with facing and a double-thickness collar.
• Cut out the undercollar on the bias, as shown. Cut the over collar with the center back on a fold. Add 3/8" (1 cm) seam allowance at all edges. Cut the facing following the lines of the front, also with 3/8" (1 cm) seam allowance. Mark center back and shoulder seams on the collar, and center back and center front on the neck opening. Cut interfacing (without seam allowances) for the over collar, and for the front edge, 2-2¼" (5-6 cm) wide at the bottom and slanting up to the shoulder, as in fig. C. For double-breasted coats, cut the facing wide enough to accommodate both sets of buttons and buttonholes.
• Press or baste the interfacing to the facing and over collar. Sew the over collar and the facing together from the shoulder markings forward. If there is a lining, sew it to the front edge and neck now (see Linings, p. 163). Sew the undercollar sections together at center back, and press the seam open. Pin and sew it to the neck edge with right sides together, matching markings. Press the seam open. Pin the facing/over collar to the undercollar/front edge, with right sides together, matching the seamlines of the over collar and undercollar precisely at the front. When sewing the notches of the lapels, use the same number of stitches on each side, so the two sides will match perfectly. Sew the facings as described on p. 150.

open. Turn the facing. If the collar is to be worn turned down, roll the facing slightly outward when the edge is basted and topstitched, so that it lies better. Pin the facing to the back of the neck and shoulder and machine- or slipstitch it down.
• For a single-thickness collar with a hemmed edge, cut a notch 3/8" (1 cm) deep in the seam allowance at the point of the greatest outside curve. Turn under double, baste, and press the edge. Stitch the edge and press again.
• For a single-thickness collar to be trimmed, see p. 152.

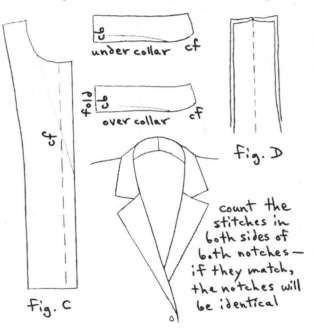

under collar   cf

fold   over collar   cf

cf

fig. D

Fig. C

Fig. C

count the stitches in both sides of both notches — if they match, the notches will be identical

• Trim all corners and press the seam allowances open. To press into the corners, fold on the diagonal so a point is formed, with the seamlines over one another. Turn the over collar/facing right side out and pin then baste the outside edge. For the collar to lie easily, the over collar and the part of the facing that turns out for the lapel, should be shifted slightly to give more fullness to that layer. Sew a single or double row of topstitching around the edges. Zigzag the seam allowances of the over collar and undercollar at the neck edge, and sew to the seamline of the neck edge, from the outside. Slipstitch the facing to the shoulders. If desired, stitch the layers together 1¼-2" (3-5 cm) in each side, sewing from the outside in the seamline. Fold the lapel back and press lightly. If the layers slip, tack by hand directly under the fold. Pin and sew this only after the lapel has been folded back, so that the top layer doesn't pull upward.

THE PATTERNS

D — FULL SKIRT

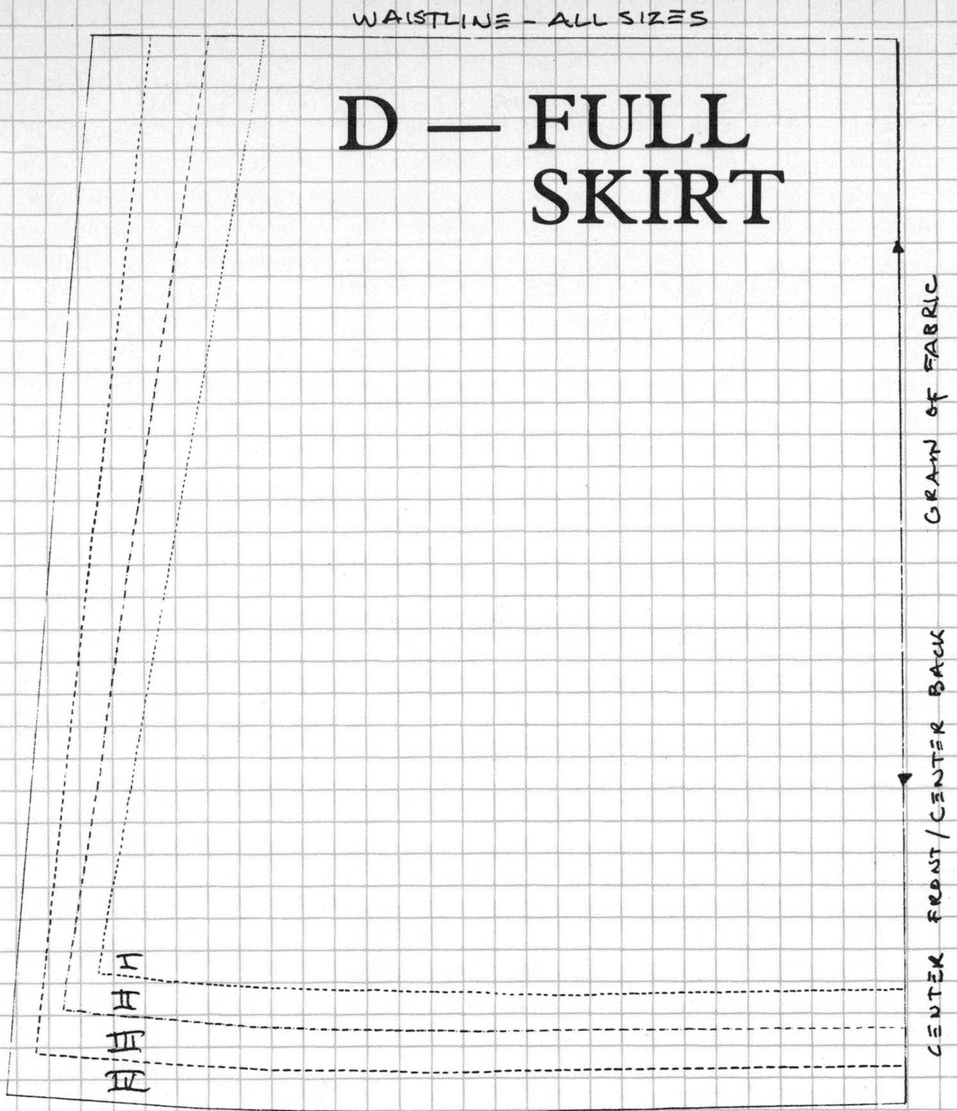

WAISTLINE - ALL SIZES

GRAIN OF FABRIC

CENTER FRONT / CENTER BACK

1 square = 1 inch

I
II
III
IV

FULL-SIZED PATTERNS AVAILABLE

The producers of *Easy Style* are pleased to offer a special Pattern Package, containing the pattern pieces shown in this section, all enlarged to actual size and ready to use. This valuable package contains all 35 pieces, plus extra copies of the collar and pocket pieces, and includes a convenient size chart. The patterns are printed on heavy white paper so they can be used repeatedly.

For each Pattern Package send a check or money order made payable to Lark Books for $9.95 plus $2.50 postage and handling (in Canada, $9.95 plus $4.50 postage and handling) to:

EASY STYLE Pattern Package
c/o Lark Books
50 College Street
Asheville, North Carolina, U.S.A. 28801

Please allow 2-3 weeks for delivery. Your satisfaction is fully guaranteed.

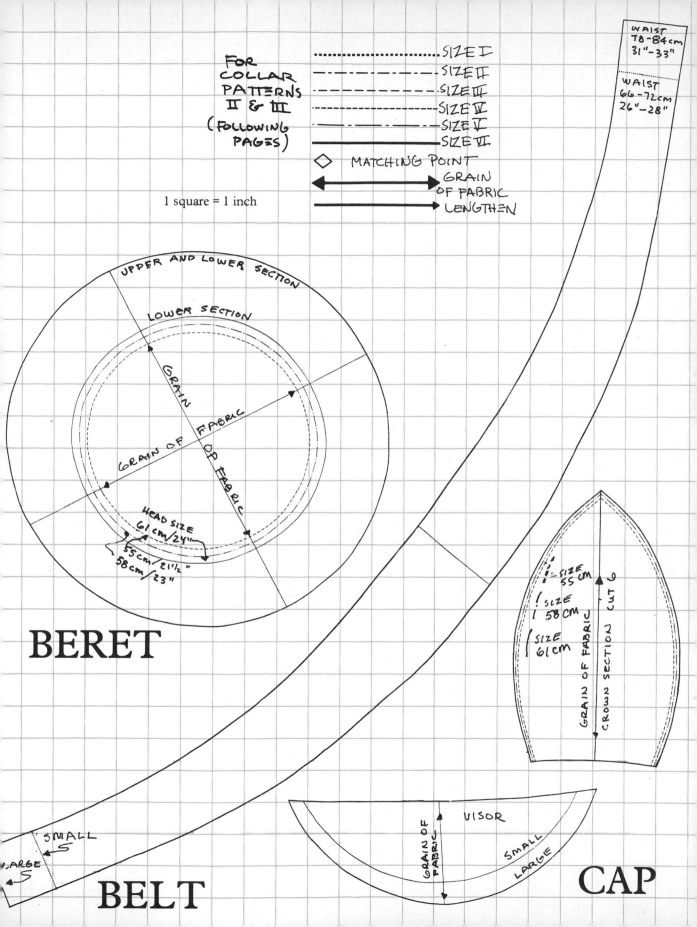

FOR
COLLAR
PATTERNS
II & III
(FOLLOWING
PAGES)

··· SIZE I
—··—··—··—··—··—··—··— SIZE II
— — — — — — — — — SIZE III
- - - - - - - - - - - SIZE IV
——————————— SIZE V
———————————— SIZE VI
◇   MATCHING POINT
←——————→   GRAIN OF FABRIC
———————→   LENGTHEN

1 square = 1 inch

WAIST
78-84cm
31"-33"

WAIST
66-72cm
26"-28"

UPPER AND LOWER SECTION

LOWER SECTION

GRAIN OF FABRIC

GRAIN OF FABRIC

HEAD SIZE
61 cm/24"
55cm/21½"
58cm/23"

BERET

SIZE
55 CM
SIZE
58 CM
SIZE
61 CM

GRAIN OF FABRIC

CROWN SECTION CUT 6

SMALL
LARGE

BELT

VISOR

GRAIN OF FABRIC

SMALL
LARGE

CAP

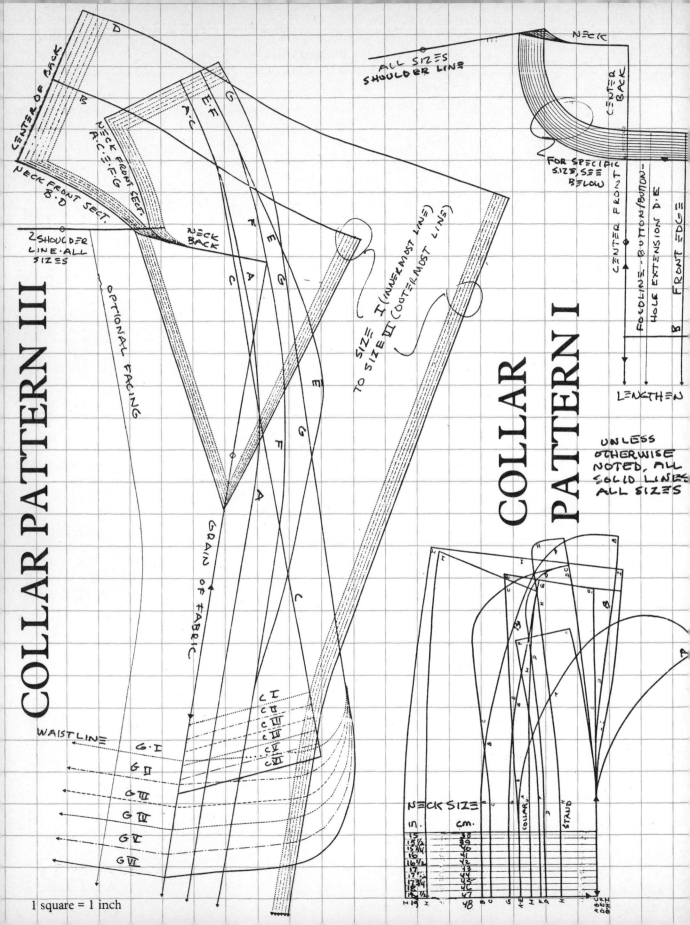

COLLAR PATTERN III

COLLAR PATTERN I

COLLAR PATTERN II

1 square = 1 inch

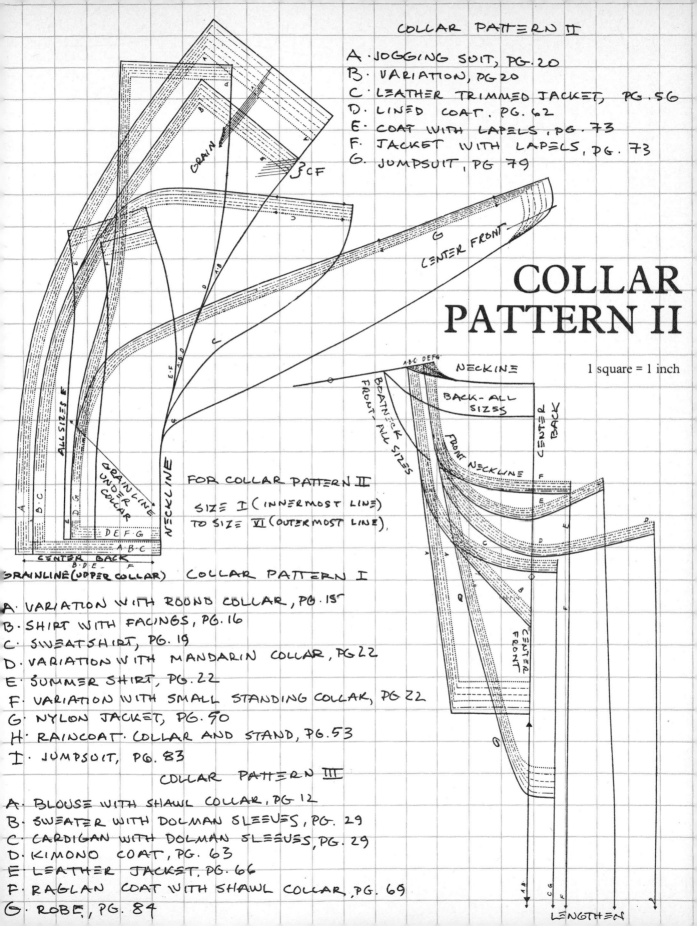

COLLAR PATTERN II

A. JOGGING SUIT, PG. 20
B. VARIATION, PG 20
C. LEATHER TRIMMED JACKET, PG. 56
D. LINED COAT, PG. 62
E. COAT WITH LAPELS, PG. 73
F. JACKET WITH LAPELS, PG. 73
G. JUMPSUIT, PG 79

COLLAR PATTERN II

1 square = 1 inch

FOR COLLAR PATTERN II

SIZE I (INNERMOST LINE)
TO SIZE VI (OUTERMOST LINE).

GRAINLINE (UPPER COLLAR)   COLLAR PATTERN I

A. VARIATION WITH ROUND COLLAR, PG. 15
B. SHIRT WITH FACINGS, PG. 16
C. SWEATSHIRT, PG. 19
D. VARIATION WITH MANDARIN COLLAR, PG. 22
E. SUMMER SHIRT, PG. 22
F. VARIATION WITH SMALL STANDING COLLAR, PG. 22
G. NYLON JACKET, PG. 50
H. RAINCOAT COLLAR AND STAND, PG. 53
I. JUMPSUIT, PG. 83

COLLAR PATTERN III

A. BLOUSE WITH SHAWL COLLAR, PG. 12
B. SWEATER WITH DOLMAN SLEEVES, PG. 29
C. CARDIGAN WITH DOLMAN SLEEVES, PG. 29
D. KIMONO COAT, PG. 63
E. LEATHER JACKET, PG. 66
F. RAGLAN COAT WITH SHAWL COLLAR, PG. 69
G. ROBE, PG. 84

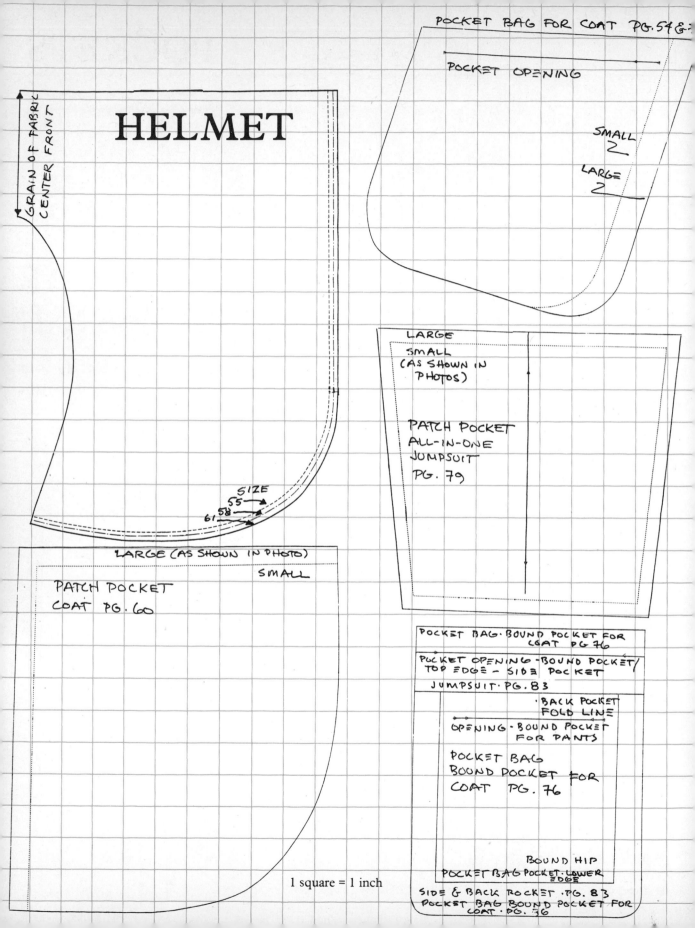

HELMET

GRAIN OF FABRIC
CENTER FRONT

SIZE
55
58
61

POCKET BAG FOR COAT PG.54 &

POCKET OPENING

SMALL
2

LARGE
2

LARGE
SMALL
(AS SHOWN IN
PHOTOS)

PATCH POCKET
ALL-IN-ONE
JUMPSUIT
PG. 79

LARGE (AS SHOWN IN PHOTO)
SMALL

PATCH POCKET
COAT PG. 60

POCKET BAG·BOUND POCKET FOR
COAT PG 76

POCKET OPENING-BOUND POCKET/
TOP EDGE - SIDE POCKET
JUMPSUIT·PG.83

·BACK POCKET
FOLD LINE

OPENING-BOUND POCKET
FOR PANTS

POCKET BAG
BOUND POCKET FOR
COAT PG. 76

BOUND HIP
POCKET BAG POCKET·LOWER
EDGE

SIDE & BACK POCKET ·PG. 83
POCKET BAG BOUND POCKET FOR
COAT·PG. 76

1 square = 1 inch

POCKETS

1 square = 1 inch

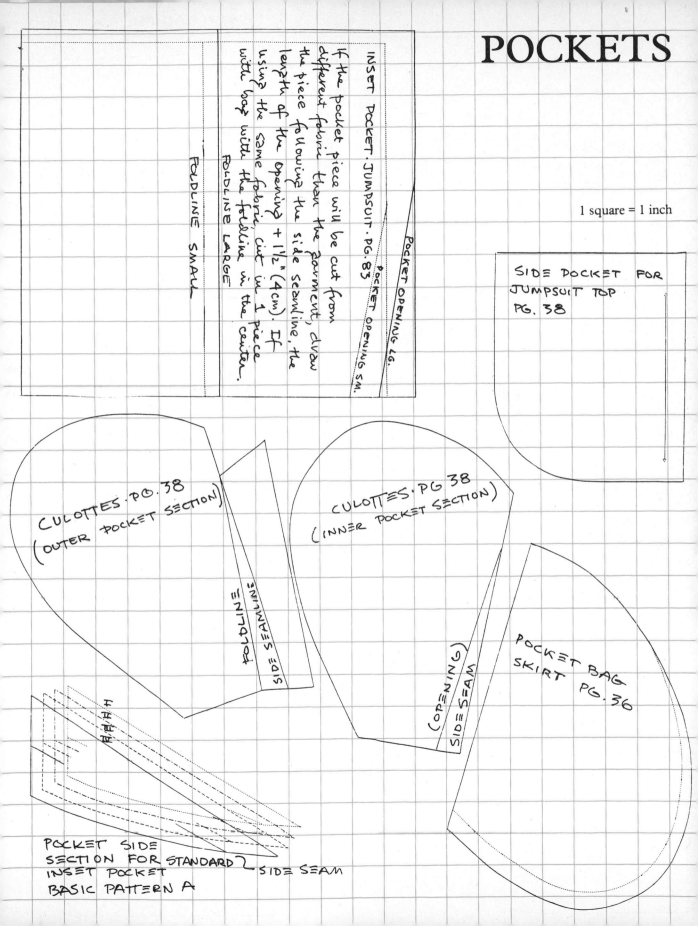

INSET POCKET. JUMPSUIT. PG. 83

If the pocket piece will be cut from different fabric than the garment, draw the piece following the side seamline, the length of the opening + 1½" (4cm). If using the same fabric, cut in 1 piece with bag with the foldline in the center.

POCKET OPENING SM.

POCKET OPENING LG.

FOLDLINE SMALL

FOLDLINE LARGE

SIDE POCKET FOR JUMPSUIT TOP PG. 38

CULOTTES. PG. 38 (OUTER POCKET SECTION)

CULOTTES. PG. 38 (INNER POCKET SECTION)

FOLDLINE

SIDE SEAMLINE

(OPENING)

SIDE SEAM

POCKET BAG SKIRT PG. 36

POCKET SIDE SECTION FOR STANDARD INSET POCKET BASIC PATTERN A

SIDE SEAM

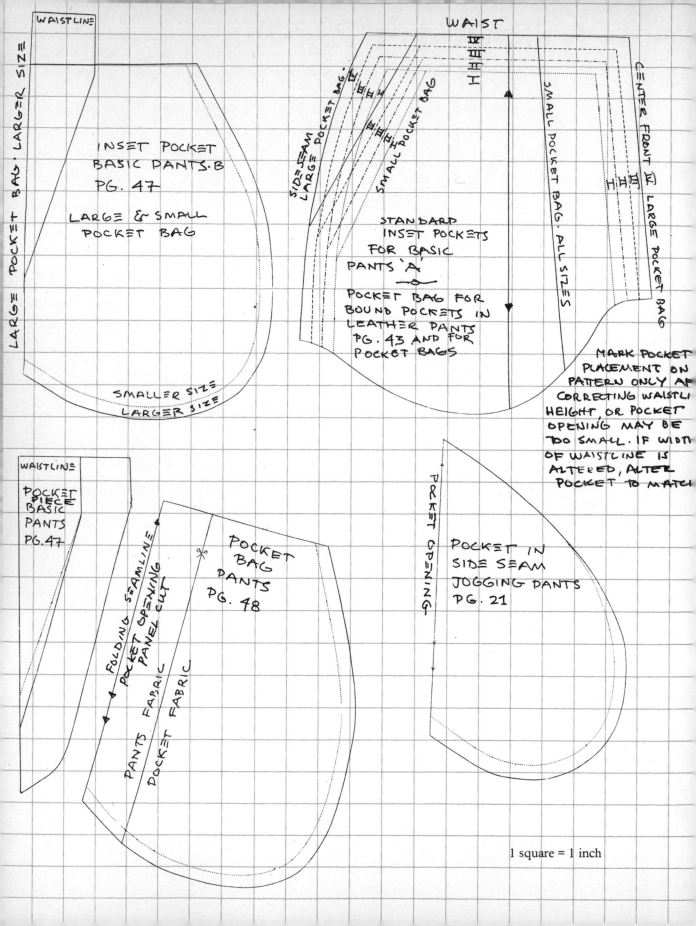

WAISTLINE

WAIST

LARGE POCKET BAG. LARGER SIZE

INSET POCKET
BASIC PANTS. B
PG. 47

LARGE & SMALL
POCKET BAG

SMALLER SIZE
LARGER SIZE

SIDE=SEAM LARGE POCKET BAG.

SMALL POCKET BAG

IV
III
II
I

SMALL POCKET BAG. ALL SIZES

CENTER FRONT IV. LARGE POCKET BAG

STANDARD
INSET POCKETS
FOR BASIC
PANTS 'A'

POCKET BAG FOR
BOUND POCKETS IN
LEATHER PANTS
PG. 43 AND FOR
POCKET BAGS

MARK POCKET
PLACEMENT ON
PATTERN ONLY AF
CORRECTING WAISTLI
HEIGHT, OR POCKET
OPENING MAY BE
TOO SMALL. IF WIDTH
OF WAISTLINE IS
ALTERED, ALTER
POCKET TO MATCH

WAISTLINE

POCKET
PIECE
BASIC
PANTS
PG. 47

FOLDING SEAMLINE

POCKET OPENING

PANEL CUT

PANTS FABRIC

POCKET FABRIC

POCKET
BAG
PANTS
PG. 48

POCKET OPENING

POCKET IN
SIDE SEAM
JOGGING PANTS
PG. 21

1 square = 1 inch

A — STRAIGHT PANTS

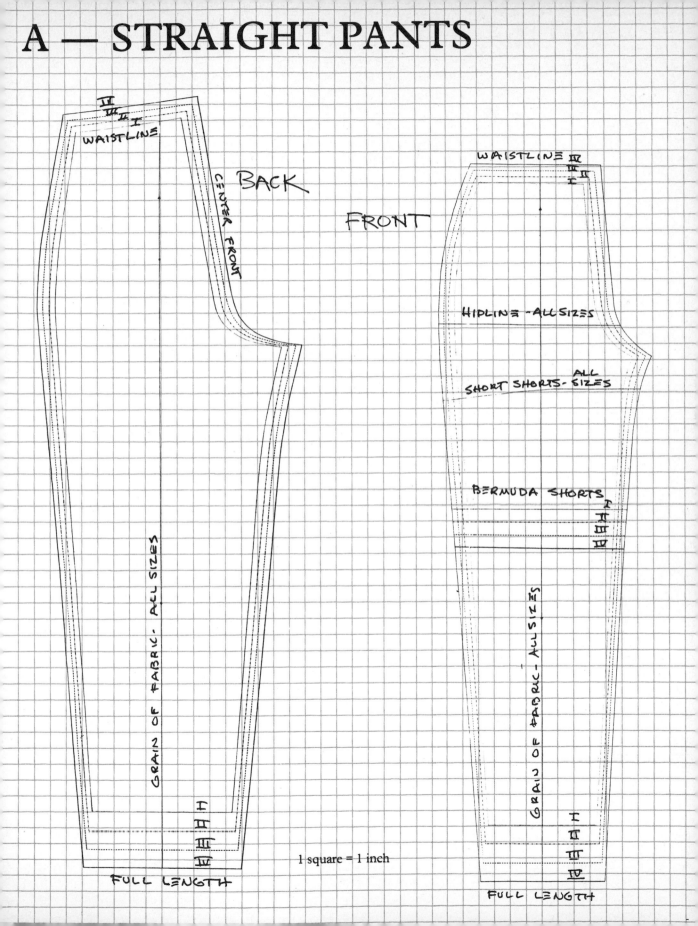

WAISTLINE

BACK

FRONT

CENTER FRONT

GRAIN OF FABRIC - ALL SIZES

WAISTLINE

HIPLINE - ALL SIZES

SHORT SHORTS - ALL SIZES

BERMUDA SHORTS

GRAIN OF FABRIC - ALL SIZES

1 square = 1 inch

FULL LENGTH

FULL LENGTH

B — FULL PANTS

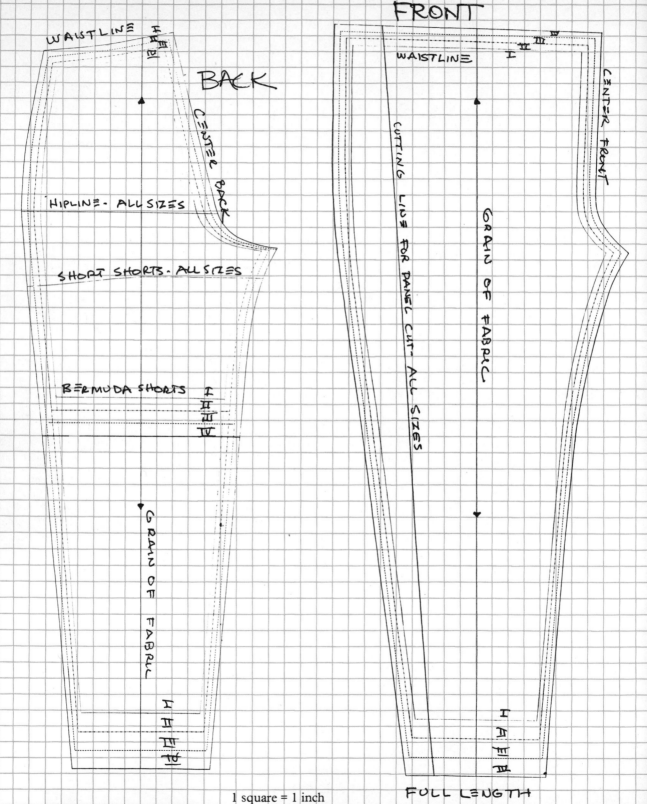

FRONT

BACK

WAISTLINE

CENTER BACK

HIPLINE - ALL SIZES

SHORT SHORTS - ALL SIZES

BERMUDA SHORTS   I
                 II
                III
                IV

GRAIN OF FABRIC

WAISTLINE

CENTER FRONT

CUTTING LINE FOR PANEL CUT - ALL SIZES

GRAIN OF FABRIC

FULL LENGTH

1 square = 1 inch

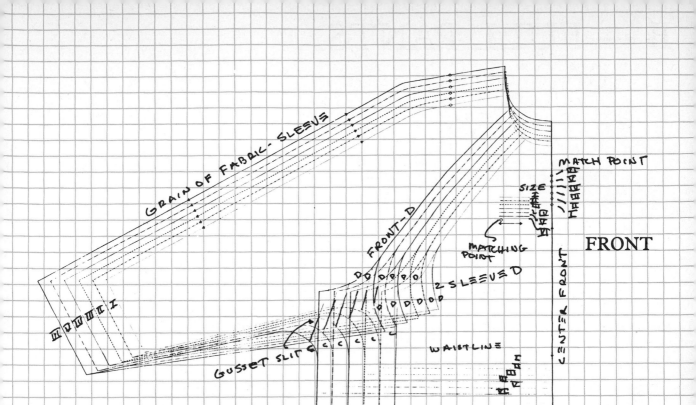

GRAIN OF FABRIC - SLEEVE

MATCH POINT

SIZE

FRONT

MATCHING POINT

CENTER FRONT

FRONT-D

2 SLEEVE D

GUSSET SLIT

WAISTLINE

HEM

BASIC TOP

C — KIMONO

D — RAGLAN

HIPLINE

SIZE

LENGTHEN/SHORTEN HERE

I
II
III
IV
V
VI

1 square = 1 inch

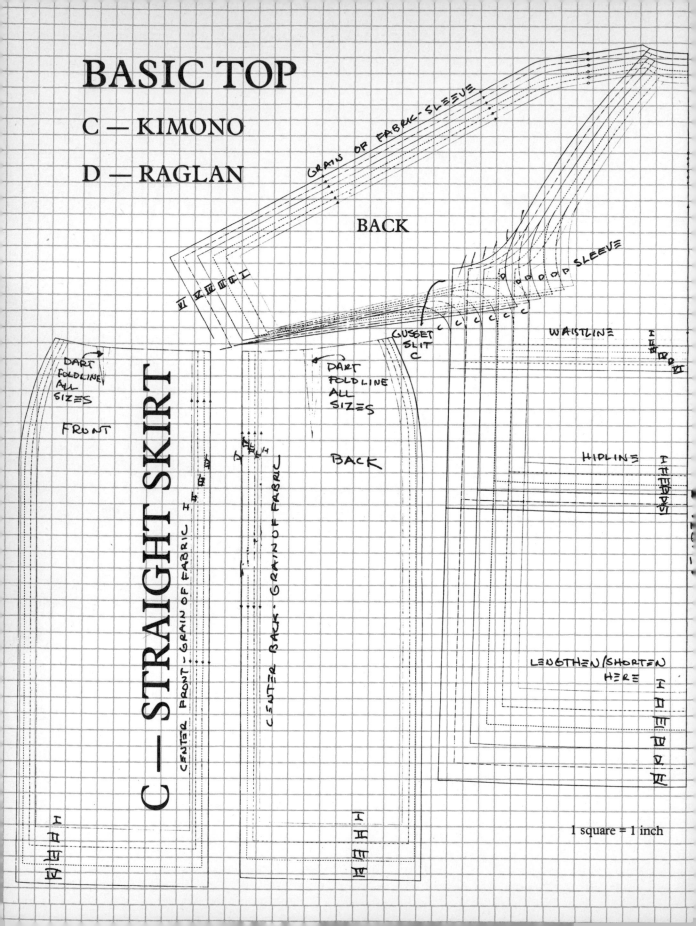

BASIC TOP

C — KIMONO
D — RAGLAN

GRAIN OF FABRIC · SLEEVE

BACK

D SLEEVE

GUSSET SLIT C

WAISTLINE

C — STRAIGHT SKIRT

DART FOLDLINE ALL SIZES

FRONT

CENTER FRONT · GRAIN OF FABRIC

CENTER BACK · GRAIN OF FABRIC

DART FOLDLINE ALL SIZES

BACK

HIPLINE

LENGTHEN/SHORTEN HERE

1 square = 1 inch

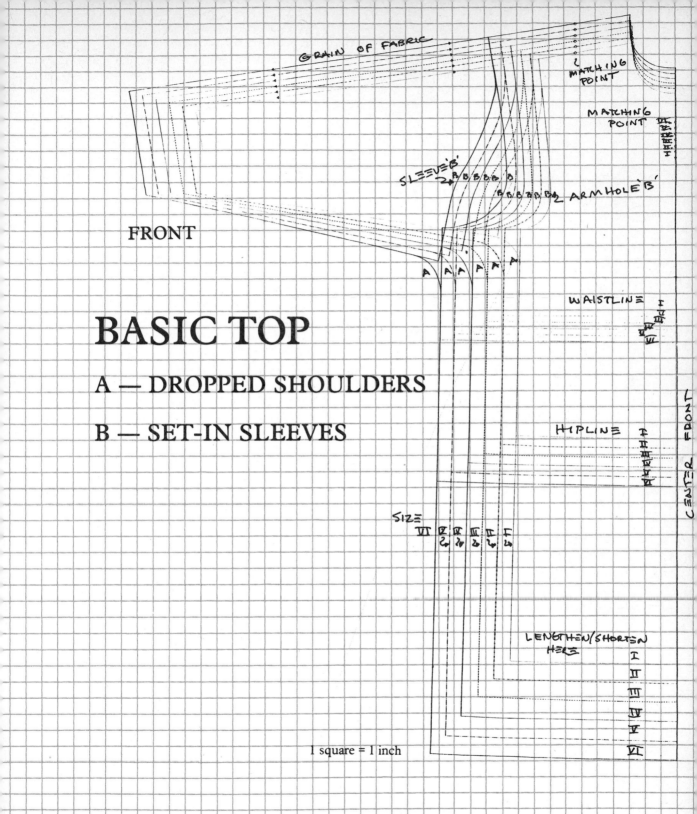

GRAIN OF FABRIC

MATCHING POINT

MATCHING POINT

FRONT

SLEEVE B'

BBBBB B

BBBBB B ARMHOLE B'

A AAAA A

WAISTLINE

BASIC TOP

A — DROPPED SHOULDERS

B — SET-IN SLEEVES

HIPLINE

SIZE

VI V IV III II I

CENTER FRONT

LENGTHEN/SHORTEN HERE

I

II

III

IV

V

VI

1 square = 1 inch

BACK

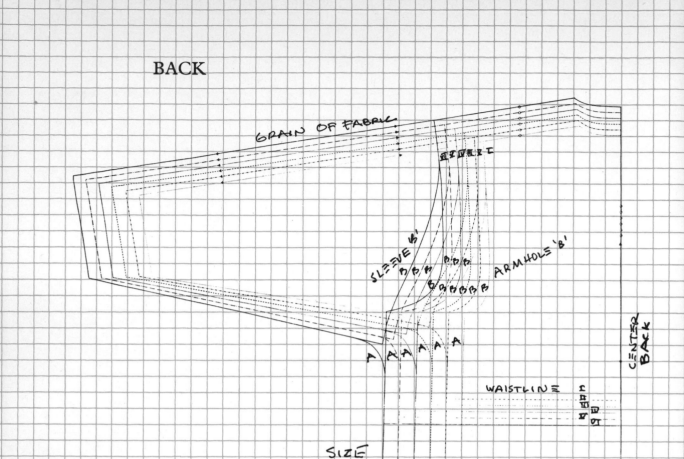

GRAIN OF FABRIC

SLEEVE 'b'

ARMHOLE 'b'

CENTER BACK

WAISTLINE

SIZE

HIPLINE

BASIC TOP

A — DROPPED SHOULDERS

B — SET-IN SLEEVES

LENGTHEN/SHORTEN HERE

1 square = 1 inch

Glossary and Index

A
Alteration of patterns, designs, 116
Alteration of sizes, 97
Applique, 136

B
Backstitch, 136
Basting, 134
Belt tabs, 168
Bias strips, 152
Bias tape folder, 152
Bias tape for trim, 152
Bound pockets, 144
Buckles, 167
To butt: to lay two edges together without overlapping them
Buttonholes, 165
   handsewn, 164
   machine-made, 164
Button extension, front button edge, 164

C
CB: abbreviation for center back
CF: abbreviation for center front
Channel: an edge, folded over and stitched, to carry elastic or a drawstring
Cleaning, 120
Collar patterns, 104
Collars, making, 175
Collar stand, 175
Combining patterns, designs, 116
Construction, 116
Cuffs, 157
   turned-up, 115
Curved seams, 136

D
Darts, 173; bust darts, 99
Dropped shoulders, 100
D-rings, 167
Dry-cleaning, 120

E
Edging, 152
Expanding patterns, 97

F
Fabrics, kinds and uses, 122
Fabric requirements, 131
Facings, 150
Flap, pocket, 83, 146
Fly, 170

G
Gathering thread, gathers, 137
Grain of fabric, 132
Gusset, 141

H
Hem, 136-137

I
Ironing/pressing, 135

K
Kick pleat, 140, 162

L
Lapels, 177
Laundering, pre-laundering, 120
Length: measurement to the lower edge of jackets, coats, etc.
Lining fabrics, jumpsuits, 160
   outerclothes, 161
   pants, 160
   skirts, 159

M
Mannequin, dressmaker's, 135
Marking the fabric, 133
Matching points, 102, 104, 114
Measurements, tables of, 96-97

N

Notch, in curved seams, in the seam
  allowance, 136

O

Outer edges: all edges not sewn into seams
Overlap: the side that lies on top when the
  garment is fastened

P

Panel cuts, 100, 101, 102, 109
Patterns, drafting/drawing, 114
  expanding, 97
  reducing, 97
Patterns in book, 94
Piecing: using two or more pieces of fabric at the
  least visible places when the fabric is insufficient
  to cut the garment section as one piece
Pinning, 134
Pin tucks, 139
Piping, 151
Plackets, 170
Pleats, 138; box, 139; double, 139
Pleats in pants, 107
Pockets, bound, 144
  hip, 147
  inset, 136
  patch, 142
  in side seams, 21, 148
Pressing, 135

R

Raglan, 103
Reducing patterns, 97
Reversible fabrics, 132
Rounded corners, 115

S

Seam allowance, 133
Seam ripper, 118, 164
Seam tape, 124

Selvage: the firm edge of woven fabrics, used to
  determine grain of fabric
Sewing directions, 116
Sewing machine needles, 120
Shawl collar, 176
Shoulder pads, 158
Sizes, 95, 97
Sleeves, set-in, raglan, 101
Slipstitch, 137
Slit facing, 173
Slit: an opening at the neck or side, or for a zipper
Stand collar, 175
Stitching down seam allowance, 137

T

Tack: to sew two layers together with a simple
  hand stitch.
Thread, 119
Topstitching, 136
Tracing, 118, 133
Trim, 152
Trying on, 134-135

U

Underlay: the side of a garment partly covered
  when the opening is fastened shut.

W

Waistband, 154

Y

Yokes, 23, 101

Z

Zigzag, 136
Zippers, in flies, 170
  hidden, 171
  separating, 171